One From Many

VISA and the Rise of Chaordic Organization

Dee Hock

16pt

Copyright Page from the Original Book

One From Many

Copyright © 2005 by Dee Hock
All rights reserved. No part of this publication may be reproduced, distributed, or transmitted in any form or by any means, including photocopying, recording, or other electronic or mechanical methods, without the prior written permission of the publisher, except in the case of brief quotations embodied in critical reviews and certain other noncommercial uses permitted by copyright law. For permission requests, write to the publisher, addressed "Attention: Permissions Coordinator," at the address below.

Berrett-Koehler Publishers, Inc.
235 Montgomery Street, Suite 650
San Francisco, California 94104-2916
Tel: (415) 288-0260, Fax: (415) 362-2512
www.bkconnection.com

Ordering information for print editions
Quantity sales. Special discounts are available on quantity purchases by corporations, associations, and others. For details, contact the "Special Sales Department" at the Berrett-Koehler address above.
Individual sales. Berrett-Koehler publications are available through most bookstores. They can also be ordered directly from Berrett-Koehler: Tel: (800) 929-2929; Fax: (802) 864-7626; www.bkconnection.com
Orders for college textbook/course adoption use. Please contact Berrett-Koehler: Tel: (800) 929-2929; Fax: (802) 864-7626.
Orders by U.S. trade bookstores and wholesalers. Please contact Ingram Publisher Services, Tel: (800) 509-4887; Fax: (800) 838-1149; E-mail: customer.service@ingrampublisherservices.com; or visit www.ingrampublisherservices.com/ Ordering for details about electronic ordering.

Berrett-Koehler and the BK logo are registered trademarks of Berrett-Koehler Publishers, Inc.

First Edition
Paperback print edition ISBN 978-1-57675-332-3
PDF e-book ISBN 978-1-60509-018-4

2008-1

Interior design and production by Detta Penna.
Cover design by Karen Marquardt.

TABLE OF CONTENTS

Foreword	xvi
Introduction	xxviii
Chapter One: Old Monkey Mind	1
Chapter Two: A Lamb and the Lion of Life	26
Chapter Three: The Bloodied Sheep	55
Chapter Four: Retirement on the Job	79
Chapter Five: The Zoo	110
Chapter Six: The House of Cards	139
Chapter Seven: Peeling the Onion	165
Chapter Eight: The Impossible Imagined	187
Chapter Nine: The Next to the Last Word	212
Chapter Ten: The Corporation or the Cane	246
Chapter Eleven: And Then There Was One	268
Chapter Twelve: Quite Ordinary People	303
Chapter Thirteen: The Victims of Success	337
Chapter Fourteen: The Golden Links	365
Chapter Fifteen: What's in a Name?	399
Chapter Sixteen: Breaking the Mold	436
Chapter Seventeen: The Successful Business Failure	451
Chapter Eighteen: The Jeweled Bearing	467
Chapter Nineteen: Out of Control and Into Order	497
Chapter Twenty: The Emergent Phenomenon	525
Acknowledgments	547
About the Author	548
Index	549

"Every now and then a book breaks through to new ground in discovery. Looking at business and innovation together, Dee Hock offers an exciting look at the role of creative thinking in a sustainable future. I was quite simply stunned at how this man broke old, staid rules in defining a new theory of social economics: accessible, personal, and deeply inspiring."
–Robert Redford

"From the military, to commerce, to the arts, our first priority is new models for effectively organizing human endeavor to match the wildly altered times. Dee Hock's *One From Many* is the most original and apt approach to organizing we have been offered so far. It clearly fits the 'must read,' 'must absorb' category for leaders in every sector."
–Tom Peters

"Entrenched, rigid bureaucracy is the common chain around mankind in the corporate, private, and public sectors. Dee Hock knows how to replace it trans-culturally with generic, adaptable structures that breathe, innovate, respond, and recover as if reality and their loftier purposes matter first and foremost. Dee Hock's book *One from Many* is an organizational revolution that the world ignores at its stagnant peril."

–Ralph Nader

"Reads as good as Ben & Jerry's ice cream tastes. If you care deeply about the future of people, place, or planet, be prepared for a surprise—as well as a real treat."

–Ben Cohen, President, Businessmen for Sensible Priorities, and Co-founder, Ben & Jerry's

"There are very few people who have changed the world: Dee Hock is one of them. His book is a celebration of the redesign of human *ego*-systems and *eco*-systems, including the most visceral and urgent form of communication—currency. There are very few books that can change one's life; this is one of them. A person with ideas that can change the world whose book can change your mind. I have read it twice, sent copies to my friends, and that is not enough."

–William McDonough, architect, designer, futurist; Principal, McDonough Consulting; and

Professor, Cornell, Stanford, and Virginia Universities

"Dee Hock, practical visionary extraordinaire, has rearranged our mental furniture. If you think you already know how we think, organize ourselves, and achieve breakthrough results, be prepared to be surprised by this remarkable book."

–Amory B. Lovins, CEO, Rocky Mountain Institute

"Dee Hock has had a profound impact on my thinking and on my view of governance and problem-solving in America. After 24 years in elective office, including two terms as governor of Oregon, I have seen firsthand the need for the kind of new organizational structures described in this remarkable book. *One From Many* is a must read for anyone who is serious about meeting the challenge of institutional failure in the United States."

–John Kitzhaber, former governor of Oregon

"Dee Hock has produced a powerful, profoundly important, and beautifully written book. It is the moving personal story of a young boy growing up dirt

poor in rural Utah, who went on to change the way the world does business. Here we see the mind behind the revolutionary global VISA model—a model that balances cooperation and competition in a way unlike anything ever seen before in commercial history.... No one knew how to approach this problem, or solve it. Someone suggested Hock. The rest is history and a rattling good story."
    —Barry Sheehy, CEO, CPC Econometrics, Inc.

"Dee Hock's work will do for organization theory in the post-industrial age what the steam engine did for the industrial age."
    —Bernard Lietaer, Chairman, Access Foundation, and author of *The Future of Money*

"*One From Many* is a book about organizational illness, sick leadership, and political cynicism. It is, thank God, even more a book about hope, social innovation, and down-to-earth, magical, organizational results. Mind-moving, playful, and beautifully written, it is also a compelling story of what mankind can be if we dare to be truly human. It has profoundly affected our students."

—Uffe Elbaek, Founder of the Kaospilot University, Denmark

"Dee Hock offers a vision that can transform any organization. His insights are brilliant and humane, his prescription is smart and workable. This is a book that aspiring leaders need to embrace."

—Alan M. Webber, Founding Editor, Fast Company magazine.

"*One From Many* is about a new organizational form (chaordic) for human systems in harmony with the principles of nature and life itself. Anyone who imagines living in such a future will be captivated by the wisdom of this book. It maps our journey to purposeful, life-affirming organizations essential for a sustainable future."

—Stephanie Pace Marshall, Ph.D., Founding President, Illinois Mathematics and Science Academy

"The originality and profundity of Dee Hock's wisdom can and does revolutionize institutions. I can bear witness to that in terms of his counsel in the creation of the United Religions

Initiative. He made it possible for URI to flourish."

–The Rt. Rev. William E. Swing, President, United Religions Initiative, Bishop, Episcopal Diocese of California

"Dee Hock's genius and vision has made it possible for organizations of all types and sizes to re-envision themselves in new ways. *One From Many* encompasses quantum physics, chaos theory, cellular biology, the butterfly effect, the natural world, and common sense. *One From Many* is a must read for anyone seeking to understand the organization of the future."

–Michael Toms, Founding President and Executive Producer/Host, New Dimensions Radio

"Dee Hock's work has become required reading for academic medicine. Once it is clear that improving patient care is the only purpose that matters, smart people begin to act smart again. Talent that had been paralyzed by dysfunctional systems becomes unleashed and is available to do the work of medicine and teaching."

–David C. Leach, M.D., Executive Director, Accreditation Council for Graduate Medical Education

"Hock is a gentle giant who successfully challenged traditional management and organization of a global industry. His 'new way of thinking' ideas can change the way all of us approach our own lives and institutional structures."

–Linda Golodner, President, National Consumers League

"Dee Hock describes a new organizational culture that might well spell the difference between a smooth, orderly transition to a more salubrious, sustainable society and the chaos and anarchy some see in our near-term future."

–Willis Harman, Founder, World Business Academy and former President, Institute of Noetic Sciences

"I highly recommend this book. There is no simpler way of learning the principles of chaordic organizations than from their inventor, Dee Hock, and there may be no more rewarding endeavor than to find out what it means to your own organizational dreams and visions."

—Karl-Henrik Robert, M.D., Founder, The Natural Steps International

"This book is a rarity! The ideas and experience in *One From Many* changed the way the world works. Read it at the risk of ending complacency and inaction. Buy a case now and save the trouble of replacing it each time you feel compelled to give your copy to someone who cares about making a difference."

—Greg Steltenpohl, Founder, Odwalla, Inc.

"Nothing is more important in today's world than for humanity to understand itself as a living system and move forward into the cooperative chaordic age Dee Hock both pioneered and interprets for us so eloquently. Read this fascinating book and take action!"

—Elisabet Sahtouris, Ph.D., evolution biologist and futurist; author of *EarthDance*

"Dee Hock did what most senior executives would consider total madness. He gave up the illusion of control in order to allow a great organization to be born. And then he had the audacity to describe his adventure in frank detail."

–Harrison Owen, creator of Open Space Technology

"Hock describes the context and chaordic processes present in the creative forces of nature that similarly apply to humankind's efforts to reach our fullest potential. In no discipline will application of this vision be more critical for achieving the interconnectivity, decision support, and transformational clinical integration needed for the 21st century than in health care. Read this book!"

–Jack Lewin, M.D., CEO, California Medical Association and Chairman, Patient Safety Institute

"The leaders of today's most outstanding schools understand that topdown leadership does not create the kind of collaborative learning teams that every school needs. Hock's seminal book should be read by everyone who wishes to create environments in which all students and teachers are successful."

–Dee Dickinson, Chief Learning Officer and Founder, New Horizons for Learning

"True brilliance is simplicity. Dee Hock understands like no one else how seemingly mundane elements like bylaws, organizing principles, and charters allow the most complex behaviors to occur in harmony. When the core is well conceived and pure, then incredible, productive activity will surround it."

–Luther Nussbaum, CEO, First Consulting Group

"*One From Many* is quite simply the most important organizational leadership book of this century. If we manage to survive this century with the Earth's ecosystems, climate, water, biodiversity, and societies intact, it will be in no small part due to the rapid adoption of the vital ideas in this book."

–Molly Harriss Olson, Founder, National Business Leaders Forum on Sustainable Development (Australia) and Founding CEO, President

Clinton's Council on Sustainable Development

"This is one of the most important books you will read in this decade. It will widen your periphery and cause you to think about how you can, and must, risk your significance."

–Dawna Markova, Ph.D., author of *I Will Not Die an Unlived Life* and *The SMART Parents Revolution*, and co-editor, *Random Acts of Kindness*

"Dee Hock is a remarkable business pioneer and a social science genius. His principles are simple and straightforward and cause the reader to view complex interpersonal dealings in a whole new light that can produce tangible and often previously unexpected results."

–Jack A. Newman, Jr., Executive Vice President, Cerner Corporation

"The relevance of Dee Hock's concepts of organizational development increases with each passing month, specifically for those who have leadership responsibilities that require dealing productively with complexity, diversity, and change. His chaordic concepts of organization have had immeasurable importance to my work in organizational governance, as a CEO, as an organizational consultant, and as a university instructor. Having the insight and tools to bring unity and a sense of oneness into the workplace and into daily practice is nothing short of mandatory."

–Richard Raymond, CEO, First Gate Energies

"Dee Hock's work represents a cornerstone in the evolution of the art of leadership and management. If you want to discover what the System is, but you want also to transform it for the benefit of all, this book is a must."

–Oscar Motomura, Founder and CEO, The Amana-Key Group, São Paulo, Brazil

"[Visa founder Dee Hock] tells the story of the conversion of a lossmaking activity into one of the fastest-growing, most successful commercial enterprises of today. Its corporate structure and rules are revolutionary. And not only is it successful and huge, it is also quite safe from barbarians, both outside and inside the gate. Anyone needing a blueprint for the successful company of the future should read this book."

 -Arie de Geus, author of *The Living Company*

"Read *One From Many* carefully! It's full of unique, intriguing, new ideas that will change the way you think about organizations and behave within them."

 –Craig A. Pendleton, Coordinating Director, Northwest Atlantic Marine Alliance

"Global organizations, like the U.S. intelligence community, are facing the classic centralize/decentralize dilemma where the trade-offs are too costly in terms of human life. It's time for a third approach and Dee Hock is the one (and maybe only) individual on the planet who has some worthy insights."

 –Verne Harnish, Founder, Young Entrepreneurs' Organization, and author of *Mastering the Rockefeller Habits*

"Dee Hock's insights and experiences provide us with the inspiration and the tools to develop organizations that are inclusive, just, and profitable."

–Jane L. Delgado, Ph.D., MS, President and CEO, National Alliance for Hispanic Health

"Organizations often suck the life out of people by treating them as expendable components of production. By contrast, Dee Hock has pioneered a new type of organization that not only breathes life into people, but provides them with a platform to realize their full potential. This kind of organization, with a fully engaged work force, could literally change the world."

–Dennis Whittle, Founder and CEO, Global Giving

"...a story of organizational growth on a global scale, from which we can all learn a great deal. Dee Hock, a foresighted entrepreneur of institutional renewal, has extracted a fundamental story that others can follow to shape the new, value-creating commons."

–Leif Edvinsson, Director of Intellectual Capital, Lund University, Sweden

To Mrs. Beautiful

***

Who made it possible, and all worthwhile.

Foreword

Peter M. Senge

Few even well-informed business leaders seem to recognize Visa as the largest business organization in the world, despite a turnover that is some 10 times that of Wal-Mart and a market value that is, conservatively speaking, more than double that of General Electric. I have often wondered why this is so. How could the world's largest business also be one of the business world's best kept secrets? It is certainly not that its product is little known, nor that it is the leader of an obscure industry. There are few companies that could claim that one-sixth of the world's people were its customers last year! Yet, over the past decade, there have been well over a thousand feature articles in *Business Week, Fortune,* and *Forbes* on Microsoft, over 350 on GE, and about 35 on Visa.

I have come to conclude that the reasons for Visa's relative invisibility are as important as those for its success.

There are virtually no feature articles on Visa International's CEO, a favorite theme of many business periodicals, because Visa's CEO makes neither the astronomical compensation nor wields the unilateral decision-making power of most CEOs—by design. There are no feature articles on its strategy because its strategy is in fact many strategies that arise from the thousands of autonomous businesses that are part of the Visa network—by design. There are no feature articles on its recent reorganization because the many regional and local Visa organizations within the network are in a continual state of evolution and therefore in no need of sweeping reorganizations by executive fiat—by design. In short, if you are a journalist interested in the latest tale of business heroes or anti-heroes, Visa is the sleepy midwest town of your profession. But, if you are interested in radical innovations in enterprise design that undermine the concentration of power in the hands of a few and enable continuous business innovation, creativity, and growth, you will regard Visa as the one of the most important organizations of the second half of the last century. I do.

In technology, historians distinguish incremental innovations that improve efficiency or cost from basic innovations like the light bulb, polymers, and digital computation, which create new industries and transform existing ones. Basic innovation is always threatening to the status quo. When it occurs in organizations and management, it threatens power relationships. It threatens established beliefs. It threatens habitual ways of doing things that, even if we do not entirely like them, are the only ways we know how to do things.

I have concluded that Visa is deeply threatening because it represents just such a basic innovation, and that is why it is impossible for the mainstream business mind-set to confront. How could a company of its extraordinary scale have only about 20,000 employees—about 5000 in Visa International around the world and then comparable numbers in several regional VISA organizations? How could it have no stockholders—and be owned by its members? How could it be organized as a network with little central authority—with member rights and responsibilities of participation rather than stock, and governed by a constitution, more like a democratic society than a business?

As a singular innovation Visa would be an interesting academic subject for study, but what makes it, and *One From Many,* important is that it is not alone. Indeed it may simply be the best business example of an emerging revolution in organizing, kin to such diverse organizations as the Internet, AA (Alcoholics Anonymous), and the worldwide air traffic control system. None has a president in control. None has owners separate from their members. Each is a network of free agents, none of whom understand the whole of the network nor do they need to, but each of whom knows the ground rules for participating. Each, like Visa, is formative and has its own set of problems. But each has grown rapidly and had large-scale impact on otherwise insoluble problems.

What is the source of this emerging wave of radical innovations in organizing? I believe it is easy but misleading to say that it lies in computers or information technology networks. This confuses enabling technology with what is being enabled. When Visa started, extended electronic data processing networks were in their infancy, as was the case with the air traffic control system, and certainly computers and IT play little role in AA. I believe the deeper source of innovation lies in the nature of the complexity we are creating around the world and the growing number of problems that exceed the power of existing institutions.

No nation-state can deal with global climate change. No single business can have an impact on the explosion of toxic chemicals in everyday products. Even the most "advanced" societies face insoluble health care crises. No one anywhere in the world is satisfied that they have a system of public education commensurate with the challenges of children growing into mature adults and responsible citizens in the twenty-first century. Global industrial development has sown the seeds for its own demise through giving rise to levels of complexity and rates of change that exceed the intelligence of the industrial age institutions that are its heirs. Consequently, on every front, we face problems for which the dominant hierarchical, authoritarian organizations are inadequate. As Dee Hock says, "We live in an era of massive institutional failure."

But new institutions require new thinking, and here is where Dee's story as it unfolds in the following pages is most important. In the midst of the chaos of a massive overshoot and financial collapse in the early years of the credit card industry, Dee had a realization. He saw clearly that it was "beyond the power of reason to design an organization" capable of coordinating a global network of financial transactions of the sort that had started to develop. Yet, he also knew that nature regularly achieves just that. Why, he wondered, couldn't a human organization work like a rain forest? Why couldn't it be patterned on biological concepts and methods? "What if we quit arguing about the structure of a new institution and tried to think of it as having some sort of genetic code?" Visa's genetic code eventually became its "purpose and principles" and its core governance processes, the details of which are spelled out in the following pages.

But none of this would have come into being without this basic shift in thinking—to abandon the "old perspective and mechanistic model of reality" and embrace principles of living systems as a basis for organizing.

The anthropologist Gregory Bateson said, "The source of all our problems today comes from the gap between how we think and how nature works."[1] We face a mounting range of insoluble problems because the DNA of our dominant institutions is based on machine age thinking, like "all systems must have someone in control" and change only happens when a powerful leader "drives" change. Yet, we all know that in healthy living systems control is

---

[1] G. Bateson, Steps to an Ecology of Mind, New York: Ballantine, 1972.

distributed and change occurs continually. But we are so habituated to the "someone must be in control" mind-set that we fail to imagine real alternatives. Dee's genius lay in imagining just that and then working out a clear philosophy and operational design capable of bringing it to life.

Visa is not a paragon and Dee Hock does not have all the answers for creating innovative 21st century institutions. "We at best got it only half right," he says. The industrial age has been unfolding for two and a half centuries, and the machine thinking that underpins it goes back even further in Western culture. We are at the beginning of a journey, and even if we are lucky it will take multiple generations. Moreover, each company or organization must make its own journey, respecting the idiosyncrasies of market, technology, people, and history.

It is in this light that I believe Dee's personal story is most helpful. It is a powerful illustration of what those of us seeking to foster such innovations must be prepared for. We will need a willingness to question our most deeply held habitual ways of seeing organizations and management. We will need a willingness eventually to embrace the seeming chaos of an organization that no one "runs" and where we all share responsibility. We will need to embrace continually mistake-making and correcting, nature's learning process. And we will need a willingness to surrender the personal need to control—"the closet Newtonian" that Dee says resides in all of us.

Lastly, I believe this book is important because it carries within it an unasked question that is crucial to our future. More and more, among my colleagues we find ourselves asking, "Could we perhaps be at the beginning of the Democratic Age?"[2] Perhaps what has been achieved in the past two hundred years can best be thought of as initial prototypes rather than final models? In particular, despite political

---

[2] P. Senge, C.O. Scharmer, J. Jaworski, and B. Flowers, Presence: An Exploration of Profound Change, New York: Doubleday/Currency Business Books, 2005.

rhetoric to the contrary, how can a nation claim to have *the answer* for democratizing other societies when most of its own institutions in the private and public sector still operate as totalitarian dictatorships? I think it is fair to regard Visa as a pioneer in showing how democratic principles can govern a business. But just as strong a case can be made for democratizing other institutions as well—for example, schools. As Debbie Meier, a revered innovator in urban education, says, "If children do not learn democracy in schools, where will they learn it?"

For Debbie Meier, as for Dee, democracy means learning how to both take a stand and to truly listen to one another, learning how to deal with conflict respectfully and without violence. It means learning how to vest authority in governing ideas rather than people and to distribute power so that no decision gets made at a higher or more central level than is absolutely necessary. It means learning how to let go of the traditional trappings of hierarchical power and position and the associated leadership styles. In short, democracy is an ongoing collective process of learning how to live with one another—much more than it is a set of feel-good values or simple mechanisms like voting and elections. It is something you do, not that you inherit. And, until this learning process penetrates a society's major institutions, claims to be a democratic society are premature.

This is not a new question. In many ways the essence of Dee Hock's vision—that the democratic age may still be in our future and that its inspiration will come from living systems—was expressed beautifully over a century ago by Walt Whitman,

> We have frequently printed the word Democracy. Yet I cannot too often repeat, that it is a word the real gist of which still sleeps, quite unawakened ... It is a great word, whose history, I suppose remains unwritten, because that history has yet to be enacted. It is, in some sort, younger brother of another

great and often used word, Nature, whose history also waits unwritten.[3]
Peter M. Senge
August, 2005

---

[3] Walt Whitman, Democratic Vistas, 1871.

Introduction

Today, before any audience in the world, I can hold a Visa card overhead and ask, "How many of you recognize this?" Every hand in the room will go up. When I ask, "How many of you can tell me who owns it, how it's governed, or where to buy shares?" a dead silence comes over the room. Something incredible happened, but what, and how?

In 1969, Visa was little more than a set of unorthodox convictions about organization slowly growing in the mind of a young corporate rebel. In 2004, its products are created by 21,000 owner/member financial institutions and used by more than a billion people to purchase *$3.2 trillion* of goods and services at 20 million merchant locations in more than 150 countries, the largest block of consumer purchasing power in the global economy. For thirty-five years, it has grown from 15 to 50 percent, compounded annually, with no end in sight.

But this book is much more than the story of the scarcely believable events that brought Visa into being and led to its extraordinary success. It is also the story of an introverted, small-town child, passionate to read, dream, and wander the woods, the youngest of six, born to parents with but an eighth-grade education. It's a story of crushing confinement and interminable boredom in school and church, along with sharp, rising awareness of the chasm between how institutions profess to function and how they actually do; what they claim to do for people and what they actually do to them. It's about three compelling questions arising from that awareness:

Why are institutions, everywhere, whether political, commercial, or social, increasingly unable to manage their affairs?

Why are individuals, everywhere, increasingly in conflict with and alienated from the institutions of which they are part?

Why are society and the biosphere increasingly in disarray?

It's a story of a lifelong search for the answer to those questions, which had everything to do with the formation of Visa. It's a story of harboring four beasts that inevitably devour their keeper; ego, envy, avarice, and ambition; and of a great bargain, trading ego for humility, envy for equanimity, avarice for time, and ambition for liberty. It's a story of events impossible to foresee, that sent a man of seventy on a journey more improbable than Visa, and infinitely more important.

Beyond all else, it's a story of the future; of something trying to happen; of a four-hundred year old age rattling in its deathbed as another struggles to be born. It is not just my story, although I am in it. It is not just your story, although you are in it. It is a story of us all.

To be confused about what is different is to be confused about everything. Thus, it is not an accident that our fragmentary form of thought is leading to such a widespread range of crises, social, political, economic, ecological, psychological, in the individual and in society as a whole.... To develop new insights into fragmentation and wholeness requires a creative work even more difficult than that needed to make fundamental new discoveries in science, or great and original works of art. Suddenly, in a flash of understanding, one may see the irrelevance of one's whole way of thinking ... along with a different approach in which all the elements fit in a new order and in a new structure.

–David Bohm

Chapter One

Old Monkey Mind

No single thing abides, but all things flow.
Fragment to fragment clings; all things thus grow
Until we know and name them. By degrees
They melt and are no more the things we know.

—Lucretius

Nine hours we have happily worked the hillside together, a sixty-five year old man and Thee Ancient One, a diesel crawler-tractor of indeterminate age and lineage. Thee roars and clanks across the ground, a squat, old creature with massive winch and rippers behind, dozer and brush rake ahead, roll cage overhead, and huge hydraulic cylinders left, right, and rear. It is more equipage than Thee was designed to bear, but she labors on nonetheless.

It was quiet and cold when we began at dawn on land savaged by a century of overcropping and abandoned decades ago to the ravages of wind and rain. Where scant soil remains, masses of poison oak and coyote brush have scabbed the land to begin the healing.

It is 1993, nine years since I abruptly severed all connection with the business world for life on the land. It is still hard to believe. After sixteen years of intense conflict with industrial age, command-and-control corporations; after thirty-five years dreaming of new concepts of organization and experimenting with them; after two impossible years bringing one of those dreams into being; after fourteen grueling years leading it to maturity—after all that, turning my back on Visa in 1984 and walking away at the pinnacle of success was the hardest thing I have ever done.

The reason is still difficult to explain, but it is not complicated. That inner voice that will not be denied, once we learn to listen to it, had whispered since the beginning, "Business, power, and money are not what your life is about.

Founding Visa and being its chief executive officer is something you needed to do, but it's only preparatory." Each time I resisted. "You're crazy! Preparatory for what, and where, and why?" there was no answer, only silence. In time the voice became incessant and demanding.

"Visa's not an end. Give it up, and the business world as well—completely—irrevocably—now! In time, you will understand." It was frightening. It was maddening. I felt a damned fool to even think about it. A rational, conservative, fifty-five year old businessman who'd never smoked a joint or dropped a drug listening to inner voices? Absurd! Throw away a lifetime of work—success, money, power, prestige—as though it had no value in the vague hope that life had more meaning? Madness!

But the voice would not be silent. This was not my lifelong friend and companion, rational Old Monkey Mind, the certified expert of logic, talking. This was another voice entirely. And I knew it was right. In 1984, I abruptly left Visa and severed all connection with the business world, offering the only possible explanation. "I feel compelled to open my life to new possibilities." No one believed it. Why should they? I could scarcely believe it myself. I hadn't a clue what those possibilities might be. But I intended to be open to them.

The nine years since Old Monkey Mind and I left Visa and opened our life to new possibilities have been good years, filled with things we deeply love—family, nature, books, isolation, privacy, the infinities of imagination—more than enough to make a fine life. From time to time, we hear that familiar inner voice with its old refrain, "This is not what your life is about. This is merely preparatory." But we dismiss it as an echo. We long ago accepted that what has occupied us these nine years past are the possibilities we were meant to realize. How can we know that before the day ends we will step on one of those tiny jeweled bearings on which life turns, which will send us spinning in a new direction.

***

It has been one of those spirit-lifting, mind-soaring, diamond days. Hands and feet fly between brakes, clutches, hydraulic levers, gearshift, and throttle; nine levers simultaneously manipulated. We are a symphony of motion, Thee and me. No sissy automatic controls for us. Thee has been a good teacher. After nine years working together, motions require no conscious thought. We are not separate things. Thee manipulates my hands and feet as surely as I manipulate her pedals and levers. We function as a single system, recognizing one another's strengths, excusing one another's foibles, communicating in ways neither of us understand, expecting no more than the other can give. We are bound to the same Earth by the same gravity. We breathe the same air. We both move by processes of combustion and dissipate our excess heat into the same space. We are a microcosm of the infinite interconnectedness of all things: at once particulate and whole, self and not-self, at one with the universe. The work seems to do itself, leaving Old Monkey and me free to roam as we will.

> Old Monkey Mind soon coaxes me into one of those deep thickets of thought we have been trying to penetrate these many years. Are machine and man inseparably connected and related in ways we can't comprehend? How and why did we begin to break everything apart in the rational mind? Is there any way to break things apart in the mind without eventually breaking them apart physically? Does the one breaking inevitably result in the other? Just who or what determines this breaking apart, locking our thoughts and lives into ever more confining boxes of specialization and particularity? Why and how did we begin efforts to make men behave like machines and to make machines behave like men? When and why did we begin to think of the Earth as separate from mankind; a warehouse of free material to make gadgets for consumption in a mechanistic money economy; a free dump for poisons and waste?

What if the very concept of separability (mind/ body— cause/ effect—mankind/ nature—competition/ cooperation—public/ private—man/ woman—you/ me) is a grand delusion of Western civilization, epitomized by the industrial age; useful in certain scientific ways of knowing but fundamentally flawed with respect to understanding and wisdom? What if our notions of separability, particularity, and measurement, useful as they may be in certain circumstances, are just momentary, mental aberrations in the mysterious evolution of consciousness?

Old Monkey and I have long chuckled at the absurd notion that mind, body, and spirit are separate things, like cogs, cams, and springs of a clock. We're certain that machines, people, and nature are not as separate as Francis Bacon, Isaac Newton, Descartes, and the science they spawned would have us believe. Science has insisted for two hundred years that the few pounds of gray matter in the bone box on my

> shoulders is nothing but electrical and chemical impulses flickering about between separate particles of matter in obedience to rigid, universal laws of cause and effect. Old Monkey and I don't think so. For all the wonders of modern science and its obsession with measurement, we believe life will never surrender its secrets to a yardstick. Body, mind, and spirit are inseparably one, and they are one with all else in the universe. We are not seduced by notions to the contrary.

Thee Ancient One and I have carefully worked our way around the half-dozen stunted Douglas fir that have found enough sustenance to begin forming a new forest. I have no design for the land. It will design itself, yet visions of how it might look covered with native grasses and flowers interspersed with groves of native trees flow through my mind. We have been laboring on these two hundred acres of pasture, hill, and forest for nine years. Early visions are already young reality.

The first fields restored are deep in grass, surrounded by groves of fir, madrone, oak, and redwood carefully transplanted as seedlings from the surrounding forests.

Within three years, air and sunlight will transform the subsurface mudstone shattered by Thee Ancient One's rippers into clay. The clay will suck nitrogen from the roots of the grasses and mix with dying stems. Thousands of gophers, mice, and moles are at work, assiduously carrying grass underground and dirt to the surface.

Billions of worms, ants, beetles, and other creatures till the soil around the clock. Trillions of microscopic creatures live, eat, excrete, and die beneath my feet. In time, larger animals and birds will return to make their contribution. Porous soil will build to absorb and distribute water from even the heaviest storms, and lateral ditches that now control runoff can be filled. Each year grasses, flowers, shrubs, and trees will be taller, thicker, more diverse, and healthy.

Could this abundance of interdependent diversity be the deeper meaning of the biblical injunction to "multiply and replenish the Earth?" Could it mean that we are here to enable the multiplication and replenishment of all life on Earth, not just our own? Is it possible that the "nature" we are destined to subdue is really our own?

Thee and I work submerged in the roar of the engine and clank of tracks. Nose-tingling clouds of dust rise, spiced with the pungency of weed and brush crushed beneath the tracks. Four red-tailed hawks scream greetings as they float high above, scribing invisible parabolas in the sky before sliding swiftly down the slope of the wind, then rising again. Five jet-black vultures spiral into view, outspread wings powered by the wind, tip feathers spread like fingers against the sky. Thee is idled as I grab binoculars to join them for a quarter hour. A bit of glass before the eye and we are one, bird observed and bird observer.

Every feather moves in intimate, intricate converse with the wind. Language is such clumsy communication compared to that between breeze and bird. Inseparability and wholeness are everywhere about. Bone and feathers, flesh and spirit, space and time—wind, bird, sunlight, Earth, man—irrevocably interconnected, defining one another. All simultaneously competing and cooperating, separate yet inseparable, a whole of parts and a part of wholes, none in control but all in order.

> Old Monkey and I are soon in another thicket of thought. Is it possible that in the deepest sense, *everything is its opposite; that all things define, thus conceive, one another.* It seems impossible to conceive of "thing" without the concept of "no thing." Is there no bird without man, and no man without bird? Are there no borders except in the mind?
>
> If the universe is truly a meaningless mechanism composed of separable, physical particles acting on one another with precise, linear laws of cause and effect as science has demanded we believe for two hundred years past, whence came these eternal questions which so fascinate Old Monkey and me? Why, at long, long

last, can't science explain such simple things as love, trust, generosity, and honor?

For decades, Old Monkey and I have puzzled over man's desire for certainty and control, his lust for science. It led to a fascinating question. What would it be like if one had perfect ability to control?

It would be necessary to know every thing and every event that had ever happened, for how could one know what total control meant without infinite knowledge of past events and their consequences?

It would require omniscience about the future. Knowledge of every entity that could ever be and every event that could ever occur; when and how it would happen and every nuance of what the effects would be. One could never control that which could not be known until it happened. Mystery and surprise would be intolerable.

Even perfect knowledge of past, present, and future would not be enough for total control. It would be necessary to know the thoughts, emotions, and desires of every human being including self—all their hopes, joys, fears, and urges. And not just those other folks. It would be necessary to know everything that self might ever think, feel, know, or experience. Even beyond that, it would be necessary to be rid of all such emotions, feelings, beliefs, and values, for such things catch us unaware and affect our behavior. Compassion must go, love must go, admiration, envy, desire, hate, nostalgia, hope, along with every aesthetic sensibility. Perfect control would require absolute knowledge of everything that came before every before, and everything to come after every after, and so on ad absurdum.

But all this reveals nothing. It still leaves the question unanswered. *What would it be like to be the possessor of total, infinite, absolute control?* The first thought is that it would be akin to being a god, at least as gods are normally perceived. With a good deal more thought and more intuition, it hit Old Monkey and me like a bolt from the blue. *It would be death. Absolute, perfect control is in the coffin.* Control requires denial of life. Life is uncertainty, surprise, hate, wonder, speculation, love, joy, pity, pain, mystery, beauty, and a thousand other things we can't imagine.

Life is not about control. It's not about getting. It's not about having. It's not about knowing. It's not even about being. *Life is eternal, perpetual becoming, or it is nothing.* Becoming is not a thing to be known, commanded, or controlled. It is a magnificent, mysterious odyssey to be experienced.

At bottom, desire to command and control is a deadly, destructive compulsion to rob self and others of the joys of living. Is it any wonder that a society whose world view; whose internal model of reality is the universe and all therein as machine should turn destructive? Is it any wonder a society that worships the primacy of measurement, prediction, and control should result in massive destruction of the environment, gross

> maldistribution of wealth and power, enormous destruction of species, the Holocaust, the hydrogen bomb, and countless other horrors? How could it be otherwise when for centuries we have conditioned ourselves to ever more powerful notions of domination, engineered solutions, compelled behavior, and separable self-interest?
>
> Tyranny is tyranny no matter how petty, well intended, or cleverly rationalized. It is that to which we have persuaded ourselves for centuries, day after day, month after month, year after year in thousands of subtle ways. It need not have been so in the past. *It should not be so now. It cannot be so forever.*

I am yanked back into the moment by a gust of wind laden with icy drops of rain. While we have wandered, the sky has darkened, the wind has picked up, and daylight has dimmed. No doubt of it, we're in for a heavy storm. Better hurry. Rain will soon saturate the soil and work will be impossible. A flick of the throttle and Thee Ancient One roars to life. We crawl across the land pushing a huge pile of brush toward the ravine. Unconsciously I slip out of harmony with my surroundings to take control of the situation. One hurried pass, then another and a third. Faster, faster—fifteen minutes more and the job will be done.

Thee Ancient One screams with metal on metal, bucks, and stops to the hammering of drive-wheel spokes jumping the track sprocket. Damn and double damn! Idiot! Fool! *I would try to impose control* and demand more than the situation required, or Thee could give. I shut down the engine and sit quietly in the rain as anger and frustration slowly drain away. I begin to grin. Plus one for Thee, ancient one. Minus one for you, old man.

I sit motionless for ten minutes, gradually returning to harmony with the whole, enjoying the sound of gusting wind, the first drops of cold rain, the ocean restless under darkening clouds, trees and grass in a supple dance with the wind. Everything is in its ancient, seamless rhythm of conflict and cooperation. The Earth, each blade of grass, each tree, the man, the tractor, the storm, each a whole of parts and a part of wholes, acting on and acted upon. Everything both infinitely understandable and infinitely mysterious, including an old man sitting on a tractor, smiling and running a hand over a stubble of whiskers on a crooked jaw.

Jogging the half mile downhill to the equipment barn, I slip into boots, rain pants, slicker, and hood. Into the back of the truck go steel crowbars, hydraulic jack, four-foot crescent wrench, shovel, and smaller tools. Rain is misting the windshield as I drive back to Thee Ancient One, silent on the hillside. Kneeling in the mud, positioning thirty pounds of crescent wrench to turn the huge nut controlling tension on the track is no piece of cake. Arms and shoulders are cramping before the track tension is released. Another half hour passes swiftly as wind and rain increase, alternately raising the front with the dozer blade and the back with the hydraulic jack until the ton of track hangs slack an inch above the mud.

With six-foot steel bars I leverage the massive track away from the frame and in line with the drive wheel. With a satisfying clank, the track settles into the sprockets front and back. Grinning, I struggle for three-quarters of an hour restoring tension to the track, removing blocks and throwing muddy tools into the truck. I drive down the half-mile hill to the barn in the rising fury of the storm.

Truck and tools safely parked in the barn, I call Ferol to assure her I will be at the house within the hour and extract a promise to turn on the sauna. Sucking a bloodied knuckle, staggered by gusts of wind, water sloshing in my boots, I laboriously climb the half mile of hill to where Thee Ancient One sits silent in the dark. She rumbles to life with the first revolution of the starter. Engaging the clutch, I revel in diamond slivers of rain dancing through the headlight as we roar down the hill to the dry barn while cold settles to the bone, making thoughts of the sauna grand.

***

At the house, rain-soaked clothes and boots are left draining in the mudroom. Shivering in a towel, I make a quick stop in a poor boy's dream realized. Four walls of books—several thousand volumes—leather chair, fireplace, and study with picture windows overlooking forest, valley, village, and ocean. In a stack of unread books, my eye is taken with the black jacket of a small volume in the center of which, bursting with light, is the picture of a small sand dune above a single word: *Complexity.*

Cold seeps from the bone as I lie in the heat of the sauna, book propped on a towel on my chest, scanning the introduction. I haven't the slightest idea that another of those tiny, jeweled bearings on which life turns has been placed in my path. Two chapters later, I set the book aside, shower, then settle into bed to read it through with growing fascination.

It is the story of a number of prominent scientists from several disciplines who formed a small institute to pursue their shared awareness that a new science might emerge from the study of complex, self-organizing, adaptive systems, which they refer to as "complexity." They seem intrigued by the notion that the two-hundred year old scientific attempt to explain the universe and all it contains as mechanisms operating with precise, linear laws of cause and effect may be inadequate. Concern that pursuit of specialization, separability, and particularity may have led to a blind alley in ultimate understanding has brought them to a new, more inclusive way of thinking. Constrained by the specialization within universities, they felt compelled to set up a separate institute to pursue the "new science."

They speculate that there is something about the nature of complex connectivity that allows spontaneous order to arise, and that when it does, characteristics emerge that cannot be explained by knowledge of the parts. Nor does such order seem to obey linear laws of cause and effect. They speculate that all complex, adaptive systems exist on the edge of chaos with just enough self-organization to create the cognitive patterns we refer to as order.

It is not so much the concepts that fascinate me. They seem like old, familiar friends. Many sentences and paragraphs contain language similar to that which I've used for years. They echo beliefs about concepts of societal organizations based on nature's way of organizing that I have developed and argued for decades. What fascinates me is that such concepts are now emerging in the scientific community in relation to physical and biological systems.

> Nearly four decades ago, three questions emerged from the constant dialogue with Old Monkey Mind. They were fascinating then. They are compelling today. They had everything to do with the origins of Visa. Time and time again they return, always more demanding.
>
> *Why are organizations, everywhere, political, commercial, and social, increasingly unable to manage their affairs?*
>
> *Why are individuals, everywhere, increasingly in conflict with and alienated from the organizations of which they are part?*

Why are society and the biosphere increasingly in disarray?

Today, it doesn't take much thought to realize we're in the midst of a global epidemic of institutional failure. Not just failure in the sense of collapse, such as might occur to a building or a business, but the more common and pernicious form: organizations increasingly unable to achieve the purpose for which they were created, yet continuing to expand as they devour resources, demean the human spirit, and destroy the environment.

Schools that can't teach

Unhealthy health-care systems

Corporations that can't cooperate or compete

Universities that are far from universal Welfare

systems in which no one fares well Agriculture

that destroys soil and poisons water Police that

can't enforce the law

Unjust judicial systems

Governments that can't govern

> Economies that can't economize.
>
> Such universal, ever-accelerating, institutional failure suggests there is some deep, pervasive question we have not asked; some fundamental flaw in the ordering of societal relationships of which we are unaware. It suggests that intractable problems can only get worse until we ask the right questions and discover the flaw. Is this the great new frontier that awaits? Is this the societal odyssey that cries out to us all?

In the deep silence of the early morning hours, a chapter or two from the end of the book *Complexity*, I become frustrated by the long strings of adjectives, "autocatalytic, nonlinear, self-organizing, complex, adaptive, holistic," with which the scientists attempt to explain their supposed new science. I rise and descend to the library to search through various lexicons looking for a suitable word. Nothing emerges. Why not invent a word? Since such systems are believed to emerge in the edge of chaos with just enough coherence and cohesion to result in order, I borrow the first syllables from chaos and order, combine them, and *chaordic* emerges. I begin to write a definition, trying to merge lifelong love of nature, sixteen extraordinary years creating such an organization, thoughts from the book, and conviction about the nature of institutions into a single, simple adjective.

> **chaordic**\kay'ord-ick\adj. [fr. E. *cha'os and ord'er*] 1. The behavior of any self-organizing and self-governing organism, organization, or system that harmoniously blends characteristics of chaos and order.
> 2. Characteristic of the fundamental, organizing principle of nature.

I return to bed to finish the final chapters. My last thought before switching off the light is noted in the margin: "The hubris of science is astonishing. It will come as quite a surprise to countless poets, philosophers, theologians, humanists, and mystics who have thought deeply about such things for thousands of years that complexity, diversity, interconnectedness, and self-organization are either new, or a science."

It is past midnight and the storm front has passed when memory takes me by the hand, leading me back to the origin of such thoughts. It was a very long time ago.

Chapter Two

A Lamb and the Lion of Life

The striking of a match is every bit as wonderful as the working of a brain; the union of two atoms of hydrogen and one of oxygen in a molecule of water is every bit as wonderful as the growth of a child. Nature does not class her works in order of merit; everything is just as easy to her as everything else: she puts her whole mind into all that she does ... [she] lives through all life, extends through all extent, spreads undivided, operates unspent.

—Stephen Paget

It is 1934, and I am five years old, wild with excitement, trotting back and forth, peering around overall-clad legs bulging with muscle as neighbors with crowbars strain alongside my father to move the frame cottage a quarter mile down the cement highway, on rollers made of old telephone poles, to an acre of land purchased from a neighboring farmer. With the cottage on site and a man on either end of a ten-foot crosscut saw, the poles are soon bucked into short sections. They are buried on end under the jacked-up house, which is slowly lowered, creaking as it comes to rest a foot above the ground on the wooden foundation.

Two hours later, with a four-foot-square wooden porch and steps nailed front and back, we pour into our new house, as beds, chairs, and table are moved from the rented, crumbling, brick house across the lane. There, six children were born, and two of them died, along with a tubercular aunt. In the dusk of the summer evening, the wood-burning iron stove that will do double duty for cooking and heating is installed against a partial wall dividing the single room into cramped sitting and kitchen space. One by one, the neighbors shoulder their tools and trudge into the night to shouts of "thanks" and replies of "welcome."

Later, as the vast, velvet night and billions of stars arc over our acre, my sisters and I christen the new house with a game of kick-the-can as our parents prepare supper. Three hours later, dinner over and dishwater flung out the back door, six people edge their way onto wall-to-wall beds on the screened porch. I tumble into the iron crib, which seems to have shrunk by half since I was a baby, forcing me into a curl of comfortable sleep.

The next morning, I trot happily behind a tall, god-like father a quarter mile through fragrant locust trees to the neighbor's flowing well, breathing the pungency of crushed peppermint snatched from the ditch bank. The five-gallon can is slowly filled and shouldered by my father for the return trip, as he proudly explains that there'll be no stale, piped water in our house. We'll have "walking water" from an artesian well. "Nothing finer."

That winter, screens of the sleeping porch have been replaced by glass. Outside, icicles hang from eaves to snow-covered ground. I often weigh an extended bladder and cramping bowel against a fifty-yard dash between three-foot snowbanks to the icy outhouse. "Nothing finer," according to my mother. Teaches one to "attend to business and not dawdle."

Earlier this evening, with great fanfare, my mother produced her special treat, "rich man's soup." Hot water, bread, salt, pepper, and a dollop of melting butter. "Nothing finer," of course. No food "spoiled with fancy sauces" for this lucky bunch. It is years before realization dawns that there may have been no other food in the house.

A hint that we are not the most fortunate of people and a hundred homilies lurking in the parental mind leap out to assault my ears. "Riches are not in the number of possessions, but the fewness of wants." "Pretty is as pretty does." "Wish not, want not." "Money's manure, no good unless you spread it." "The road to hell is paved with good intentions." They buzzed about like flies and I hated them. Very much against my will, the intuitive wisdom of centuries was being handed down.

It was there, in that tiny cottage in the small farming community at the edge of the Rocky Mountains, that the three great loves of my life arose—literature, nature, and a lovely girl with beautiful brown eyes. They would have everything to do with the unorthodox ideas that led to the creation of Visa, although I could not know so at the time.

When and how I learned to read is lost to memory. Ours was not a bookish family. My parents considered themselves lucky to have graduated eighth grade before pride and necessity drove them to earn their own living. Where the books came from, I have no idea. Probably from people who knew "the Hock boy's a little strange. He'll read anything."

One of the most powerful memories of those early years is countless hours curled on my side in my favorite place—the floor in the corner next to the warm wood stove—face propped up on my left hand, right hand turning pages of a book. The radio is muttering across the room and the family to one another as they crowd around it. I've gone to another place and hear nothing.

Night after night my mother pulls me from the pages of a book, opens the oven door, removes a round, fifteen-pound rock, wraps it in flannel, carries it to my bed, and slips it between the sheets. "Nothing finer," of course, than an icy room and cold feet on a hot rock for a kid anxious to again disappear in the pages of his book.

It is easy to know where the second grand passion, love of nature, came from. The west face of the Wasatch Range of the hundred-mile-wide Rocky Mountains dropped precipitously to the strip of farmland, orchards, tiny village, and our cottage nestled on the foothills below the towering peaks. West of the cultivated land, miles of alkali marshes stretched flat and unbroken until they met the barren shores of the Great Salt Lake.

Rivers and streams of fresh, cold water from snowbanks deep in the mountains tumbled and fell through boulder-strewn canyons bisecting the sheer, mile-high face of the mountains. They slowed as they met the alkali flats, picking up silt until they became turgid, brown sloughs imperceptibly wandering westward to merge with the Great Salt Lake. The whole of it was a haven for wildlife.

Vast hours and days in the midst of such magnificence, often wandering alone, are impossible to describe, nor can words convey the abiding love of nature and deep, intuitive sense of connection to the Earth and all therein that were aroused.

Love me as they will, there is a growing feeling of estrangement from family; a feeling of not belonging. No one shares my passion for reading or wandering alone. No one directs them either. I live largely in a private world of nature, ideas, and imagination. There was a completeness to life then. An inarticulate sense of the universe and all it contained as a living, breathing, fragrant whole. Money was scarce, but value was ample. Getting was hard, but sharing was easy. Possessions were scant, but love was abundant. Is that when the seeds of obsession with relationship and connection were sown? Is that where aversion to rational, mechanistic ways of thinking sprouted and took root?

There was no way then to know how the passion for literature and love of nature would sustain me through years in the ticktock world of business, or how they would shape beliefs about institutions and the people who hold power within them. But they did.

Nothing in my first six years prepared me for the shock of institutions. With school and church came crushing confinement and unrelenting boredom. To a child passionately in love with nature who lived in imaginary worlds, the reality of institutions was pure misery. I had no words for it at the time, but the feeling was powerful, often overwhelming. It was as though everyone began to shed wholeness and humanity at the door of institutions, along with their coats and overshoes. Adults suddenly turned in a mob to confront one; "Alright kid, you've had the joy of life for six years. That's enough. Grow up. Learn what life is all about." Failure to conform brought discipline, accepted without realization it was often a form of abuse. One day in particular is burned in memory.

***

Sunday, 1941, I walk along the road on a bitter-cold winter morning, blown snow swirling like fine white sand as the wind works assiduously to build drifts. I am on the way to church to serve sacrament with other deacons, preteen boys on the first step of the patriarchal lay ladder of church officials. At the crossroads, diminutive, crotchety old Joe in his white apron is alone behind the counter and half-dozen stools in the warmth and light of his one-room café. Along with a two-pump gas station and small grocery, it passes for the center of town. Moments later he turns, a smoking plate of eggs, ham, and hotcakes in hand. **"Eat!"** I'm not the smartest kid in my class, but eat is something I do understand. Momentary panic—I have no money. Does he expect me to pay? This is no time for indecision. He said eat and I do, with a vengeance.

"Hey kid, get in here!" Old Joe is standing in the doorway, scowling in my direction. **"Get in here. I can't keep the damned door open all day!"** Oh my God, he means me! What have I done? This is not a town or a time for disrespect of elders, let alone disobedience. I reluctantly cross the street and enter, engulfed by warmth and the smell of hot food. Joe is busy at the grill, scowling over his shoulder as he snaps, **"Sit down."**

"On your way to church?"

"Yup."

"Uh-huh. Thought so. Well, if you're gonna spend all morning with hypocrites, you'll need all the strength you can get. Have another hotcake." As the last bite disappears, he throws open the door and barks, **"Get movin', you're gonna be late."** The storm seems more friendly as I climb the hill, looking back to see Joe's dwindling figure scowling through the window.

An hour later, we are lined in the back aisle of the church, the organist pumping out a hymn as an elder blesses the sacrament, bits of bread and small paper cups of water on glass plates suspended from wire handles. We march forward to be handed a plate and fan out down the aisle to pass them through the congregation. Ancient Mr. and Mrs. Jones sit on the bench that is my lot. He is enjoying a wee nap, jaw drooping, as spittle leaks from the corner of a slack mouth. She accepts the plate, partakes, elbowing him in the ribs as she turns. His eyes fly open, his hand flies up and it happens. In the deep silence of the church the plate crashes to the floor. In a flash, the elderly Mrs. Jones snatches the handle from the midst of shattered glass and bits of bread and shoves it into my hand.

Every eye in the church turns to stare. The silence speaks. "Guilty! You have smashed the sacrament! The evidence is in your hand!" In that frozen moment, no one knows what to do. A friend loses his cool and giggles. The church fills with suppressed guffaws. But the unctuous, rotund superintendent of the Sunday school is not smiling. He is slowly swelling with the wrath of God. Days seem to creep by before the sacrament is finished, the handle is out of my hand, and the organist has launched a march, signaling the congregation to move to classrooms in the back of the building.

Practicing invisibility in a corner of my class is no protection. The door bursts open and the rotund superintendent enters. He fixes me with an icy stare as the tirade begins. "Blasphemy!—flesh of the father trampled—nothing humorous about—on your knees to pick up—lack of respect—should have this, should have that." His bladder of righteousness is bursting as he spews words of condemnation. It would hurt less if he used a whip. I say nothing and endure, but questions *will* rise. Why wasn't he on his knees picking up after it happened? Why does he turn a reprimand into a performance? Why did he not then behave as he now commands? Has he no interest in what actually happened—does he care nothing about the truth?

Walking the mile home in sullen, burning silence, something in the back of my mind began to simmer, which over the years boiled over. What is this chasm between how most institutions profess to function and how they actually do; between what they claim to do for people and what they actually do to them? What makes people behave in the name of institutions in ways they would never behave in their own name? Church, school, government—all the same. What is this difference between Joe and the Super? Joe in his tiny café, crotchety and generous. The Super in church, unctuous and abusive.

Nothing in nature feels like church or school. There's no black bird "principal" pecking away at the rest of the flock. There's no "super" frog telling the others how to croak. There's no "teacher" tree lining up the saplings and telling them how to grow. Something's crazy! Is it me? I can't begin to think about it in a coherent way, let alone understand the resentment, confusion, and doubt. But the sense that something has gone awry is powerful. I look up at the massive, mountain peaks under their mantle of snow towering a mile into the pale winter sky. They are not troubled. The turmoil gradually subsides.

Mind and body returned to the church from time to time, but heart and spirit—never! To Joe's we returned whole and happy many times, until the day of his death, and beyond.

> Over the years, as Old Monkey and I puzzled over an ancient, fundamental idea, the idea of community, memory of those early years was ever present. In time we came to believe that the essence of community, its very heart and soul, is the nonmonetary exchange of value. The things we do and the things we share because we care for others, and for the good of the place. Community is composed of things that we cannot measure, for which we keep no record and ask no recompense. Since they can't be measured, they can't be denominated in dollars, or barrels of oil, or bushels of corn—such things as respect, tolerance, love, trust, generosity, and care, the supply of which is unbounded and unlimited. The nonmonetary exchange of value does not arise solely from altruistic motives. It arises from deep, intuitive, understanding that self-interest is inseparably connected with community

interest; that individual good is inseparable from the good of the whole; that all things are simultaneously independent, interdependent, and intradependent—that the singular "one" is inseparable from the plural "one."

The nonmonetary exchange of value is the most effective, constructive system ever devised. Evolution and nature have been perfecting it for thousands of millennia. It requires no currency, contracts, government, laws, courts, police, economists, lawyers, or accountants. It does not require anointed or certified experts of any kind. It requires only ordinary, caring people.

In a true community, unity of the "singular one" and the "plural one" applies as well to beliefs, purpose, and principles. Some we hold in common with all others in the community. Some we hold in common with only part of the community. Others we may hold alone. In true community, the values others hold that we do not share we nonetheless respect and tolerate—either because we realize that our beliefs will require respect and tolerance in return, or because we know those who hold different beliefs well enough to understand and respect the common humanity that transcends all difference.

True community also requires proximity—continual interaction between the people, places, and things of which it is composed. Throughout history, the basic community, the fundamental social building block, has always been the family. It is there that the greatest nonmonetary exchange of value takes place. It is there that the most powerful nonmaterial values are created and exchanged. It is from the community called family, for better or worse, that all other communities are formed.

Without any one of the three—nonmaterial values, nonmonetary exchange of value, and proximity—no true community ever existed or ever will. If we were to set

> out to design an efficient system for the methodical destruction of community, we could do no better than our present efforts to monetize all value and reduce life to the tyranny of measurement. Money, markets, and measurement have their place. They are important tools indeed. We should honor and use them. But they do not deserve the deification their apostles demand of us, before which we too readily sink to our knees. *Only fools worship their tools.*

At thirteen, I rebelled. Not the overt, in your face, rebellion so common today. At that time and in that place, it would have been rewarded with a choice between two years in reform school or four years in the army. It was persistent, stubborn, at times stupid refusal to accept orthodox ideas, be persuaded by authoritarian means, or seek acceptance by conformity.

Much as I detested confinement and rebelled against it, it was in a fifth grade classroom that my third great passion and greatest of good fortune came. In the way of all young boys craving attention from girls, I slyly slipped my hand onto the desk behind, to tip her books to the floor. Without so much as acknowledging my presence or the slightest change of expression in her magnificent brown eyes, with her fingernails, she put four bloody, crescent moons in the back of my hand. We've been together every step of the way since. Whether, without Ferol, I would be writing this book is very much in doubt. One thing is certain, I would not wish to be.

The years passed alternating between the magnificent mysteries of nature, the imaginative joy of books, the dull reality of institutions, and work, work, work. From time beyond memory, both Ferol and I had chores to contribute to the welfare of our families. At ten, I was hand-harvesting fruit and vegetables at a penny the pound while Ferol labored to help her father on a small, hardscrabble farm. At twelve, I was at stoop labor thinning sugar beets at twenty dollars the acre. That was followed by a first salaried job at farm labor for twenty cents the hour. The first nickel raise to a quarter was a proud moment, remembered still.

At fourteen, a forged baptismal certificate claiming sixteen brought a job dumping slop in a canning factory. Summer and after-school jobs came one after the other: mucker at a dairy, hot-tar chain dipper under 100-degree sun, orchard spray-truck operator, hod carrier, laborer in the offal department of a slaughterhouse. None of it seemed demeaning. It was life. It was making a living. It was what proud men did, without whining. "Root, hog, or die" was the homily of the day.

***

Hunting and fishing were also a way of life, and major source of food. Deer, elk, pheasant, ducks, geese, and rabbit continually found their way to the table, and I was only too willing to be the gatherer. In the fall of my fifteenth year, two pals and I carefully planned the opening day of duck season. We would drive in the dark to the end of a dirt road in the middle of the marshes bordering the Great Salt Lake and wait for dawn. As it grew light, flocks of ducks and geese would rise from the lake and head east across the marshes to feed in the farmland. We would be waiting.

When we gathered in the cold, dark morning, we were four, not three. My pals had invited a new boy who had moved to an adjacent farm only a week before, loaning him a doubled-barreled, twelve-gauge shotgun. Full of excitement and laughter, we drove west in a dilapidated farm truck. My pals would work farther into the marshes in one direction; Ralph, the new boy, would row the boat down the slough in another; and I would keep pace along the shore.

It was a cold, clear morning as light gathered over the mountains far to the east, gradually revealing the vast, flat miles of salt grass and bullrushes that stretched in every direction. There was splendid, absolute silence except for the occasional creak of oars and crunch of my footsteps on a skiff of frozen snow. A flock of ducks rose far to the west and moved swiftly in our direction. I called softly to Ralph, pointing them out. He rowed hurriedly to the far bank. They were moving steadily toward us as he leaped from the boat, turned quickly and reached for his gun, grasping it by the barrel and jerking it toward him. The hammer flipped on the side of the boat. **WHAMM!** The sound of the shot echoed and reechoed over the deathly silence of the marsh. He dropped the gun and grabbed his left hand with his right, clutching both to his chest. My mind flashed. "My God! He shot off his hand!"

Straightening, he screamed, *"I got it, boy, I got it,"* took four staggering steps up the muddy bank, and pitched onto his face. Blood cascaded down the bank. It wasn't his hand. An ounce and a half of lead shot had shredded his heart.

As I tore frantically at bulky boots and clothing, a figure appeared moving swiftly down the far bank, racing toward Ralph. The stranger brought Ralph across the slough in the small boat in the midst of a universe paralyzed by the sound of the gun. He quickly left to report the accident, trotting across the vast, flat expanse until he dwindled away to nothing.

In the vast, silent expanse of the barren marsh, time froze under that clear, cold morning sky. Nothing existed, not a single thing, except a boy standing alive, staring at a boy lying dead.

An eternity later, small figures appeared in the distance, growing larger as they ran toward us, gathering around the boat, among them a father and mother sobbing inconsolably as they bent over their only son. I knew him for only three hours, one alive and two dead. It was not apparent then, but in those three hours everything changed. The relevance and importance of everything shifted. Never again could I think a thought, ask a question, or hear an answer in quite the same way. Answers became less important, while questions grew in profusion. The need to know slowly dissolved into desire to understand. An inward eye began to open.

> Old Monkey and I don't remember if that is when our lifelong dialog

began in earnest. But we do often return to the events of those days when asking our endless questions about the nature of community and the nonmonetary exchange of value. In time, we came to realize that there can be no civil society worthy of the name without true community. In fact, there can be no life without it. All life, all of nature, all earthly systems, are closed cycles of nonmonetary exchanges of value, save only the gift of energy that comes from the sun. There can be no life whatever without balanced cycles of giving and receiving.

When we attempt to monetize all value we methodically replace the most effective system of exchanging value for the least effective. Because we cannot mathematically measure the nonmonetary, voluntary exchange of value, we cannot prove to our rational mind the efficiency of the whole or the parts. Nor can we engineer or control that which we cannot measure. Nonmonetary exchange of value frustrates our craving for perfect predictability and control that monetary exchange always promises but can never deliver.

When we monetize value, we have a means of measurement, however misleading, that allows us to calculate the relative efficiency of each part of the system. It doesn't occur to us that we are destroying an extremely effective system whose values we can't calculate in order to calculate the efficiency of an ineffective system. It doesn't occur to us that attempting to engineer mechanistic societies and institutions based on mathematical measurement may be fundamentally flawed. As the popular dictum declares, "What gets measured is what gets done." Perhaps that's precisely the problem.

Giving and receiving can't be measured in any meaningful sense. A gift with expectation is no gift at all. It is a bargain. In a nonmonetary exchange of value, giving and receiving is not a transaction. It is an offering and an acceptance. In nature, when a closed cycle of receiving and giving is out of balance, death and destruction soon arise. It is the same in society.

When money's rant is on, we come to believe that life is a right, which comes bearing a right, which is the right of getting. Life is not a right. *Life is a gift which comes bearing a gift which is the art of giving.* And community is the marketplace where we give our gifts and receive the gifts of others. When our individual and collective consciousness becomes receptive to new concepts of organization which that way of thinking suggests, societal organizations may yet come into harmony with the human spirit and the biosphere. Is that the voice that sings to us now? Is that distant song beginning to be heard throughout the land?

Like most young boys of the time, sports filled part of my life, although hampered by lack of aggression and aversion to the braggadocio, butt-slapping bonhomie of the locker room. The good fortune of a leg muscle damaged at football, along with a perceptive high school dean, brought me to debate with enough success to have some idea of both what it means and what it costs to excel. The state high school debate tournament, arguing alternate sides of a proposition, affirmative and negative, for sixteen consecutive wins and the state championship, brought a strange mixture of disbelief that it could have happened to me, and elation that it did.

It also brought a certificate from tiny Weber Junior College for an annual remission of tuition in the amount of $50. Incredible! I went. The first of my family to advance beyond high school. Ferol could not. She was the eleventh of twelve children raised in a three-room cottage on that small, hardscrabble farm. Only one child had gone beyond high school. Her father died of cancer during her final year of high school. In spite of twelve years of perfect 4.0 grades, she set aside dreams of university and took work as a seamstress in a clothing mill to support a widowed mother and younger sister.

At college, another dean put me in the way of the classics and some understanding of both the powers and limitations of the human mind. At the same time, increasing conflict with the college and other organizations inflamed a growing preoccupation with the paradoxes inherent in institutions and the people who hold power within them.

No doubt those early years in a small mountain town, the intense love of nature, and the shock of institutions began the slow, lifelong process of unraveling some of the paradoxes then tying my life in knots. The seeds of many of the perceptions that shaped my life, some now grown to convictions, were planted then. Events of those high school and college days remain much more vivid and clear than the embryonic thoughts then in gestation. Sharp among them is college graduation.

***

It is 1949. Officials of the tiny, two-year Weber Junior College are ambitious for increased stature as a four-year school, with a new campus. They are obsessed with impressing the legislature about the ability of the institution and the acumen of its products. The graduation ceremony is planned with meticulous care to impress a plethora of state officials who are to attend.

At commencement, my parents, numerous relatives, and Ferol, the love of my life, are in the packed auditorium to watch the first member of the family to attend college receive an AA degree. Graduates line up in the corridor outside, waiting their turn to cross the stage. Far to the rear someone yells, "Hey, Hock!" Thinking there is ample time, I bolt from the line for a reunion with friends who graduated the previous year. We are rudely interrupted by officials racing down the hall hurling accusations of egregious error and malignant intent for failure to appear as my name was called, over—and over—and over again to an empty stage and ghastly silence. They insist I make an appearance at the end of the line. Nooo way! One thing I *have* learned is to let bad enough alone. I slip away into the night, later to face the utter devastation of my parents and listen sullenly as my father snaps out the inevitable homily, "Well, there's no point in being stupid unless you can show it."

Thus, at twenty, newly married, unemployed, eager to learn but averse to being taught, emerged an absurdly naive, idealistic, young man—an innocent lamb hunting the lion of life. The hungry lion was swift to pounce.

Chapter Three

The Bloodied Sheep

> *Begin the morning by saying to thyself, I shall meet the busybody, the ungrateful, arrogant, deceitful, envious, unsocial. All these things happen to them by reason of their ignorance of what is good and evil.*
> —Marcus Aurelius Antonius

> *A society of sheep must in time beget a government of wolves.*
> —Bertrand de Jouvenal

In the summer of 1951, the lamb fell into a job at a small, floundering branch office of a consumer finance company. Within months, the manager departed and his lot fell to the lamb. Protected by remoteness, anonymity, and insignificance, four lambs, whose average age was twenty, trashed the company manual, ignored commandments, and did things as common sense, conditions, and ingenuity combined to suggest. Within two years, business tripled and the office was leading the company in growth, profit, and quality of business. Anonymity was gone and the blind fists of corporate power and orthodoxy began pounding for conformity. How much better the lambs could do if they conformed to central mandates. Even if they could be trusted with freedom to use their ingenuity, others could not. Exceptions could not be made without risking anarchy.

It was too much for a lamb already dreaming of greener pastures. He transferred to another division and slipped away to open a new office in a small, remote Oregon town, hoping that the pressure to conform was an aberration of former division management, not the true nature of the company. There, the pattern repeated itself. Using the same iconoclastic concepts and ideas, the new office was in the black by the third month, with business and profit increasing rapidly. It soon attracted the iron fist of corporate power and the itchy fingers of centralized bureaucracy. Confrontation with superiors grew frequent and intense.

In little more than a year came an "invitation" to visit the head office, where a transfer, skillfully veiled as a promotion, was arranged, ostensibly to handle branch development companywide. Three weeks later, on the twelfth floor of a gray, granite headquarters in a maelstrom of smog, traffic, and noise in the heart of Los Angeles, I was taken in tow by a charming man, Dick Simmons, an experienced employee in the marketing department, who was to familiarize me with the work. He was extremely literate. Exceptional intelligence and perception lay behind the literacy, and more than a little cynicism. He detested his job. We swiftly became friends.

Several weeks into the work, a summons came to step into the office of Brown, head of the marketing division, a diminutive, rotund fellow, pleasant enough, though pompous with subordinates and unctuous with superiors. Visitors, he told me solemnly, were occasionally confused about location of the senior executives' offices.

I was to attend to the matter and keep him informed.

Back in the office shared with Simmons, I asked for the name of sign companies with whom we customarily dealt.

"How do you intend to handle it?" he asked.

"Call a sign company, see what's available in brass, either freestanding or wall-hung, and have it installed," I replied. His hands went up in mock horror as he came down hard on every other word. "That will *never* do. You've been assigned a *project.* It will already be in the department project *control log,* flagged as important because it involves *senior executives.* Important projects *always take time.*"

"Yeah, sure, Dick, funny, funny," I replied, reaching for the telephone. His hand closed over mine.

"Am I not responsible for your indoctrination? Trust me. This will be fun, and you'll learn something as well." At lunch he explained.

"What you don't understand is that in companies like this, procedure is more important than purpose, and method more important than results." He carefully went over a list of officers, deciding on those who would be most likely to have an opinion on signs, and how to make an innocuous approach.

During the weeks to follow I received a fascinating education about both human nature and the nature of organizations. Bored to death and disillusioned with the company, one of the most intelligent people I had ever met casually extracted opinions about "the sign problem" from various officers, each opinion different and duly admired by him. I listened as he told Brown about "the sign problem" and aroused concern that no one "upstairs" be offended by what we did. He obtained diverse sketches, samples, and prices from suppliers, exposing them to officers in idle moments to elicit conflicting opinion and avoid decision. Brown's inquiries were skillfully turned aside with allusions to things "going well," or "about wrapped up," then digression to other subjects.

Fascinated, I watched as he manipulated situation after situation. He suggested a story for the company magazine about executive secretaries, causing a muddle of childish maneuvers by middle managers over who would be identified as "executive" by inclusion of their secretary and who insulted by exclusion. He organized a move to new quarters and induced months of bickering over allocation of space, layouts, furnishings, and windows. Not once was a lie told or a person misled. Simmons had more integrity and skill than that. He simply left murky minds unclarified and petty minds free to fuss.

Caught up in a bureaucratic command-and-control organization that would not allow him to use his ability constructively on substantive matters, he skillfully honed it on complicating trivial matters to no end at all other than his own amusement. The difference between Simmons and millions of others trapped in mechanistic, industrial age organizations is that he chose to be undeceived, either by self or others. He refused to demean his talent by not using it to the maximum, even for trivial ends.

He soon left the company and the world of business, quietly determined there must be a place where he could use his ability constructively among kindred spirits. I hope he found it.

***

I have never forgotten Simmons. Countless times over the years I have asked diverse groups of people to reflect very carefully on their work within organizations and to make a simple balance sheet. How much time, energy, and ingenuity did they spend obeying senseless rules and procedures that had little to do with the results they were expected to achieve? How much did they devote to circumventing those rules and procedures in order to do something productive with the remainder? How much was wasted interpreting such rules and enforcing them on others? How much time and talent did they simply withhold due to frustration and futility? It's a rare person who arrives at a sum less than 50 percent. Eighty is not uncommon.

A few years ago, I was asked to spend three days in no-holds-barred discussion of chaordic concepts in a major U.S. Army command. The first day was with the Audie Murphy Club, the best and brightest noncommissioned officers on the lowest rungs of the hierarchy. The second day was with senior commissioned officers of the command, and the third with sergeant majors; grizzled veterans on the top rung of the noncommissioned ladder charged with the day-to-day operation of the Army.

The young noncoms were apprehensive when asked to make the assessment of wasted time, energy, and ingenuity. It took considerable reassurance before they would accept that they could safely speak of such things. After considerable discussion and some thought, the estimates emerged. They ranged from 45 to 85 percent of time spent unproductively.

The senior commissioned officers were more solemn and deliberate but gradually got into the spirit of it. Their estimates were lower—ranging from 20 to 40 percent. Not surprising, since people with power to write and enforce rules rarely spend much time following them. The third day was the surprise.

The sergeant majors didn't take long to make the assessment. Some were as low as 5 percent, none above 20. I pointed out the discrepancy between the three groups and asked for an explanation. The toughest-looking cookie in the crowd looked through me as though I was the dumbest recruit to crawl from under a rock and roared,

"Hell, that's easy. We been gittin' around dumb rules all our lives, and we damned well ought to know how to do it without wastin' time. If a new rule comes down, it don't take ten minutes to figure out how to look good and still do things our way. The young pups haven't learnt how yet, and the brass is too busy tryin' to get promoted to care." Raucous laughter.

"Well, how do you do it? I'd like to know. Can I get a copy of the sergeant major's manual that explains it?" More laughter.

"There ain't no manual. Any sergeant major calls me and needs something, he gets it, no questions asked or answered. I need something and call another sergeant major, I get it. Same deal."

"OK, but you can't con a country boy. There's more to it than that. How can I find out what really happens?" Laughter again.

"No problem. Go to the sergeant major war college. Don't worry too much about classes. Take plenty of beer money and don't expect much sleep. If the bunch gets to like you and you're not too dumb you'll learn plenty."

"Sounds like there are two armies. The official Army and the real one. The explicit and the implicit organization. What might happen if the two ever came together?"

"Hell, I don't know about that explicit, implicit crap but I do know the Army. It's been this way since war was a pup. Ain't none of us gonna live long enough to see it change." One look around the room is enough to convince me that knowing more about the real army will have to wait. No way could I hold my own on a beer bust with these boys.

Unfortunately, what the sergeant majors intuitively knew, what Simmons was trying to teach, the lamb was not then ready to learn. It took him decades to synthesize the lesson. In industrial age organizations, purpose slowly erodes into process. Procedure takes precedence over product. *The doing of the doing is why nothing gets done.* Simmons had elevated the doing of the doing to an art form until virtually nothing got done.

At twenty-five, for all his rebellious, unorthodox ways, the lamb was too naive, too well-indoctrinated, too enamored of rising in the company to see the realities. He thought he saw a bitter, brilliant man damaging a decent company. What he did not see was a mechanistic, command-and-control company demeaning and discouraging a capable man.

The lamb stepped eagerly into the jaws of the beast. He wanted to believe in the company. He wanted it to be different. He wanted to make it better. It's an old, old story. The lamb was determined to change the company; the company was determined to corral the lamb. It was no contest. Within the year, a badly mauled lamb was out the door, much wiser in the ways of hierarchal, command-and-control organizations, and the people who hold power within them.

> Old Monkey Mind and I have long puzzled where mechanistic organizational concepts originated, and why we are so blind to their reality. Their genesis reaches back to Aristotle, Plato, and even beyond. However, it was primarily Newtonian science and Cartesian philosophy that fathered those concepts, giving rise to the machine metaphor. That metaphor has since dominated our thinking, the nature of our organizations, and the structure of industrial society to a degree few fully realize. It declared that the universe and everything in it, whether physical, biological, or social, could only be understood as clock-like mechanisms composed of separable parts acting on one another with precise, linear laws of cause and effect. It asserted that if we could dissect and understand all the parts and the laws governing them, we could reconstruct the world and all therein into predictable, controllable mechanisms,

presumably much more to our liking than the world had ever been.

For nearly three centuries we have worked diligently to structure society in accordance with that concept, believing that with ever more reductionist scientific knowledge, ever more specialization, ever more technology, ever more efficiency, ever more linear education, ever more rules and regulations, ever more hierarchal command and control, we could learn to engineer organizations in which we could pull a lever at one place, get a precise result at another, and know with certainty which lever to pull or for which result. Never mind that human beings must be made to behave as cogs and wheels in the process.

For more than two centuries, we have been engineering those institutions and pulling the levers. Rarely, very rarely, have we gotten the expected results. What we have gotten is all too obvious: obscene maldistribution of wealth and power, a crumbling ecosphere, and collapsing societies.

Just as the machine metaphor was the father of today's organizational concepts, the industrial age was the mother. Together, they dominated the evolution of all institutions. The unique processes of the age of handcrafting were abandoned in favor of mechanistic, command-and-control organizations. To produce huge quantities of uniform goods, services, knowledge, *and people,* those organizations amassed resources, centralized authority, routinized practices, and enforced conformity. This created a class of managers expert at reducing variability and diversity to uniform, repetitive, assembly-line processes endlessly repeated with ever-increasing efficiency. Thus, the industrial age became the age of managers.

It also became the age of the physical scientist, whose primary function was to reduce holistic ways of understanding to specialized knowledge through uniform, repetitive, laboratory processes endlessly repeated with ever-increasing precision. In time, universities obtained an oligopoly on accreditation and production of both classes.

It has led to one of those immense paradoxes of which the universe is so infinitely capable, one that is having profound societal effect. The highest levels of management in all organizations, commercial, political, social, and educational, are now formed of an interchangeable, cognitive elite with immense self-interest in preserving existing forms of organization and the ever-increasing concentration of power and wealth that they inevitably bring.

At the same time, those organizations are spawning an incredible array of scientific and technological innovation; immense engines of change that create enormous diversity and complexity in the way people live, work, and play. This, in turn, demands radically different concepts of organization that can more equitably distribute power and wealth, unshackle human ingenuity, and restore harmony between societal organizations, the human spirit, and the ecosphere.

The essential thing to remember is not that we became a world of expert managers and specialists, but that the nature of our expertise became the creation and management of uniformity and efficiency, while the need has become the understanding and coordination of variability and complexity, the very process of change itself.

It is not complicated. The nature of our organizations, management, and scientific expertise is not only increasingly irrelevant to our enormous economic, societal, and environmental problems, it is a primary cause of them.

Loss of the job was a crushing experience. Ferol and I were friendless in a massive city we hated, breathing air so polluted it seared the eye and blotted out everything beyond a few blocks—smog so thick we could see the bluish haze within our apartment. We had money for a month's groceries, no savings, considerable debt, two toddlers, and another baby about to be born. Pride prevented mentioning our plight to relatives, let alone seeking their help. We had been raised to believe that shame was the companion of need, and pride the companion of self-sufficiency. We had worked for clothes and spending money since we were ten, thought nothing of it, in fact, derived our sense of self-worth from doing so. "Root, hog, or die" had set the tenor of our days.

One event is seared in memory. The feeling returns as sharp as a throbbing tooth. A few days after the severance, we were desperate to know what to do. We had no idea when I might find a job or receive another paycheck. We agreed I must apply for unemployment. The next morning, deeply depressed, I drove through massive traffic and blinding smog to the nearest unemployment office. A line of people extended out the door and down the sidewalk.

Sitting in the car across the street, looking carefully at the faces of the people, I could not make myself open the door. One moment, I imagined myself in the line, the next, explaining to a concerned wife why I had not done so. I told myself that refusal to get out of the car was ridiculous, just false pride. I was entitled to the compensation. The feelings would probably vanish as soon as the application was filled out and I'd realize how silly such feeling were. *But I could not get out of the car.* Something deep inside said, "No! Take me there and I will die." Sick at heart, I drove slowly home to explain to a bewildered, pregnant young mother of two that entering that line was something I could not do. I did not know why then. Still don't.

The next morning I began a frantic search for work; any kind, anywhere, doing anything. Within the month, a miserable job at pitiful pay appeared. I grabbed it, giving us momentary breathing room. We were determined never again to be in such a vulnerable position. We swore that, with the possible exception of a home mortgage, we would never again have more debt than cash in the bank. Within a month, I took two more miserable jobs. None of the three required regular hours or confinement. The sprawling city was an advantage. I could work three jobs without any employer knowing of the others. It is amusing now to remember how we shredded every credit card in our possession, swearing never to have another. And for the next fourteen years, we did not. Be careful! Vengeful spirits have an affinity for oaths.

With Herculean effort, we paid our debts in a year and a half and put a small sum in the bank. I abandoned two jobs to concentrate on the best of the three, a tiny investment company in serious trouble due to corrupt management, since departed. The sole owner, a wealthy, thin-lipped, dour man, refused much in the way of salary but gave solemn assurance of freedom to use unorthodox methods and a substantial share of the profits if success followed. He kept the first promise.

Five years later, the lamb sat down with the owner to divide a handsome profit from the sale of a successful company, only to come face-to-face with naked greed and an astonishing display of accounting and contractual legerdemain. Although worth millions from a variety of businesses, he claimed that the profit he had promised to share must include years of losses that preceded my arrival. Therefore, there was no profit to share, even though the company fetched a huge premium when sold. He was adamant. If the lamb didn't like it, he could sue.

It was a severe dilemma. Throughout his years in the financial services business, the lamb had strong aversion to litigation, taking great pride in never repossessing mortgaged property without the customer's consent and never suing a customer to collect a debt or enforce a contract. Everything had been accomplished by collaboration and persuasion. It was a defining moment.

It was no longer a lamb, but no less a bloodied sheep, that looked deeply into those dead, expressionless eyes, drew a deep breath, and with a tinge of pity and a mountain of contempt softly said, "Keep the money. You apparently need it more than I do!"

The dead eyes did not blink. The thin lips never moved. The expressionless face was frozen. The beast, avarice, had devoured him completely. The sheep turned and walked out the door. They never saw or heard from one another again.

***

The sheep wandered north to Seattle to supervise the entry of a financial conglomerate into the consumer lending business. Don't hold your breath. Yes, it happened again: conflict between iconoclastic, innovative concepts of organization and management, and the iron fists of corporate power and orthodoxy, and with the same, painful result. Just another hunk of unemployed mutton bruised and bleeding on the sidewalk.

After sixteen years of unorthodox management and unblemished results, the sheep, by the standards of industrial age command-and-control organizations, was a failure. In truth, those with whom the sheep battled and lost were not without merit. The words they used to inflict so many wounds were not without some justification: "stubborn, opinionated, unorthodox, rebellious." The power of those words to wound came from elements of truth each contained; their weakness from the fact that none contained the whole of it. The sheep's unorthodox ways and inability to swallow whole and fully practice the gospel of industrial age management were seen as invitations to battle.

It would be a comfort now to claim that the sheep never accepted or practiced industrial age beliefs and practices, but it would be a lie. He did so often and well. But that was also part of the learning, for the aftermath inevitably brought distress and shame for the damage inflicted on self and others.

During those years the sheep was torn apart by internal conflict. He was filled with desire for acceptance in the world as he found it, for his piece of the American dream. He wanted to believe and belong; to rise to a place among the powerful, rich, and famous. But he was also filled with a multitude of things he would not do to get there. Side by side with a compelling desire to excel in the world as he found it was equal desire to behave in accordance with the world as he wished it to be. Shoulder to shoulder with desire for power, fame, and fortune was longing for solitude and contemplation. Hand in hand with the urge to excitement and action was the call to contemplation and beauty.

The sheep did not fully realize how thoroughly he was being torn apart by a society that was methodically pulling itself apart, or how rapidly it was pulling apart the biosphere. Nor did he see clearly who was doing the pulling, or why. But he felt the pain and saw it everywhere around him. And he was slowly learning.

Throughout the sixteen years of successful business failure, the sheep continued to read avariciously—poetry, philosophy, biography, history, biology, economics, mythology—anything and everything that satisfied his curiosity about connectedness and relationship. He mastered nothing, nor did he wish to, but new ways of seeing old things began to emerge and new patterns slowly revealed themselves. The preoccupation with organizations and the people who hold power within them became an obsession. It was then, in the 1960s, out of the maelstrom of experience, study, and stress, that the three questions emerged, softly at first, then more demanding and compelling.

Why are organizations, everywhere, whether political, commercial, or social, increasingly unable to manage their affairs?

Why are individuals, everywhere, increasingly in conflict with and alienated from the organizations of which they are part?

Why are society and the biosphere increasingly in disarray?

The vague shape of some answers had begun to form, but the sheep had no idea what to do with them. Sheared, bloodied, and once again unemployed, he lost heart and wandered into a slough of despond.

Chapter Four

Retirement on the Job

How can a part know the whole? Man is related to everything that he knows. And everything is both cause and effect, working and worked upon, mediate and immediate, all things mutually dependent.
—Blaise Pascal

For prosperity doth best discover vice, and adversity doth best discover virtue.
—Sir Francis Bacon

It was in 1965 that the heart went out of me. Four years before, partially from concern we would never be able to educate three children on my earnings alone and partially to fulfill a thwarted dream, Ferol had decided she would begin university.

With three young children, a heavily mortgaged house, no job, little money in reserve, and Ferol in her final year at university, it was impossible to stay out of a dismal swamp of depression. Day after day, I walked the woods in misting Northwest rain. My constant companion was an overwhelming feeling of failure. What was wrong with me? Why constant inability to climb the corporate ladder? Why continual conflict with superiors? Extraordinary effort and exceptional results had come to nothing. It seemed impossible to act consistent with my beliefs and succeed in the corporate world. Yet, there seemed no way to escape from it without putting the welfare of family at risk. That I could not do.

Ferol was well on the way to a degree in education and speech and hearing therapy. Our children were doing well in school. We liked the Pacific Northwest. Another move was foolish. We made a firm decision. Ferol would obtain her degree and take a job helping children with speech and hearing impairments. I would make no more effort to climb the corporate ladder.

There would be no more intense commitment to work. Instead, I would take up the most common career in modern organizations, "retirement on the job."

My victim would be one of the local banks where a modest living could be had at the cost of a pleasant demeanor, conformity and fractional ability or effort. There would be no cheating. A creditable job would be done. But they would get no great bargain. Henceforth, my life would be family, books, oil painting, gardening and nature. I began looking.

The Seattle First National Bank was disheartening. Endless, inane forms to fill out. Interminable interviews with officers housed in a rabbit warren of offices in a pretentious, high-rise building. Years of interviewing people for loans had left me skilled at extracting information. It was not difficult to induce several officers to depart from programmed praise of the bank and confide a litany of complaints.

The National Bank of Commerce was different. On the fourth floor of a modest building, elevators opened into a large, open space with windows across one wall. After stating my business to a gracious receptionist, I was quickly greeted by a man who rose from one of several desks spread across the room, Ron McDonald, senior vice president in charge of personnel. Soft spoken and pleasant, he ushered me into a tastefully furnished sitting room. We were soon in a deep conversation ranging far beyond banking and finance. This was not an interview; it was an interesting conversation.

In a quiet way, he made it plain that although the bank filled management positions from within, it was not a sacrosanct policy. It was merely a sensible thing to do. Within the hour, after asking if I had time to meet the president of the bank, he escorted me to another of the desks in the open room. A tall, thin man with a kind face and shy smile rose to greet me.

"Dee, this is Maxwell Carlson. Max, this is Dee Hock. Dee has an interest in the bank. I thought you two should meet." McDonald excused himself and I enjoyed a pleasant hour with Maxwell

Carlson. It was, once again, easy to forget my need of a job and become engrossed in conversation. An hour later, I left with nothing but assurance they would reflect on our discussions. I was certain nothing would come of it, but such gracious treatment was heartening.

Ron McDonald's call was unexpected and perplexing. There were no open positions commensurate with my experience at the bank. They had no idea when there might be. However, they felt the people at the bank might enjoy working with me, and I with them. They would be happy to have me join the bank. We could get acquainted through temporary assignments. In time, something consistent with my experience and interest might be found. No title was offered. No promises were made. The salary was little more than half of that to which I was accustomed. Not a scrap of paper had been filled out. Not a test had been taken.

But whoa Nellie! Back up a minute. For the first time in sixteen years, there would be nothing to manage. There would be no title. There would be no assurances of what the future might hold. At thirty-six, I would be a trainee, a nobody. We couldn't live on the salary. If a significant job and better salary did not come within a year, our savings would be gone. *But I really liked these decent people.*

With hand over the telephone mouthpiece, the circumstances were quietly conveyed to Ferol. She urged me to rely on my feelings about the people, not salary or position. For the first time, I abandoned logic, tossed old barren reason in the trash, and made a career decision on intuitive feeling and faith. A deep breath!

"Yes, I will be pleased to join the Bank." A day later I was having second thoughts. Retirement on the job was not going to be all that I had hoped. The burdens of loss of identity, uncertainty, and inadequate income would be added to depression and gnawing self-doubt. The flames of self-respect guttered, but they didn't wink out. I decided to stick with the decision.

***

The next nine months were worse than imagined. Shunted from one department to another—the credit department, a branch office, the real estate department, the commercial loan department—and given little of substance to do, there was nothing to challenge mind or body. People were kind and considerate, but they didn't know what to make of the situation, let alone what to do with such a stranger. My days were filled with menial work that I could have done in my sleep. This was retirement on the job with a vengeance. But it was not without compensation. It brought time to read, reflect on the past sixteen years, and dive even deeper into the obsession with organizations and the people who hold power within them.

> Old Monkey Mind and I found ourselves exploring simple words we thought we knew well, such as lead and follow. They were not so simple after all. The more we thought, the more we began to understand our constant conflict with institutions. As

that year passed, and many years to follow, it became increasingly clear.

leader\\'le-d^r\\ A word used to describe so many different forms of behavior that it has become relatively meaningless. A favored definition of the author, attributed to a centuries-old Scottish dictionary, will be used throughout this story. **Lead**\\'led\\ to go before and show the way

Leader presumes follower. Follower presumes choice. One who is coerced to the purposes, objectives, or preferences of another is not a follower in any true sense of the word, but an object of manipulation. Nor is the relationship materially altered if both parties accept the dominance and coercion. The terms *leader* and *follower* imply the continual freedom and independent judgment of both. A true leader cannot be bound to lead. A true follower cannot be bound to follow. The moment they are bound, they are no longer leader or follower. If the behavior of either is compelled, whether by force, economic necessity, or contractual arrangement, the relationship is altered to one of superior/subordinate, manager/employee, master/servant, or owner/slave. All such relationships are materially different than leader/follower.

Educed behavior is the essence of leader/follower. Compelled behavior is the essence of all the others. Where behavior is compelled, there lies tyranny, however petty. Where behavior is educed, there lies leadership, however powerful.

educe\eh-duse\ A marvelous word seldom used or practiced, meaning, "to bring or draw forth something already present in a latent, or undeveloped form."

It can be contrasted with **induce**, too often used and practiced, meaning, "to prevail upon; move by persuasion or influence—to impel, incite, or urge."

Educe will appear often in this story.

Leadership is not necessarily constructive, ethical, or open. It is entirely possible to educe destructive, malign behavior and do so by corrupt means. Therefore, clear, meaningful purpose and compelling, ethical principles evoked from and shared by all participants should be the essence of every institution.

The problem is how to ensure that those who lead are constructive, ethical, open, and honest. The solution is to follow only those who behave in that manner. It comes down to both an individual and collective sense of where and how people choose to be led. In a very real sense, followers lead by choosing where to be led. Where a community will be led is inseparable from the shared values and beliefs of the individuals of which it is composed.

True leaders are those who enable the unconscious values and beliefs of every member of the community to emerge, transmitted and consciously shared—who epitomize in their own behavior the general sense of the community—who symbolize, legitimize, and strengthen behavior in accordance with the sense of the community—who enable that which is trying to happen to come into being. The true leader's behavior is educed by the behavior of every individual who chooses where and how they will be led.

The important thing to remember is not that leading can be either constructive or destructive depending on purpose, principles, and method, but that true leadership is based on educed behavior and has an affinity for good, while false leadership is based on compelled behavior and has an affinity for evil.

Over the years, I've enjoyed discussions with hundreds of groups at every level in different organizations about any subject of interest to them. Nearly always it is management:

either aspirations to it, dissatisfaction with it, or confusion about it. To avoid ambiguity, I ask each person to describe the single most important responsibility of any manager. The incredibly diverse responses always have one thing in common. All are downward looking—having to do with exercise of authority; with selecting employees, motivating them, training them, appraising them, organizing them, directing them, and controlling them. That perception is completely mistaken. In chaordic organizations it must be stood on its head, as it should in all organizations.

The first and paramount responsibility of anyone who purports to manage is to manage self—one's own integrity, character, ethics, knowledge, wisdom, temperament, words, and acts. It is a never-ending, difficult, oft-shunned task. The reason is not complicated. It is ignored precisely because it is incredibly more difficult than prescribing and controlling the behavior of others.

Without exceptional management of self, no one is fit for authority no matter how much they acquire. In truth, the more authority they acquire the more dangerous they become. The management of self should have half our time and the best of our ability. In the process, the ethical, moral, and spiritual elements of managing self are inescapable.

Asked to identify the second responsibility of any manager, again people produce a bewildering variety of opinions, again downward-looking. Another mistake. The second responsibility is to manage those who have authority over us: bosses, supervisors, directors, regulators, ad infinitum. In an organized world, there are always people with authority over us. Without their support, how can we follow conviction, exercise judgment, use creative ability, achieve constructive results, or create conditions by which others can do the same? Devoting a quarter of our time and ability to management of superiors is not too much.

Asked for the third responsibility, people become a bit uneasy and uncertain, yet their thoughts remain on subordinates. Mistaken again. The third responsibility is to manage one's peers—those over whom we have no authority and who have no authority over us—associates, competitors, suppliers, customers. Without their respect and confidence, little can be accomplished. Peers can make a small heaven or hell of our life. Is it not wise to devote at least a fifth of our time and ingenuity to managing peers?

Asked for the fourth responsibility, people have difficulty coming up with an answer. They are now wary of thinking downward. They eventually again focus on managing subordinates for there is nothing else left. This time they are right. The fourth responsibility is to manage those over whom we have authority. The instinctive response is that one's time will be consumed managing self, superiors, and peers. There will be little or no time left to manage subordinates. Exactly!

Select people of good character, introduce them to the concept, go before and show them how to practice it, and encourage them to educe the process from their so-called subordinates. If those over whom you have authority properly manage themselves, manage you, manage their peers and replicate the process with those they employ, what is there to do but see they are properly recognized, rewarded, and stay out of their way? *It is not making better people of others that management is about. It's about making a better person of self. Income, power, and title have nothing to do with that.*

The obvious question then always erupts. How can you manage bosses, peers, regulators, associates, customers? The answer is equally obvious. You cannot. But can you understand them? Can you persuade them? Can you motivate them? Can you disturb them, influence them, forgive them? Can you set them an example? Of course you can, provided only that you have properly managed yourself. Eventually the proper word will emerge. Can you **lead** them?

There are no rules and regulations so rigorous, no organization so hierarchal, no bosses so abusive that they can prevent such use of your energy, ability, and ingenuity. They may make it more difficult, but they can't prevent it. The real power is yours, not theirs. Forget management! Strike the word from your dictionary! That's not what I've been writing about at all.

Lead yourself, lead your superiors, lead your peers, employ good people, and free them to do the same. All else is trivia.

If you move down this path, there is no reason to be discouraged by shortcomings. Success, while it may provide encouragement, build confidence, and be joyful indeed, often teaches an insidious lesson—to have too high an opinion of self. It is from failure that amazing growth and grace so often come, provided only that one can recognize it, admit it, learn from it, rise above it, and try again. True

> leadership presumes a standard quite beyond human perfectibility and that is quite alright, for joy and satisfaction are in the pursuit of an objective, not in its realization. The only question of importance is whether one constantly rises in the scale.

Retirement on the job at the National Bank of Commerce was not all reflection. One day stands out. I had been sent to a suburban office to learn branch banking. The manager turned me over to a crusty woman who was to train me as a teller. The very soul of courtesy to customers and a genius at her work, she was, nevertheless, of choleric disposition, not at all improved by tenuous relations with men. When she turned away from attending to a customer, she could be a veritable bear, and I was raw meat. At the close of a trying day she brought me to my knees.

The branch was closed at the end of the day and empty of customers. The lady and I could not balance the day's receipts and disbursements. More than an hour passed as we checked everything time and again without success. Clearly, this was not something to which she was accustomed. The likely source of the problem was standing at her side. She turned to me with an order, beneath which there appeared a glint of sadistic humor.

"It must be a lost deposit. Go down to the basement, look through the garbage, and see if you can find it." Speechless, I descended to the basement visualizing a single can of crumpled paper. There, neatly in a row, were eleven fifty-five-gallon cans stuffed with far more than paper—cigarette butts, ashes, chewing gum, rotting remnants of leftover lunches, and other disgusting detritus.

My neck grew hot with anger. This ripped it! After managing businesses since the age of twenty, this was preposterous! Language learned working my sixteenth summer in a slaughterhouse poured out. Damned if I was going to spend the night grubbing though garbage for a lost deposit, and double-damned if a snotty bank teller was going to order me about, and triple-damned if I was going to spend another day at the National Bank of Commerce.

At the worst and the best of times, the ridiculous has always tickled my funny bone. As anger and expletives diminished, laughter came pouring out. Sure, I'd been climbing the corporate ladder for sixteen years, but before that I'd done stoop labor, picked beans, thinned sugar beets, mucked out dairy barns, cleaned offal, and dumped slop. I'd been proud to be a boy able to do a man's work and never felt demeaned by a minute of it. Hell, I'd worked for sadistic bosses who made this woman look like the tooth fairy. Words spoken a thousand times to employees came swinging back to clout me in the back of the head. *"There isn't any poor work; there's only work poorly done, poorly recognized, or poorly paid."*

Pride is pride. This work was not going to be poorly done. Off came coat, tie, and shirt as I upended the first can and dove into the garbage. If there was a lost deposit, I would find it if it took all night. Then, they'd learn what they could do with this *#X*X#* job.

As we worked in that dismal basement, Old Monkey and I were soon happily in the magical forest of fascinating questions. What is pride? How can there be such a thing as pride without humility? How can there be such a thing as humility without pride? Humility would be impossible to conceive without the notion of pride. One defines the other. They are integral, one and the same, different faces of the same coin. Were not both pride and humility dancing seamlessly through me then and there? What made me think of them as separate? What made me want to choose one and deny the other?

Was someone shuffling papers and making trash at an expensive desk in a luxurious room high up in an imposing building with a sign on the door saying "President" a superior form of humanity to someone sorting trash in the basement? Was his activity intrinsically "better"? Whence came the craving for one rather than the other?

> Where did all this superior, inferior nonsense come from? By what method could one possibly know? By what possible measurement and what standards could one judge the value of climbing a ladder of power, wealth, and fame, other than the pronouncements of those who lust after them? Could such desires amount to no more than a basement full of mental trash? Isn't all life a seamless blending of opposites? If so, why do we think to separate one thing from another and elevate it to the status of a deity? On and on the questions darted and whirled as time lost all dimension.

Two hours and ten cans later, my boss came down the stairs to take away my desired victory, smiling smugly as she said,

"I found the error. We're in balance. It wasn't a lost deposit after all." Had I been had by this diabolical woman? I could not know, but no matter. If I'd been had, it was a masterful piece of work. The next day, as we worked frantically in the teller's cage to keep up with a flood of customers, she casually turned. As though it were a rhetorical question, she abruptly said, "I need you to run down to the drug store and pick up a prescription for me. You can bring me a cup of coffee on your way back." I gave it to her like a man.

"Run your own #X*&#*X errands. I'm not your personal servant." She didn't take it like a woman, but gave it back in kind.

"And I'm not here to clean up your *X#*X# mistakes." We stood nostril to nostril, eyeball to eyeball, breathing fire as we stared each other down. Later, in a slack half hour, both defeated and laughing, we went on the errands together.

It did not seem so then, but now it seems a matter of perspective whether sorting trash in the basement of the branch was the high or low point in my retirement on the job at the National Bank of Commerce. The year provided ample time for reading and reflection, along with days wandering forests, mountains, and ocean shores. Better yet, was reconnection to the suppressed, yet incredible spirit and creativity of the managed—the many who day in, day out, do the ordinary work of the world from which the wealth, power, and fame of the few is extracted. These were my people. It was where I belonged, although I denied it then and longed to escape.

Years before, words by Emerson had leaped from the page to stick in my mind like a cocklebur in a long-haired dog. *"Everywhere you go you take your giant with you."* He was writing about the insatiable desire to escape the present and seek paradise in the new and different—new places, new stations in life, new possessions—a futile quest to escape self. No matter how hard I had tried to escape my giant, he always returned. The country kid, the two-room house, manual labor, no university degree, estrangement, a raging sense of inferiority. It was then that I had the guts to turn, look my giant in the eye and say,

"You're an ugly cuss and you scare the liver out of me, but if we're going to be forever linked we might as well get to know one another and live civilly together." My giant and I are not yet buddies, but we're working at it.

> Old Monkey and I did not find it difficult to test our growing belief that all else is trivia if you properly lead your self, lead your superiors, lead your peers, and free all employees to do the same. Reflect a moment on group endeavors of which you are observer rather than participant. If your interest runs to ballet, you can undoubtedly recall when the corps seemed to rise above the individual ability of each dancer and achieve a magical, seemingly effortless performance. If your interest runs to sports, the same phenomenon is apparent. Teams whose performance transcends the ability of individuals. The same phenomenon can be observed in the symphony, the theater, in fact, every group endeavor, including business and government.
>
> Every choreographer, conductor, and coach, or for that matter, corporation president, has tried to distill the essence of such

performance. Countless professors, consultants and other "experts" have joined in the effort to reduce to a mechanistic, measurable, controlled process that which causes the phenomenon. It has never been done and never will be. It is easily observed, universally admired, and occasionally experienced. It happens, but cannot be deliberately done. It is rarely long sustained but can be repeated. It arises spontaneously from the relationships, interaction, and convictions of those from whom it is composed. Some organizations seem consistently able to do so, just as some leaders seem able to cause it to happen with consistency, even within different organizations.

To be precise, one cannot speak of leaders who *cause* organizations to achieve superlative performance, for no one can *cause* it to happen. Leaders can only recognize and modify conditions that prevent it; perceive and articulate a sense of community, a vision of the future, a body of principle to which people are passionately committed, then encourage and enable them to discover and bring forth the extraordinary capabilities that lie trapped in everyone, struggling to get out.

Without question, the most abundant, least expensive, most underutilized, and constantly abused resource in the world is human ingenuity. The source of that abuse is mechanistic, industrial age, dominator organizations and the management practices they spawn.

In the deepest sense, distinction between leaders and followers is meaningless. In every moment of life, we are simultaneously leading and following. There is never a time when our knowledge, judgment, and wisdom are not more useful and applicable than that of another. There is never a time when the knowledge, judgment, and wisdom of another are not more useful and applicable than ours. At any time that "other" may be superior, subordinate, or peer.

Everyone is a born leader. Who can deny that from the moment of birth they were leading parents, siblings, and companions? Watch a baby cry and the parents jump. We were all leaders until we were sent to school to be commanded, controlled, and taught to do likewise.

People are not "things" to be manipulated, labeled, boxed, bought and sold. Above all else, they are not "human resources." We are entire human beings, containing the whole of the evolving universe. We must examine the concept of superior and subordinate with increasing skepticism. We must examine the concept of management and labor with new beliefs. We must examine the concept of leader and follower with new perspectives. Above all else, we must examine the nature of organizations that demand such distinctions with new consciousness.

It is true leadership; leadership by everyone; leadership in, up, around, and down this world so badly needs,

> *and dominator management it so sadly gets.*

Within days of my wrestling match with the garbage cans and confrontation with my crusty-lady boss, Maxwell Carlson leaves a message. He has something he would like to discuss with me. Well, here it comes. My vows of conformity and a pleasant demeanor have been broken and the consequences must be borne. No matter, for it was not the kind of retirement on the job I had imagined. What's one more failure? Just another arrow of confrontation stuck in my gizzard.

Mr. Carlson smiles and waves me toward the small conference room near his desk. When I am comfortably seated, he assumes his accustomed position, one leg wound around the other, toe of one foot hooked behind the ankle of the other, thumbs parked in the pockets on either side of his vest looking thoughtfully down. He is ever quick to the point.

"It was kind of you to arrange time to see me this morning. There are a few things happening at the bank which you may find interesting." It breaks my stride. Kind of me to see Mr. Carlson? Interesting things? Does he mean it? This is a strange way to begin a reprimand. I hold my tongue as he continues.

"Since you once lived in California, you are no doubt aware of the credit card program of the Bank of America. You also know that Seattle First National has entered the business with their Firstcard. A good many of our senior officers think credit cards are unsound, and I'm not certain I disagree with them. Nevertheless, Bank of America has decided to franchise BankAmericard and we have agreed to take a license. We would like to be in business within ninety days. Bob Cummings is to head the program. He is an experienced branch manager. However, he has no experience with credit cards and little with consumer lending. He could use your help. We would like to borrow you to assist him. What do you think?"

Silent thoughts flow swiftly. Is this some sort of disguised punishment—what a strange way to offer an assignment or induce acceptance—who is Cummings—ninety days is a ridiculously short time to launch such a venture—senior officers don't wish it well and will undercut it—I'm fed up with the bank anyway. Might as well get it over with. But how to say no to a kind, gracious man without offense? Candor begets candor.

"Mr. Carlson, there are a couple things you should know. I've been managing businesses since I was twenty and would be a terrible assistant anything. And I have absolutely no use for credit cards. All I had were destroyed fourteen years ago. I've not had one since and want none in the future." Well, that should take care of that! I'll soon be out the door. He reflects for a scant moment. A suppressed smile tugs at his face and wins. Grinning, he softly replies,

"Well, young man, if that won't bother you too much, I expect it won't bother me either. Why don't you have lunch with Mr. Cummings and see if the two of you can work it out?" What is left to be said after one has thrown their best verbal pitch and watched it effortlessly hit out of the ballpark?

It will be months before I realize Mr. Carlson never "promotes" anyone. He "borrows" them for new assignments so that they can withdraw without feeling a failure if the new situation is unsuitable. If it proves productive, titles and rewards soon follow.

But Cummings was something else again.

Chapter Five

The Zoo

*I experienced under the sun that
The race is not to the swift,
Nor the battle to the strong;
Wise men lack an income,
Prophets do not have riches,
The learned lack wealth,
And time and chance overtake them all.*

—Koheleth

Over a lunch of smoked oysters, Bob Cummings and I verbally circled and sniffed one another like two strange dogs deciding whether to fight or form a pack. We soon discovered four things in common. We didn't like one another. We didn't want the jobs we had been offered. We didn't know why we had been selected. We had high regard for Maxwell Carlson.

Bob had come up through the ranks of commercial lending at the National Bank of Commerce. He seemed a traditional, conservative branch manager. He believed that credit cards were nothing but another form of banking. The thought of being burdened with an assistant who was an unorthodox, consumer-credit outsider was appalling. I believed that credit cards were nothing but high-volume, unsecured, consumer lending. The thought of being burdened with a conservative banker boss was appalling. I knew it wouldn't work. Bob knew it wouldn't work.

In the end, it came down to Maxwell Carlson. Since we were both "borrowed" to get it started, either or both could walk away when the inevitable rupture occurred. Right now, Mr. Carlson had asked for our help. Neither of us could deny him that. We agreed to give it a shot.

Within two weeks, Bob and I were in San Francisco for training at the Bank of America Service Corporation, along with representatives of five other licensee banks. The first day left the two of us extremely uncomfortable. As the meeting droned through presentation after presentation, it all boiled down to "mass issue hundreds of thousands of unsolicited cards, sign every merchant in sight, and all will come right in the end." Questions were either brushed aside or answered with another marketing harangue. We were puzzled that the instructors were all marketing people, none of whom had experience in the Bank of America card operation. In the hotel that night, we shared our concerns.

"Bob, either I never learned anything about consumer credit in sixteen years or these people don't know what they are talking about. All they talk about is mass marketing, mass marketing, mass marketing. It's individuals who earn income and pay debt, not mobs." Bob was equally uncomfortable.

"I feel the same about their claims of how much traditional banking business we can get from issuing cards to consumers and signing merchants who are customers of other banks, then cross-selling them our bank services. When it's all over, I don't think much banking business will change hands." I was inclined to openly challenge the training, but Bob disagreed.

"I'm worried that we don't know enough to argue about what we're being told."

"Yes, but I'm more worried about what they may not be telling us. I learned a long time ago that listening to what people don't say is often more important that listening to what they do." A small light came on.

"Bob, I've met a couple of people in their card center. Why don't you attend the training sessions while I quietly disappear and dig into operation of the center? At night, we can compare notes and see if what we're being told by the service corporation squares with what's actually being done in their operating center, and if either makes sense." Bob agreed.

The next night as we shared experience of the day, little squared and less made sense. There was bad blood and limited communication between the BankAmericard center and the licensing corporation. They reported to different segments of the bank. Worse yet, the bank's own card center had no capacity to comply with rules prescribed in the licensing agreements. Our bank, The

National Bank of Commerce, had already made a public announcement of its BankAmericard program. It had a forty-year correspondent banking relationship with the Bank of America. Founders of both banks have been close friends. There was no way to reverse the decision our bank had made. Bob and I were in deep trouble.

On the flight home we cooked up a plan. The next day, in the midst of an airline strike, we set off across the country flying catch-as-catch-can to spend each day at a different credit card company, cramming ourselves with their diverse experience. There was something to learn from each, yet none fit our circumstances well enough to emulate completely. We made deals to share experiences in the months ahead. Within a single week, our original belief that the BankAmericard franchise would provide a well-marked, expeditious road to the future had been shattered by what we had learned.

***

There was no choice but to design our NBC BankAmericard program out of our collective experience, knowledge of our market, and what we could glean from the diverse experience of others. Most of the Bank of America training material went into the trash. Worse news began to pile up. There was no empty space in our bank building to house the operation, and none readily available in the vicinity. Preliminary calls to suppliers of imprinters, card stock, card embossers, point-of-sale material, and other essentials brought solemn warnings of shortages and limited capacity, along with pressure to order immediately. Were we being honestly advised or hustled? There was no way to know.

    The situation was screaming for the unorthodox concepts of organization and management in which I deeply believed, but had tried to suppress during my year of retirement on the job. I had come to know Bob fairly well in the preceding two weeks. His mind was quick. He was decisive. Lurking below the surface was a quirky sense of humor. Hints had come along that "Bob is not your traditional branch manager." Could I smell a closet rebel? Restraint went into the garbage can as I pleaded with Bob to abandon tradition, throw detailed planning to the winds, rely on a clear sense of direction, a few simple principles, common sense, trust in the ingenuity of people, and let the answers emerge.

"Bob, we only have ten weeks. We'll make endless mistakes. If they are mistakes of commission and we recognize them, they can be fixed. But there will be no remedy for mistakes of omission. You know banking and the Washington State market cold. I know consumer credit and unorthodox management. If we ask enough crazy questions, answers will emerge." It took little persuasion. He was quickly there.

The next day we picked up the telephone and ordered a thousand imprinters at $35 each. Another two calls, and we were on the hook for two hundred thousand plastic cards and several expensive card embossers. I don't remember the sum, but it was huge for the time and circumstances. The same day we commandeered the bank auditorium next to the cafeteria.

Within the week, we had rifled bank departments and storage warehouses for spare file cabinets, massing them on the stage. We "liberated" all the desks we could find, rented others, lining them end-to-end across the floor of the auditorium in rows four feet apart. Electrical and telephone cords were taped to the floor along the front edge of each row of desks. We "borrowed" all willing, unassigned employees, and all those who could be spared for ninety days, no questions asked. Ads went in the paper for credit analysts, merchant sales representatives, collectors, and other essential personnel not readily available in the bank. It wasn't quite send me "the wretched refuse of your teeming shores," but it was similar.

Within two weeks, the auditorium was a beehive of people, laughing, interviewing, ordering supplies, planning advertising, and attending to hundreds of other tasks. It was out of control. It was chaos. But bit by bit, order was emerging. Word had moved like lightning through the bank. No one passed on their way to lunch in the bank cafeteria without poking their head in the auditorium door to observe the frenzy, shaking their head, and laughing as they walked away. Within days, we were dubbed "The zoo." Not inappropriate, for it was pure lamb's milk and monkey's bananas.

Three days and you were trained. A week brought competence. Two weeks produced an "expert." A month made an "old hand." Hours became meaningless as the days swept by. Each week knocked 8 percent off the time to launch. We tried to keep the executive office informed but it was difficult, for we often surprised ourselves. We kept an eye out for the corporate iron fist. It rarely came down. When it did, we ducked. The staid old bank seemed unusually malleable. Either that or everyone was happy to stand aside while Cummings and Hock dove off the bridge into a few inches of water. We became blood brothers on a crusade. The zoo was only the beginning.

***

Within the month we are in the last of many grueling meetings across the state, in an effort to qualify 120,000 bank customers for credit cards within two weeks. In front of us are several dozen veteran commercial bankers, not at all thrilled with the notion that the bank is entering the credit card business. The room reeks of skepticism and hostility. By now, our act is well rehearsed.

Bob begins the meeting, grumbling about his new assignment, drawing on his credibility as a branch manager to gain sympathy and confidence. The veteran bankers are not reluctant to unload. "Ridiculous business—unconscionable to lead people into continual debt—our customers don't need or want credit cards—only irresponsible people use them—this is worse than financing cars—credit cards should be outlawed—the bank will lose its shirt." The litany pours out while we nod and sympathize. We've heard it all before. Suddenly, Bob throws both arms in the air and abruptly stops the tirade.

"Hold it! Hold it!" Knowing what is coming, I struggle to hold a straight face as he continues.

"Get out your wallets. Come on, all of you. That's right, get them out and lay them on the table. Now open them and take out everything other than checks and cash that you use to buy stuff—come on, out with them—all your charge cards—gas, merchandise, airline tickets, entertainment—all of them." The room begins to look like a giant poker game as cards cover the tables.

"Good! Now fan them in your hand like a deck of cards—go ahead—use both hands if you're having trouble. Good! Now hold them over your head." A few faces break into grins as the hands go up and they glance around the room. It looks like an overplanted flower garden in the summer sun. There is not an empty hand in the room.

"Wonderful! Now, while you hold them up, we'll listen as long as you want to talk about the evils of credit cards and the irresponsible people who use them!" The room erupts in laughter as arguments break out about who is the most reckless spender in the crowd.

"OK," Bob continues, "Now, let's get down to it and figure out how the National Bank of Commerce is going to enter the credit card business in a sensible, responsible way. You're the people who can make that happen, and we're going to rely on you."

We already know that every branch will come up with different but similar plans. Every officer with lending authority in each branch will work together in the evenings reviewing a computer printout of every checking account, savings account, and loan customer of the branch. A "yes" from any officer without dissent from any other officer and a card will be issued with no further investigation. A "no" without dissent and a card will not be issued. We will rely entirely on the integrity of our people and their knowledge of customers. If a customer is not well known one way or the other, a credit report will be drawn and a decision made later. Every customer selected will receive an advance mailing so that they can accept or decline a card.

We will make the same careful preparation for enrolling merchants. No major promotions outside the bank will be made until our own customers have been properly served. The results are spectacular. The people in each branch self-organize the work, and within the month, letters are on the way to 120,000 customers, offering them a card.

> As the ninety days we had been given to launch the card program flew by, Old Monkey and I never stopped thinking about the nature of organization. The Yakima Branch officers were only one of dozens of groups of people coming together, agreeing on things to be done, doing them, then dissolving into other sets of relationships. Nothing we were doing had any resemblance to the way the bank had operated before. Its traditional structure, processes, and procedures had little effect on what was happening. What is the essence or organization anyway? When Bob and I met over a plate of smoked oysters and agreed to work together, did that alone constitute an organization?
>
> Is it possible the most concise definition of organization is simply

"agreement"? Wherever there is need for agreement, there has to be either ambiguity or differing points of view, else there is nothing to agree about. There also has to be desire for clarity about and reconciliation of the differing views. When two people engage in such a process and "agree," is that the essence of organization, however small in scale and transitory in time? Agreement contains the essence of both difference and commonality. If there is no difference, there is nothing about which to agree. With agreement comes at least some degree of commonality. If two individuals meet and agree, the agreement contains the essence of organization. They are, no matter how briefly or for what purpose, "organized." Agreement also contains the essence of self-governance, for each must rely on the self-induced behavior of the other to act in accordance with the understanding.

Agreement is always dynamic, imperfect, and malleable. Language, with all its vagaries and nuances, is the primary tool with which to reach agreement. Its use is complicated by the fact that every word uttered or written is conditioned in the mind of the originator by one set of beliefs, emotions, expectations, and experiences, and conditioned in the mind of the recipient by quite another. Reaching and sustaining agreement is a continual process, as alive as the people involved. It does not admit of certainty or perpetuity, especially in the particulars. Relationships between even two people who live or work together is far too complex to allow agreement much beyond intent, sense of direction, and principles of conduct.

This reveals other essential elements of agreement, tolerance, trust, and mutual caring. One must accept that the behavior of another can never be reduced to the kind of specificity that science proposes and contracts attempt to provide, or that the behavior of another can ever conform entirely to any single understanding of words, sentences, and paragraphs. No agreement can provide for all particulars, and particulars will never conform to any agreement. Yet certainty and conformity are what present institutions, in fact, the whole of society, have been organized to try to create.

In the constructive sense of the word, governance can be based only on clarity of shared intent and trust in expected behavior, heavily seasoned with common sense, tolerance, and caring for others as fellow human beings. This is not to say that contracts, laws, and regulations do not serve a purpose. Rather, it is to point out that they can never achieve the mechanistic certainty and control we crave. Rules and regulations, laws and contracts, can never replace clarity of shared purpose and clear, deeply held principles about conduct in pursuit of that purpose.

Principles are never capable of ultimate achievement, for they presume constant evolution and change. "Do unto others as you would have others do unto you" is a true principle, for it says nothing about how it must be done. It presumes unlimited ability of people to evolve in accordance with their values, experience, and relations with others.

True governance is based on understanding that even simple societies are far too complex to expect agreement in the particular. Systems of self-governance, in the individual and at every scale beyond, are based on understanding that ordinances, orders, and enforcement deal with an absence of true governance. They are an attempt to compel the kind of behavior that organizations fail to educe. Ordinances, orders, and enforcement are simply different words for control, command, and tyranny. Force is the ultimate tool of tyranny. Those who rise in a tyrannical world are those least capable of self-governance, whether of themselves, or inducement of it in others, else they would not engage in tyranny. When they rise, it is axiomatic that self-governance will decline and government will gradually be for the benefit of the few and subjugation of the many. It will inexorably become destructive. Ultimately, there will be no limit to that destruction, for there appears to be no limit to the ability of science and the rational mind to create devices to alter or destroy all life forms and all aspects of the physical world.

There is no way to give people purpose and principles, yet there can be no self-organizing self-governance without them. The only possibility is to evoke a gift of self-governance from the people themselves. It is there that a true leader may be useful, perhaps even essential. There is a choice to be made. We now live in a world of such complexity, diversity, and multiplicity of scales that there is little possibility of achieving constructive, sustained governance with existing concepts of organization. People everywhere are growing desperate for renewed sense of community. Deeply held, commonly shared purpose and principles leading

> to new concepts of self-organization and governance at multiple scales from the individual to the global have become essential.

It is nearing the end of 1966, and we are but two weeks from launch, faced with major problems and no margin for failure. One hundred thousand card mailers in huge rolls arrived today, along with special machinery for feeding them into computer printers and cutting and folding them as they emerged. The printing contractor is standing to one side, admiring the gleaming new machinery he has installed to the front and back of the bulky printer.

To the side is the large mainframe of the IBM 1401 computer. A long row of tape drives, each as tall as a man, stare at us with plate-sized eyes of spooled magnetic tape. A labyrinth of cables connects them to punch-card readers that feed them and high-speed, mechanical printers each the size of three desks, which they in turn feed. Dozens of spools of magnetic tape lie waiting, filled with the names, addresses, and essential data of a hundred thousand bank customers who are to receive a small rectangle of blue-white-and-gold polyvinyl chloride emblazoned **National Bank of Commerce, BankAmericard.** I am awed, almost worshipful in this temple of technology. No one there can imagine that all the computing power in that room will, in three decades, reside in a five-pound laptop computer costing less than a thousand dollars.

We have carefully calculated the ten hours required to print, cut, and fold the card mailers. Processing of all other bank work has been suspended at great risk to give us sole use of the computers until seven in the morning—twelve hours. Two hours to spare. No more time available. It's now or never.

The grinding work of entering the card business over the past three months has occupied only part of my mind. Imagination is seething with what this all means to the world of organizations. It has led me into computer and programming classes, a few dozen books, and several "crazies" on the fringes of the computer world willing to share their dreams. Giving people another way to borrow money interests me not at all. What credit cards might become is something else again.

> As the machinery is being set up to print the mailers, Old Monkey and I drift into the world of imagination. What is the meaning of the marriage of money and computers? How does that meaning change if they get a bit polygamous and wed telephone lines, radio waves, television? Where does software fit in? What is the nature of money in computer memory? What is the difference between the "bone boxes" running about on every pair of shoulders in the computer room and the "black box" of the computer immobile on the computer floor? Aren't both processing information? Is there some cosmic beat to all this?
>
> Awareness rises. This whole thing is not about banks or merchants or credit or cardholders. It's not about data or information or computers. It's

> about connections! No, no, it's about more than connections. It's about massive change in interconnectivity. No, no, it's got to be deeper than that. It's about dissolution of the notion of boundaries between separate, connected things—it's about—it's about—it's about—there are no good words. Could it be about relationships and growth, about all things growing from one another and everything growing from some indefinable essence *that is,* about all things inseparably interrelated? Could it be about some flaw in the very concepts of separability, particularity, and linearity? Is there some analogy between the industrial machine age as an extension of muscle, and the computer age as an extension of mind and memory?

Old Monkey and I are rudely jerked back into the computer room. Something is sadly awry. The form-feeder cannot be synchronized with the printer. Both machines constantly jam. As mailers flow erratically from the printer, cutting and folding machinery slices some in half and crumples others. Technicians are bent over, heads and hands deep in the machinery. The supplier soon confesses. The whole setup is untested. They've never used it before, and it's an abysmal failure.

Bob and I walk away to a quiet corner near a supply closet to console one another. There is no possibility of another block of time on the computer. Without mailers by morning, the whole thing is off. How can we explain our failure to Maxwell Carlson, a hundred thousand customers waiting for their promised cards, and hundreds of merchants waiting for those customers? Our minds are racing in a hundred directions seeking a way out. Bob is leaning on the handle of a push broom.

Inspiration is often the child of desperation. Could he be leaning on the answer? We quickly unscrew the handle, rush to the stack of mailers and shove it through a roll. With a heave we lift it—might even be able to hold it for half an hour at a stretch, maybe more—or prop it up on cabinets. The broom handle makes a decent axle.

With a third person to guide forms into the computer and enough three-person crews, it might work. Other crews could wind mailers on broom handles as they came from the printer. With enough crews we might get mailers printed. We can worry about cutting and folding another day.

We call everyone in the area together, printing company executives, bank officers, programmers, operators, janitors—everyone. There is no need for blame. Will they work the night—no bosses—no procedures—just grab a piece of the problem and get it done? Need help, ask—want to help, offer. Yes? Good! Two people lift a roll of mailers and the printer begins to chatter. Two others grab a second broom handle and begin to roll up mailers as they emerge. Ideas pour out from everyone and someone is instantly on the way to attend to each. "Search the building and steal broom handles." "Get food and drinks sent in." "We'll need gloves." "Round up relief crews." "Rig a backup printer." No one knows all that is happening and no one has time to care. We must trust.

The last roll comes off the printer at six in the morning. An exhausted, happy band of brothers and sisters head home to catch a few hours of sleep before the next ordeal begins. As we labored through the night, someone had not only claimed ownership of every aspect of the night's work, but future work separating and folding mailers to get the project back on track. Is that how the future happens? Ingenuity? Passion? Spontaneous order out of chaos? It seems so, as long as control is kept on a leash.

***

With but days left until launch, there remains an immense problem to which we have no solution. More than a hundred thousand mailers are ready to receive newly embossed NBC BankAmericards. Each card must be proofread against the printed mailer, hand-inserted, and bundled for delivery to the post office. It must be done in three days. It is far beyond the capacity of the small staff of the card center. We need a mass of clerical workers motivated to do an excellent job. The ingenious solution is Bob's.

Who are the best at the work to be done—the real experts? Clerical employees and keypunch operators on the bottom rung of the bank ladder of course. Good! They will be the "leaders." The ingenious part we explain to Andrew Price, Maxwell Carlson, and Robert Faragher, chairman, president and executive vice president of the bank. It is fiendishly simple. They "borrowed" Bob and me to help get the card program launched in an impossibly short period of time. Now we need to "borrow" them to get the mailers out in an impossible short period of time. Will each of them join us for dinner at the center at five in the afternoon for three days, then report to their clerical "leader" and work until nine or ten in the evening proofreading and stuffing a share of the cards? If so, other senior officers will be "invited" to join them and participate in the work. With acceptances in hand from senior officers, we will offer the same opportunity to every officer and manager in the bank. No pressure. First come, first served.

No records kept. The marvelous part is that all are exempt employees, not hourly workers subject to overtime. Meals will be catered by the bank cafeteria. Aside from extra compensation and overtime for the "leaders," it will cost almost nothing. It is outrageous. It is common sense. It catches fire.

One after another, executive officers agree to be "borrowed." Within hours of the bank-wide communication, we are oversubscribed. No one wants to miss this upside-down party. We have to ration time, allowing no officer more than a single night. Those late in calling are seriously put out at being rejected.

It is some party, not without wonderful moments. In the midst of fifty intensely concentrating people, there is a crash and all eyes turn to stare. Bob Faragher, executive vice president, has knocked his tray of cards off the desk, scattering them across the floor. In a flash, his boss, little Nancy Smilinich, card-embossing operator, is at his side to help and console.

"Never mind, it could happen to any of us." They are both smiling as they kneel together to straighten out the mess. At the end of three nights, one hundred thousand cards are on their way to customers and the program is launched.

Bob Cummings grew to love his job and was, in turn, loved by the people. I thought he would be there for years, if not the remainder of his career. I expected to work until the center was well established, then get back to retirement on the job. Shortly after the first anniversary of the launch, Ron McDonald, senior vice president in charge of personnel asked if I could come by to speak with him. I assumed he had a new assignment in mind. To my surprise, he told me there was a need to "borrow" Bob for another assignment, which Bob was eager to accept. That would not be possible unless I was open to becoming head of the credit card department at a significant raise in pay.

It appeared Bob would be denied something he wanted if I were to decline, nor did our family finances make it prudent to say no. Yes, of course. I accepted. Bob repeatedly told me how happy he was that I had accepted and how pleased he was with his new assignment.

It was fifteen years later, at Bob's retirement party, when Ron finally told me the truth. Bob had walked into his office and abruptly announced, "Ron, get me out of this job. Dee needs and deserves it. I'm just in his way."

If Bob Cummings had not made such a magnificent gift of the job he loved, the extraordinary events of the next chapter would never have come to be.

Chapter Six

The House of Cards

Taking a new step; uttering a new word is what people fear most.
—Fyodor Mikhailovich Dostoyevsky

Early in 1966, within months after Bank of America let it be known that it would license its BankAmericard program and five California banks announced a joint MasterCharge program, the banking industry was seething with speculation and rampant with rumors: "Citicorp has committed millions to develop proprietary card technology to force an industry standard controlled by them"—"American Express is buying a bank and will blanket the country with American Express bank cards"—"Bank of America's licensing program is a cover-up they will use to promote deposit accounts nationwide"—"Citicorp and Chase Manhattan are going to license proprietary cards"—"Banks in a dozen different regions are forming groups modeled after the California

MasterCharge association"—"Independent bank cards are forming a network using a common interbank logo"—"Legislation is being introduced to give the Federal Reserve System a monopoly for the clearing of sales drafts between banks"—"The federal government is going to pass a usury law to preempt all state laws governing credit card rates"—"The federal government is going to forbid mass mailing of unsolicited cards."

Bankers found the rumors hard to believe. But that changed when many rumors were confirmed by surprise announcements and aggressive marketing. Thousands of vendors, suppliers, and consultants leaped into the feeding frenzy, playing one bank against the other, exaggerating everything and dreaming up credit card marketing and operating schemes, none so bizarre that they failed to find takers.

Within months, there was no rumor so wild and no claim of success so exaggerated that it was without believers. It was the great Oklahoma land rush magnified a thousandfold.

Whoever got there first and got their stake in the ground would win. Whoever got there last would come home in a broken wagon with empty hands. Fence-sitting bankers did an about-face. The risks of getting into the business seemed small compared to the risks of staying out. Doubts were swept under the rug and the panic was on.

***

    Stories of the banking madness of the time are legendary. In the beginning, there was no magnetic strip on the card and no electronic card readers at point of sale. Cards were placed in the bed of a manual imprinter, a four-part sales draft placed on top and a lever pulled or pressed to create an impression. They were dubbed "zip zap" machines. Imprinters were purchased by banks for a few dollars and rented to merchants for handsome monthly fees. Many banks were incensed when imprinters they had supplied were used to serve cardholders of competitors. Determined to stamp out this injustice, one major bank reissued all their cards with a hole in the center and installed a steel peg in the bed of their imprinters to shatter the card of other issuers. No sharing of point-of-sale devices for this rabid competitor.

Merchant service representatives of a southern bank engaged in creative marketing. They leased imprinters to merchants at a reduced rate and carried away imprinters of their competitor with assurance to the merchant that all was understood between the banks. Where the liberated imprinters went was a bit murky. The bank's market research proved faulty, for the local sheriff turned out to be a loyal customer of their competitor. He swiftly rounded up the innovative merchant representatives and threw them in the slammer.

Advertising slogans knew no bounds. "The Card With A Heart." "The Captain America Card." "The Everything Card." A prominent bank in a southeastern state entered the business with a huge mass mailing of cards, plastering their market with billboards and saturating it with television screaming, "THE CARD YOU WON'T GO BERSERK WITH." It was a challenge the bank's cardholders accepted with enthusiasm. The earnings of the bank were soon sadly depressed, shareholder dividends reduced, and the price of shares plummeted.

The system for clearing sales drafts between banks was primitive, cumbersome, and impossible to fully describe—nor is it necessary to the story to understand this brief summary. There were no electronic data entry or clearing systems. Each merchant-signing bank accepted all transactions regardless of the issuing bank, crediting the merchant account for the total, manually sorted the transactions by issuing bank, and reimbursed themselves by drawing a clearing draft on each issuing bank through the Federal Reserve System. When the clearing draft reached the issuing bank, it was posted to a suspense ledger while waiting for the merchant bank to keypunch the sales drafts and send them through the U.S. mail.

Meanwhile, the merchant bank, having already been paid and under immense pressure to handle its own cardholder transactions, had no incentive to process foreign transactions and get them to the issuing bank for billing to the cardholder. Since each bank was both a merchant-signing bank and a card-issuing bank, they began to play tit-for-tat, while back rooms filled with unprocessed transactions, customers went unbilled, and suspense ledgers swelled like a hammered thumb. It became an accounting nightmare.

Criminals sensed a bonanza. Within months, large quantities of plastic cards not yet embossed with cardholder names and numbers began to disappear from manufacturers' warehouses, shipping companies, and bank storage facilities. A few thousand dollars for embossing machines, some organized pilferage of account numbers from discarded copies of sales drafts, and the crooks were in the counterfeit card business.

Counterfeit cards were soon more than matched by cards stolen wholesale on their way through postal departments, pilfered from mailboxes by thieves, snatched by pickpockets, and "forgotten" by customers, with assistance from conniving store clerks. Thousands of counterfeit and stolen cards were soon on the black market, selling for as little as $50, each card swiftly used to purchase and resell thousands of dollars of merchandise before being abandoned.

Sham merchants appeared, depositing large quantities of fraudulent sales drafts during the weeks it took banks to process them through the system, then vanishing with the money as complaints piled up.

There were no electronic systems for authorizing transactions. Each merchant had a floor limit, beneath which no authorization was required. It took criminals no time at all to pattern such limits and accurately assess the degree of risk in each merchant location. A transaction over the floor limit required that a merchant employee telephone the bank with which they had contracted. An employee of the merchant bank then made a long-distance call to the card-issuing bank, where an employee manually looked up the customer's account in huge, computer-printed, paper ledgers, determined if the sale could be authorized, gave an authorization number to the inquiring bank, who passed it along to the merchant. Meanwhile, the customer waited angrily or was required to return later. The card-issuing bank posted a hold on the customer account for the amount of the sale, to be released when the sales draft appeared weeks, often months, later.

Merchants swiftly realized it was prudent to obtain an authorization in advance for every potential sale, however slight the chance it would be completed. Customers' lines of credit were swiftly absorbed by holds for sales never completed and they were denied credit they should have had. System authorization costs soared since merchants made local calls, while banks absorbed all long-distance bank-to-bank calls.

There was no Internet, no electronic entry of data, no CRT screens for electronic examination of accounts, and no dispersed computing power. All data entry required keypunching each digit of information (every letter and every number) into a four-by-six inch piece of cardboard by a clunking mechanical punching typewriter the size of a large refrigerator. The punched cards were then put through an elongated card reader twice the size of the keypunch machine to capture the data on magnetic tape, then fed into a van-sized computer for posting to customer accounts. The data were returned to tape and finally sent into a large mechanical printer to produce huge binders of customer records.

Primitive and cumbersome as the system was, it performed well enough to allow the massive outpouring of cards to gain considerable consumer and merchant acceptance. As acceptance skyrocketed, the number of transactions flowing between banks exploded. The clearing system swiftly disintegrated under the volume.

***

Very few bankers had sound experience in the management of unsecured consumer credit, and fewer had knowledge of credit cards. The most experienced and best-qualified people outside the banking industry were repelled by the methods and madness of the industry, nor did they find the mediocre salaries common to banking attractive. However, there was no shortage of those with questionable ability and experience. They came forward in droves. Most were quickly snapped up.

Within the banks, similar problems appeared. Most bankers looked down their noses at the card business, placing it lower on the scale of respectability than auto dealer financing, only then gaining scant acceptance by banks. Few banks really wanted to be in the card business. Few bankers wanted to be assigned to it. Card operations were located in the least desirable part of the bank premises and staffed with employees who did not fit elsewhere.

It was both curse and blessing. Most credit card departments were filled with an eclectic mixture of bankers and outsiders, pragmatists and dreamers, liberally laced with iconoclasts, renegades, and incompetents. Isolated and disdained, they were lashed by top management to launch a poorly understood, massive business in an impossibly short time in the midst of competitive frenzy. Strangely, however, the eclectic mix of people contained more than enough of the innovative, adventurous spirits that the resulting disaster required. Many of those who survived would later emerge as a major force in bank management.

By 1968, the fledgling industry was out of control. No one knew the extent of the losses, but they were thought to be in the tens of millions of dollars, a huge sum for the time and for the size of the system. Drawing on Greek legend, *Life Magazine,* then in its glory days, ran a famous cover story depicting banks as Icarus flying to the sun on wings of plastic, one a BankAmericard, the other a MasterCharge. Below was a blood-red sea labeled "losses." The magazine predicted banks would soon plunge down, wings melted, and drown in a sea of red ink.

> In the midst of the credit card maelstrom, Old Monkey Mind and I could not escape the three questions that had emerged from our sixteen years of institutional life. The

difference between our experience creating the National Bank of Commerce card program and the disaster the industry had become increased our obsession with institutions and the people who hold power within them. Again and again the same questions returned, demanding an answer:

Why are institutions, everywhere, whether commercial, political and social, increasingly unable to manage their affairs?

Why are individuals, everywhere, increasingly in conflict with and alienated from the institutions of which they are part?

Why are society and the biosphere increasingly in disarray?

Slowly, bit by bit, our old perspective dissolved, new perceptions arose, and a pattern began to emerge. The answer to those questions was deeply embedded in compression of time and events. Some readers may recall the days when a check took a couple of weeks to find its way through the banking system. Bankers called it "float." Not float in the sense of a corked bottle floating on water, but in the sense of the time it might take a bottle in the ocean to float from one place to another, or the time it might take for something to change from one form to another, such as a log changing from wood to heat, ashes, and smoke as it burns. The time between when a check was written and the time it was finally presented for payment at the customer's bank could be considerable, and a great many people and small business used it as a form of interest-free capital. Today, we are all aware of the incredible speed and volatility with which money moves throughout the world and the profound effect it has on us. Money "float" has virtually disappeared.

However, we ignore vastly more important reductions of float, such as the disappearance of "life float." The first life forms appeared approximately 4.5 billion years ago. It took evolution about half that time, 2.2 billion years, to make the first tiny step from the nonnucleated to the nucleated cell. It took only half that time, another billion years, to create the first simple vertebrate, then only a half billion years to produce primitive fish and reptiles. Then, in only 200 million years, evolution produced dinosaurs, birds, and complex plants, then mammals in only 100 million years. Each change reduced by more than half the time required to produce the next exponential leap in the diversity and complexity of organisms, right on through to the creature writing this book. There is no reason to believe this exponential reduction of time to create more complex, diverse organisms will not continue. In fact, with the advent of genetic engineering, the time required for creation of new species—"life float"—may literally collapse.

The same pattern is apparent with respect to information float. As the futurist James Burke pointed out, it took centuries for information about the smelting of ore to creep across a single continent and bring about the

Iron Age. During the time of sailing ships, it took decades for that which became known to become that which was shared. When man set foot on the moon, it was known and seen in every corner of the globe 1.4 seconds later. Yet that is hopelessly primitive by today's standards. Countless events anywhere can be instantly heard and seen everywhere.

Even more important is the disappearance of scientific and technological float: the time between the discovery of new knowledge, the resultant technology, and its universal application. It took centuries for the wheel, one of the first bits of technology, to gain universal acceptance—decades for the steam engine, electric light, and automobile—years for radio and television. Today, countless microchip devices sweep around the Earth like the light of the sun into universal use.

The same is true of cultural float. For the better part of recorded history, it took centuries for the customs of one culture to materially affect another. Today, that which becomes popular in one country can sweep through others within weeks. Nor is language an exception. Words from one language used to require generations to take root in another. Common words now emerge from the global culture simultaneously in all languages, while English is rapidly becoming a universal tongue, as anyone who has listened to pilots and controllers at any airport in the world is bound to note.

It is no different with "space float." Within a couple of long lifetimes we went from the speed of the horse to the speed of interstellar travel. Men and material now move in minutes where they used to move in months, while services based on information do so in a fraction of a second.

This endless compression of float, whether of life forms, money, information, technology, time, space, or anything else, can be combined and thought of as the disappearance of "change float"—the time between what was and what is to be—between past and future. Only a few generations ago, the present stretched relatively unaltered from a distant past into a dim future. *Today, the past is ever less predictive, the future ever less predictable and the present scarcely exists at all. Everything is accelerating change, with one incredibly important exception.* **There has been no loss of institutional float.**

Although their size and power have vastly increased, although we constantly tinker with their form, although we constantly change their labels, there has been no new, commonly accepted idea of organization since the concepts of corporation, nation-state, and university emerged, the newest of which is several centuries old.

Much as Old Monkey and I loved such ideas and wished every moment was free to pursue them, events would not leave us alone. It was good that they did not, for they were shattering our old perspectives, emptying us of much that we had

> accepted as truth and allowing space for new thoughts to rush in.

In the midst of the credit card mess, the Bank of America Service Corporation called a meeting of licensee card program managers to discuss operating problems plaguing the system. Jim Cronkhite, operations officer of our card center, and I flew to Columbus, Ohio, to join one hundred twenty others from across the country. We were surprised to find that top officers of the BofA Service Corporation had apparently not thought it important to attend. Others were no less surprised. The meeting was to be conducted by Hal and Don, both pleasant and capable bank operations officers assigned to the Service Corporation to work with licensee banks.

The meeting droned on for most of the first day, many licensees sharply critical of what they perceived as the Bank of America's lack of awareness of the problems, and inability or unwillingness to deal with them. The Bank representatives were no less critical of their licensees. By the end of the day, accusations, denials, and counter-accusations were flying about the room. Licensees were attacking one another as well as the Bank of America. Jim and I debated whether to return to Seattle rather than waste another day in the midst of the squabble, but decided to remain.

The next morning was worse. By midday, the meeting disintegrated in acrimonious argument. Shortly before lunch, in evident desperation and without prior discussion with those named, Hal and Don announced appointment of a committee of seven licensee card-center managers, of which I was one, to which they intended to refer a couple of the more critical operating problems. We were to study the assigned problems and suggest solutions. If BofA found the suggestions agreeable, they would attempt to impose them on the licensee banks.

I thought such a committee would be an exercise in futility. During the lunch break, I asked Hal and Don for a few moments in private, thinking to persuade them to appoint another in my place. Hal, sweating and face flushed beneath his shock of red hair, was angry and beleaguered. Don, tall and reserved, was no less disturbed. Both listened defensively.

"Look, I don't want to make things more difficult than they already are. If you insist, I'll do this committee thing, but I'd rather not be involved. It would be a big favor if you'd get someone else."

Hal's reply is abrupt and sarcastic. "You guys seem to think everything we try to do is wrong, so here's your chance to do it right."

Don is a bit more reserved but equally concerned. "Dee, why not? Do you have a problem with the idea of the committee itself, or is there some other reason?"

There is no reason to hold back. "Don, it's a waste of time. By the time the committee can meet and agree on anything, there'll be a dozen more problems. No one really knows how many problems there are or how serious they might be. Nothing a committee could suggest would satisfy everybody. The way your license agreements are written, if a bank refuses to go along with the rules, your only choice is to kick them out of the system. BofA won't do that and we all know it. It would jeopardize too many banking relationships. I just don't want to waste my time." Hal and Don stare at me in silence. What the hell, they are friends and we are speaking in private. It might as well be on the table.

"Don, you can't renegotiate every license every time you want to change operating procedures, and that's essentially what your licensing agreements require. Besides, this mob hasn't the chance of snow in the desert of reaching agreement on anything, let alone sticking to it. And if you think you can get banks to surrender enough authority to the Bank of America to let you make rules and enforce them, you've fallen down the rabbit hole with Alice and are wandering in Wonderland. We all know that BofA would swallow our banks like a snake swallows a mouse if branch banking law didn't prevent it." Neither Hal nor Don can prevent a grin.

Hal gives it back in kind. "Yeah? Well, I'm not a snake and you're not a mouse, so what do you suggest?"

"If you're going to form a committee," I reply, "why not give it responsibility for creating some way to examine all problems in a systematic, continuous way? What's the point in trying to correct any problem if we're constantly guessing about its importance, what else needs to be done, and how they all connect and affect one another? And why mill around yapping at one another out of ignorance?" We're soon in intense discussion. The more we talk, the more they warm to the idea, but not without reluctance.

Don explains. "Even if we agree with you, we have no authority from the bank to set up such a committee. And even if we did, there's no way we're going to suggest it. If it comes from us, it'll be suspect."

"Don, I don't think so. Most licensees would welcome such a suggestion from the Bank of America. We all know the system is in trouble and any coordinated, self-organizing effort would be welcome, even if it came to nothing."

"Dee, we can't do it without approval from the Bank."

"Why not? You called the meeting and asked us to come to discuss system problems. Didn't the Bank trust you to run the meeting? Don't they trust you to act in their best interest and the interest of the system? All I'm suggesting is that you ask the committee you've appointed to find the best method to do just that. There's no risk. The committee has no authority. It can't commit the Bank to anything."

Hal and Don are obviously on the horns of a dilemma. I know their difficulty without asking. They like the idea and know they should support it. They don't want to say no, but they clearly don't want the responsibility. They're trapped by the same old paradigms of predictability and control. They want to know how things will end before they begin. They don't want to create the conditions for solutions to emerge without being able to control what the solutions might be. They're enmeshed in a command-and-control organization and fear how it will respond if they obey their own common sense, creativity, and judgment. I try to ease the situation.

"Look, I don't want to put you on the spot. It's not my affair. Just announce that I have other commitments, appoint someone in my place, and get on with it. I think it's a mistake, but so what? I'm not going to say anything unless someone asks, and they won't." But Hal and Don won't let it go, puzzling over what to do. I offer them a way off the hook.

"Is this a Bank of America meeting, or is this a licensee meeting that the Bank just happened to call? Is there anything in the license agreements that forbids licensee banks to meet anytime they want, anywhere they want, to talk about anything they want? If my suggestion makes sense, maybe you have an obligation to tell the group about it. You don't have to take a position. Attribute the idea to me, if you want. Just give them the option and ask them what they want to do. What's the big deal? Just do it or let it die." It's plain their decision is reluctant, as Hal responds.

"Well—okay, but we won't suggest it. It's your idea and you'll have to present it."

"Look, it's your meeting and I don't want to mess with it. If it's the right thing to do, you should take the lead. That's what the group will expect." But Hal and Don become adamant both ways. The suggestion should be made. I must make it.

***

It is a perplexed group that assembles after lunch to find one of their own on the stage. After Hal's preamble, I share my concerns about the system and suggestion that the committee address a single problem—how to create a cohesive, coherent, self-organizing effort involving all licensees to examine all problems plaguing the system. It should be an open effort committing no one, including BofA, to anything other than participation.

"How much will it cost?" someone in the audience asks.

"Nothing but some of your time and an occasional airplane ticket."

"What will it commit us to?"

"Nothing." The audience, in the way of all disorganized groups faced with a proposal creating the illusion of progress but requiring no money or commitment, swiftly agreed. The meeting disbanded and the committee of seven met. Fred James, a soft-spoken, laconic man of considerable influence from Memphis, Tennessee, was the first to speak.

"Well, I don't know what you got us into, but this is sure enough your idea. Unless somebody wants to argue, looks like you're the chairman. Any you other folks contrary-minded?"

And just so, I was elbowed into the lead with no intent but to do a bit of civic duty, never suspecting I had stepped on another of those tiny, jeweled bearings on which the future turns.

Chapter Seven

Peeling the Onion

> *To be free is precisely the same thing as to be pious, wise, just and temperate, careful of one's own, abstinent from what is another's and thence, magnanimous and brave ... To be an opposite of these is the same thing as to be a slave ... So it comes to pass that the nation which has been incapable of governing and ordering itself and has delivered itself up to the slavery of its own lusts is itself delivered against its will to other masters, and whether it will or not, is compelled to serve.*
> —John Milton

There was no time for the new licensee committee to do more than get acquainted and agree to meet two weeks hence. On the flight home, Jim Cronkhite and I ripped a map of the United States from the airline magazine and began dividing the country into sections, minds buzzing with a multitude of questions. What might best define areas of operational, political, cultural, and banking interests? What might provide equitable balance of number of licensees and volume of BankAmericard business? What might keep travel time and costs to a minimum? What might include a healthy mix of differing interests, yet not be so diverse as to make agreement impossible?

We arrived in Seattle with a rough concept of multiple, self-defined regions, each with four functional committees—operating, marketing, credit, and computer systems. Every card-issuing bank within each region would have a right to appoint a representative to each of their regional committees. A regional executive committee would be composed of the chairmen of the functional committees and any other individuals the four chairmen selected. Five national committees would be composed of the chairman of each committee in the seven regions. Everyone would be heard but no one could dominate.

Within the week, the concept was expanded to a set of proposals. The licensee committee appointed by BofA met in Atlanta, Georgia. After a day of discussion and modification, agreement was reached. The seven regions became eight. Each member of the group would return to his region, host a meeting of all licensee banks to share the concept, and, if successful, coordinate self-organization of regional committees. In the event the concept was not acceptable to all regions, the effort would be abandoned. If the effort were successful, the regional committees would elect their respective chairmen, each of whom would become a member of a comparable national committee. The present committee, selected by the Bank of America, would be replaced by the national executive committee.

The concept was cumbersome but it had the advantage of including every card-issuing licensee bank. Each would not only be acting on its own behalf, but on behalf of hundreds of merchant-signing banks that had been sublicensed in accordance with rights granted in their license from BofA. We identified issues to be addressed. A tentative schedule was set for the national committee meetings, at which regional information and suggestions would be synthesized into a comprehensive picture of the whole.

We hoped that the committee structure would not only develop preliminary data about fraud, credit, operating, and technology problems, but assign priority to them and propose solutions to the most vexing. Bank of America would have an exofficio member on each national committee. As sole owners of the service marks and the franchising company, BofA would have responsibility for implementing any proposals. Whether BofA could or would, and how, was anyone's guess.

Within six months, the complex of regional and national committees had self-organized. In the process, I was asked to serve as chairman of the Pacific Northwest regional executive committee and chairman of the national executive committee as well. It was thankless, unpaid, often unpleasant work that added substantially to the time already heavily committed to the management of the National Bank of Commerce card operation. So much for retirement on the job!

The complex of committees had but one redeeming quality: It allowed organized information about problems to emerge. It took only two cycles of meetings to realize that the problems were enormously greater than anyone imagined—far beyond any possibility of correction by the existing committees or the licensing structure—and growing at an astonishing rate. Losses were not in the tens of millions, as everyone had thought, but in the hundreds of millions and accelerating.

Suddenly, like a diamond in the dirt, there it lay. The need for a new concept of organization and a precarious toehold from which to make the attempt.

> The thought was enough to send Old Monkey Mind and me leaping joyously back into thoughts about institutions. In our effort to diagnose the epidemic of institutional failure sweeping the world, we often returned

to an ancient bit of philosophy that served us well.

Understanding events and influencing the future requires mastering of four ways of looking at things; as they were, as they are, as they might become, and as they ought to be.

We knew a good deal about the financial services industry and credit cards. How they were we had pretty well mastered. How they are was literally killing us. How they might become was even worse. But what about *how they ought to be?*

Could this be an opportunity to *reconceive* in the most fundamental sense, the very ideas of bank, money, and credit card—even beyond that to the essential elements of each and how they might change in a microelectronic environment? But how could we do that unless we understood in the deepest sense the essence of organization itself? We had to go back a long, long way.

Imagine yourself a *Homo sapiens* in that shadowy world that preceded corporations, institutions, tribes, perhaps even family. A thinking animal in a world teeming with carnivores rich in tooth and claw, seeking to fill their bellies with tender flesh. Experience would soon teach you, if common sense did not, that failure to differentiate between the nature of a cobra and a rabbit, or a lion and a gazelle, would result in a short, nasty life. *If you did not understand the nature of the beasts, it would be of little use to know the mechanics of their anatomy.*

Today, we are living in a world in which the filling of bellies by tooth and claw has been enormously diminished through the use of institutions—family, city, county, state, nation, church, corporation, school, association—millions of every size and description, accepted with as little thought as we accept the changing seasons. Yet, those institutions can demean, damage, or destroy us as certainly and capriciously as any saber-toothed tiger. And they do so with technological, psychological, and economic instruments infinitely more destructive than tooth and claw

Institutions are not a law of nature, nor did they spring full-blown from the head of Zeus. In the great sweep of evolution they are, for all their size and complexity, newly born, primitive, aberrant, and often uncivilized. People are not the creatures of institutions; institutions are the creations of people, yet they increasingly seem as much beyond our control as the turning of the Earth and the burning of the sun. We endlessly tinker with their anatomy and bear up under their abuse, but how well do we understand the intrinsic nature of the institutional beast?

Not well at all. The problem arises from the pervasive habit of perceiving an institution as a tangible, physical reality, such as a building or a machine. When anyone began to talk or act as though a company had such reality, I would assure them that it was a fiction, that it did not exist. Most would argue vociferously that it certainly did. I would test their convictions with a simple exercise in which you, the reader, can easily engage. Fix the company you work for, or any other organization of which you are part, firmly in your mind. Not its physical manifestations such as its name, employees, or offices, but the company itself. Put all other thoughts aside and *fix the organization itself* firmly in your mind.

Surely you have seen it. What color is it? No? Well, then you must have smelled it from time to time. Describe its odor. No? Then surely you've tasted it. Is it sweet or sour, tart or bland? You don't know? Well, you must have touched it often. Is it hot or cold, hard or soft? No? Then, without doubt you have heard it. Make its sound. No? Can you perceive the company you work for, or any other organization, whether political, social, or commercial, with any of your senses? Obviously not. If you can't perceive an organization with any of your senses, does it have any reality at all? Perhaps it's a fiction. Perhaps it doesn't exist. But you're not going to accept that explanation.

The truth is that a corporation, or for that matter, any organization has no reality save in the mind. It is nothing but a mental construct to which people are drawn in pursuit of common purpose; a conceptual embodiment of a very old, very powerful idea called community.

All organizations can be no more and no less than the moving force of the mind, heart, and spirit of people, without which all assets are just so much inert mineral, chemical, or vegetable matter, by the law of entropy, steadily decaying to a stable state.

Healthy organizations are a mental concept of relationship to which people are drawn by hope, vision, values, and meaning, along with liberty to cooperatively pursue them. Healthy organizations educe behavior. Educed behavior is inherently constructive.

Unhealthy organizations are no less a mental concept of relationship, but one to which people are compelled by accident of birth, necessity, or force. Unhealthy organizations compel behavior. Compelled behavior is inherently destructive.

Since the strength and reality of every organization lies in the sense of community of the people who have been attracted to it, its success has enormously more to do with clarity of a shared purpose, common principles, and strength of belief in them, than with money, material assets, or management practices, important as they may be.

When an organization loses its shared vision and principles, its sense of community, its meaning and values, it is already in process of decay and dissolution, even though it may linger with the outward appearance of success for some time. Businesses, as well as nations, races, and tribes die out not when defeated or suppressed, but when they become despairing and lose excitement and hope about the future.

Without deeply held, commonly shared purpose that gives meaning to their lives; without deeply held, commonly shared ethical values and beliefs about conduct in pursuit of that purpose that all may trust and rely upon, communities steadily disintegrate, and organizations progressively become instruments of tyranny.

To the direct degree that clarity of shared purpose and principles and strength of belief in them exist, constructive, harmonious behavior may be educed. To the direct degree they do not exist, behavior is inevitably compelled. It is not complicated. The alternative to shared belief in purpose and principles is tyranny. And tyranny, whether petty or grand, whether commercial, political, or social, is inevitably destructive.

People deprived of self-organization and self-governance are inherently ungovernable.

Old Monkey and I, then in our middle years, were off on an extraordinary adventure. It was necessary to rethink the very nature of the institutional beasts in which we were enmeshed. To examine in the most fundamental way the functions of a bank, of money, and of a credit card; even beyond that to the essential nature of each and how it might change with full application of emerging electronic technology. We must get beyond how things had been, were, and might become into how they *ought to be.* It was slow. It was painful. It was frustrating. Several convictions slowly emerged. They were enormously exciting.

First: such zealously protected things as branches, deposits, loans, and investments were the anatomy, not the nature of banking. They were form, not function. The nature of a bank, its essential function, was the custody, exchange, and loan of money. But what was money? More digging. Money was not coin, currency, or credit card. That was form, not function. Money was *anything* customarily used as a measure of equivalent value and medium of exchange. But what had that *anything* become?

Coin had long since been debased. It no longer contained more than a trace of precious metal. Melt a few hundred pounds of coin from any country and you would be fortunate to get a few pennies for the resulting blob of metal. Certainly the paper on which currency and checks are printed has no significant value, nor does ink. A barrel of ink and a pulped tree turned into paper costing a few dollars would print billions of dollars worth of currency. Old Monkey Mind and I continued to peel our onion of understanding looking for the essence of money.

Realization slowly dawned that money had become alphanumeric symbols recorded and transported on valueless metal and paper. This still left a gap in understanding, for symbols themselves had no value. Anyone could write down letters and numbers; printing presses and computers could spew out infinite quantities. It eventually emerged. *Money had become **guaranteed** alphanumeric data expressed in the currency symbol of one country or another.* Thus, a bank would become no more than an *institution for the custody, loan, and exchange of guaranteed alphanumeric data.*

Even this did not satisfy us. It was necessary to know not only what money and banks had become, but what they ought to be. What actually happened when a computer was injected into the process? Certainly the metal of the coin and paper of the currency played no part in the bowels of a computer.

What was the essence of what happened when we used the telephone to authorize a credit card transaction? That was certainly a guarantee. Certainly data of some sort was being transferred by voice; by sound. But no sound was passing down that wire. The voice saying "five hundred dollars" was being turned into electronic signals and those signals were turned into sound on the other end. Such signals could pass through wires or through broadcast waves. Nothing was passing but orderly disturbance of electronic particles—waves of energy.

Peeling this onion of understanding was enough to make us cry. The essence of money seemed to be everywhere, yet nowhere. But we had to understand. More research, more digging, more connections. What was the essential nature of the computer, of the communications systems rapidly emerging, and what would happen if they became ubiquitous, as many science-fiction writers were speculating? What if most data began to move as electronic impulse—radio waves—even beams of light? Certainly everything seemed headed in that direction, and at an ever-accelerating pace. Our old perspective began to evaporate. Our perception began to change. It was as though we could now see with different eyes. Even more, with a different mind. Even beyond that: *with a different consciousness, and it was incredibly exciting.*

Money would become nothing but alphanumeric data in the form of arranged energy impulses. It would move around the world at the speed of light at minuscule cost by infinitely diverse paths throughout the entire electromagnetic spectrum. *Any institution that could move, manipulate, and guarantee alphanumeric data in the form of arranged energy in a manner that individuals customarily used and relied upon as a measure of equivalent value and medium of exchange was a bank. It went even beyond that. Inherent in all this might be the genesis of a new form of global currency.*

Old Monkey and I were stunned. If electronic technology continued to advance, and that seemed certain, two-hundred year old banking oligopolies controlling the custody, loan, and exchange of money would be irrecoverably shattered. Nation-state monopolies on the issuance and control of currency would erode. It mattered little that traditional banks or government might be the settlers of last resort—the ultimate handlers of huge, accumulated transfers of monetary value. The vast preponderance of the system would fall to those who were most adept at handling and guaranteeing alphanumeric value data in the form of arranged particles of energy.

We continued to peel the onion. Just what was the nature of the business in which we were engaged? Was credit really the nature of our business? What was the essence of the transaction when a customer presented a sliver of plastic to a merchant? Clearly, it introduced a merchant willing to sell something to a prospective customer who might wish to buy it. In that regard, it was a substitute for a driver's license, social security card, government identity card, or other means of identification. *Thus, the first primary function of the card was to identify buyer to seller and seller to buyer.*

Clearly, it guaranteed that they could safely exchange value, the merchant delivering goods or services, and the customer signing a draft that the merchant could deposit for monetary credit. The seller would receive good funds in local currency and the buyer would be billed later in the currency of their country. *Thus, the second primary function was as guarantor of the value data.*

Clearly, it warranted to both buyer and seller that the system would attend to the mechanism of exchange without either having to know the language, laws, currency, customs, or culture of the other. The fact that many card issuers allowed the customer to pay for the transactions over a period of time (in the jargon of banking, "extended credit") was really an ancillary service and not the primary function of the card. When the card was put through the imprinter, it merely created a financial message in the form of alphanumeric data—it was a substitute for pen and paper. *Thus, the third primary function was origination and transfer of value data.*

As we abandoned our old perspective and challenged our mechanistic model of reality, we ceased thinking of the jargon of banking and payment systems. We thought in a more fundamental way and another change of consciousness occurred. It seems ordinary and obvious now. It was a revelation then. We were not in the credit card business. "Credit card" was a misnomer based on banking jargon. The card was no more than a device bearing symbols for the exchange of monetary value. That it took the form of a piece of plastic was nothing but an accident of time and circumstance. *We were really in the business of the exchange of monetary value.*

Old Monkey Mind and I began to race to put more of the pieces together. If our business was to guarantee and process the exchange of value between a buyer and a seller, where at any moment in time might the buyer and the seller be? With modern transportation and the collapse of time, the buyer might be anywhere, any time, around the globe, around the clock. With evolution of catalog sales and electronic marketing, any seller might be able to present goods or services to any buyer, anywhere, at any time, without being present. The demand for the exchange of value in the form of electronic particles would be around the clock, seven days a week, at every point on the globe.

Exhilarating realizations followed one after the other. Any organization that could guarantee, transport, and settle transactions in the form of arranged electronic particles twenty-four hours a day, seven days a week, around the globe, would have a market—every exchange of value in the world—that beggared the imagination. The necessary technology had been discovered and would be available in geometrically increasing abundance at geometrically diminishing cost. But there was a problem. No bank could do it. No hierarchal, stock corporation could do it. No nation-state could do it. In fact, no existing form of organization we could think of could do it. On a hunch I made an estimate of the financial resources of all the banks in the world. It dwarfed the resources of most nations. Jointly, they could do it, but how? It would require a transcendental organization linking together in wholly new ways an unimaginable complex of diverse institutions and individuals.

Did I think it could be done? No! It was impossible! Did I think the Bank of America would give up ownership of the program? No! Did I think banks worldwide could be brought together in such an effort? No! Did I think laws would allow it? No! Did I think anyone would seriously listen to such notions or allow them the light of day even if they did? No! *But did I believe it was what ought to be?* Ah, that was another question indeed! Powerful enough to draw me on.

Absurd as it seemed, might this be an undreamed of opportunity to experiment with my beliefs about organizations and management? It seemed beyond imagining. But what could be lost by the attempt? Oh, how well I knew the answer to that question. And I was sick of being a bloodied sheep. This time, I was not going to shoot off my mouth about my beliefs, nor would I force them on others. My convictions would guide what I did. To the best of my ability, I would act in accordance with them. But, if nothing came of the effort, let them die a quiet death. If people should come to the ideas, let it be in their own time, in their own way, for their own reasons. If something of substance should result, let it emerge in the fullness of time.

One thing was certain; it was time for a talk with the boss.

Chapter Eight

The Impossible Imagined

What is a good man but a bad man's teacher?
What is a bad man but a good man's job?
If you don't understand this you will get lost,
However intelligent you are.
It is the great secret.

—Lao-Tzu

"Mr. Carlson, I'm in trouble. When I spoke up at the meeting in Columbus I had no intention of getting so involved. I agreed to serve on the committee with the thought of setting things in motion and stepping aside. Problems are much worse than we imagined. People across the country have become deeply concerned and are looking to the committees as a possible solution. There is growing expectation

I'll continue as chairman. I have a few ideas about how to proceed, but no way of knowing what might result. I'm continually being drawn deeper into the situation and should either make a serious commitment or step aside. I'm torn between the two."

Conversations with Mr. Carlson are never long. The most patient, intense listener I have ever known, his questions are inevitably short, penetrating, and singularly to the point, although often softened by looking down or away. His manner induces others to listen intently and give short, clear answers. In the habit of referring to me as "young man," that is how he began.

"Well, young man, how much of your time do you think this might take?"

"I honestly don't know. In the beginning, perhaps a quarter or more, but if something comes of the effort, it might be more than full time. There's simply no way of knowing."

"I see. If something is not done what will happen?"

"Again, there's no way to know. If the BankAmericard system fails, we'll either have to convert to a private card program or make an affiliation with another system. Either would be costly. If the industry fails, we may be dragged down with it. Worst case, we would have to call in all cards and discontinue business at substantial loss. In any event, we can't isolate our reputation from the reputation of BankAmericard or the credit card industry. It's all interconnected."

"Yes, yes, I see. Well, what about the people you work with? Could they manage without you?"

"They're good people who know how to take care of themselves and help others do the same. They don't need direction; they need reasonable resources, encouragement, and recognition from time to time. I don't think the center would miss a tick. It might do better without me." Mr. Carlson suppresses a smile.

"I understand. Would your salary and expenses be paid by the committee?"

"To this point, every bank has paid its own way. It's possible the chairmanship could be turned into a paid position funded by the banks. At the moment, there is no entity to receive or disburse money, but that could be remedied. We have been working as equals, and I'm comfortable with that. Working for the others would be quite different."

"Well, young man, what will this effort commit us to?"

"Again, I don't know, Mr. Carlson. But I do know that it can't succeed if any bank has a preferred position. The job can't be done properly unless the National Bank of Commerce is in the same position as all others. Whoever does this job must be above reproach with respect to openness and fairness. It simply can't be done without a great deal of trust and confidence, and that will be hard to develop. I don't want to attempt the work if this bank receives preferred information or treatment."

"Yes, yes. But even if that were the case, would others believe it if you were still connected with the Bank?"

"That's not the point. What others believe is their own affair. In time, I expect most would prefer the truth." There is a long pause as he looks intently down, deep in thought, thumbs hooked in vest pockets, legs intertwined with one another as is his wont. His next words are engraved in memory and in my heart. Smiling gently he looks up.

"I think I understand. Well, young man, sometimes we just have to be good citizens. Go where you have to go and do what you have to do. Treat us as you would the others. We will ask no more. The resources of the bank are at your disposal. You must have a place and position from which to do this work. You will continue as a vice president of the bank and head of the credit card department with full salary and all expenses paid. Arrange things there as you think best." Dumbfounded, I watch as he leans back in his chair and asks the question with which he closes all meetings.

"Did the meeting serve your purpose?" Did it serve my purpose! I have never been so treated in my entire life! For this man, I would do anything. Such an obligation as he has just given me is a joy that should come to everyone. Did the meeting serve my purpose? Well—well, almost.

"Mr. Carlson, there is one other matter. We're going to need legal advice and there's no money for lawyers." Without a word he picks up the telephone and dials a number. The managing partner of the bank's outside law firm answers. Maxwell Carlson is ever to the point.

"Mr. Hock is doing some work that is in the public interest. He needs legal assistance that we would like you to provide. If the costs are not paid by others, they will be paid by the bank. Please tell no one in the bank what you are doing, including me. This is a private matter between you and Mr. Hock." He listens intently for a moment, and says, "Yes, yes. Thank you kindly." Returning the receiver to the cradle, he turns to ask once more, "Did the meeting serve your purpose?"

"Yes, sir!" And it served my spirit, my confidence, my need for understanding, my belief in humanity and—well, what didn't it serve? He rises, shakes my hand warmly, smiles, and says, "Thank you so much for coming to see me. Please let me know if I can be helpful at any time."

I floated out of the place—*can't even remember if I thanked him*—determined this man should never have cause to be disappointed in what he had done. In the next two years, through some incredible events, of which you shall learn more in the next few chapters, Maxwell Carlson never once asked where I was or what I was doing. I hope with all my heart he never had cause to be disappointed. If he did, not a whisper came back to me.

***

With compelling need for a new organization, a precarious toehold from which to make the attempt, and now, the liberty to try, I suppressed my desire to control the future, and tried to create the conditions by which new concepts might emerge. How that might happen, I did not know. My learning would have to evolve in concert with others. I thought long and hard about each member of the national executive committee, settling on three, each of whom seemed to have a good sense of who they were, an open, curious mind, generous spirit, and keen sense of humor. More important, none seemed inclined to either follow or lead a mob. Each moved to a rhythm of his own.

Sam Johnson was a big, bluff, Boston Irishman with a ready smile and a thousand ideas that spilled from him like iridescent marbles from a bowl. His enthusiasm was contagious, and his huge capacity for friendship had wrapped me in its arms.

Jack Dillon was a veteran of World War II who for years had remained in the Army Reserve. He loved to talk of army life, though long removed from it. A thirty-year employee of the Bank of America, raconteur extraordinaire, connoisseur of fine food and wine, he was delightful to be around.

Fred James, from Memphis, Tennessee, was a fine storyteller in the droll southern manner. Often, in the middle of intense discussion, he would shake his head and say,

"Well, now, that's shore mighty intrestin', and I don't doubt it for a minute, but I do wonder what that little old lady in Calico Rock's gonna think about it." Whether "that little old lady in Calico Rock" owned the bank, was an archetypal customer, or just a clever way to get our attention, I never knew.

After sharing belief about the opportunity that might be hidden in the problems of the system, I asked if they would be willing to take a week or more of their time, isolate themselves completely, set aside all thought of the problems of the system and address a single question based upon a single assumption.

If anything imaginable was possible, if there were no constraints whatever, what would be the nature of an ideal organization to create the world's premier system for the exchange of value?

After a bit of head shaking and eye rolling, they became intrigued and agreed—providing I would join them. It would have been a bitter disappointment had they not asked.

***

The Altamira Hotel, tucked on a hillside in Sausalito, California, was as long-in-the-tooth and charming as its surroundings, with a thriving business in tourists, weddings, honeymoons, and enamored couples not yet ready for matrimony. The restaurant and ample outdoor dining deck provided a panoramic view across the bay to cities and hills in the east and central San Francisco to the south. It was there we hid out for more than a week.

We argued over every conceivable kind of organization for three long days and agreed on nothing. Frustration increased. Tempers flared. It would be difficult to imagine a more unlikely group in a more unlikely place addressing a more unlikely question, but there we were, and there it happened. For three nights, Old Monkey and I woke often and thrashed about, trying to see a way forward. It took us deeply into things we had been struggling with for many years.

> Over the years of reading and trying to master the four ways of thinking about organizations, *as they were, as they are, as they might become,* and *as they ought to be,* Old Monkey and I had learned to think of

"ought" in the inductive sense of a preferred, ethically better condition, rather than in the compulsory sense of an instructive command. We had also begun to sense that synthesizing those four ways of thinking about things into a compelling concept of organization more in harmony with the human spirit and biosphere can never be a singular work of genius, but is a cooperative work of genius that lies buried in everyone, patiently waiting to be educed. We began to sense that all life on Earth, consciously or unconsciously, cries out for the work to be done.

Since the past can never be more than preparatory and the present no more than a point of departure, it is the future that should have our best thoughts and energy, though it seldom does in the stress and strain of modern life. If one examines organizations *as they might become* or *as they ought to be,* the specifics of that which we know must yield to the abstracts of that which we can conceive. Perception is the primary means by which we cast up such concepts. Therein lies a serious problem.

Somewhere in the middle of perception is the fun-house mirror of perspective. It distorts everything we know, think, or imagine. Therefore, when considering the future, one's viewpoint, one's frame of reference, one's internal model of reality, in a word, the *perspective* that experience indelibly implants in each of us is all-important.

Out of the lumber of things we are taught, the gravel and cement of our experience and the nails of the things we observe, we slowly erect an edifice, an unconscious, internal temple of reality, gradually filling it with the furniture of habit, custom, preference, belief, and bias. We get comfortable there. It's our sanctuary. Through its windows, small though they may be, we view society and the world. Our internal model of reality is how we make sense of the world. And it can be a badly built place indeed. Even if it is well constructed, it may have become archaic. Everything that gave rise to it may have changed. Society and the natural world are never stagnant. They are constantly becoming.

It is our individual perspective, the view from our internal temple of reality, that constantly discolors and distorts our perception, blinding us to how things might become, or conceiving of how they ought to be. When everything changes around us and it becomes necessary to develop a new perception of things, a new internal model of reality, the problem is never to get new ideas in; the problem is to get the old ideas out. Every mind is filled with old furniture. It's familiar. It's comfortable. We hate to throw it out. The old maxim so often applied to the physical world, "nature abhors a vacuum, "is much more applicable to the mental world. Clear any room in your mind of old perspectives, and new perceptions will rush in.

Yet, there is nothing we fear more. We *are* our ideas, concepts, and

> perceptions. Giving up any part of our internal model of reality is worse than losing a finger or an eye. It seems as though part of us no longer exists. Fortunately, unlike most organs of the physical body, internal concepts of reality can be regenerated. Although it is a frightening, painful process it can, at the same time, be joyous and exhilarating.
>
> *Perspective is the Achilles heel of the mind.* And the bloodied sheep had been a long time realizing he had one, let alone what it was. And, oh how he hated to give it up!

Lying awake the fourth night, Old Monkey Mind and I knew that no bank could create the world's premier system for the exchange of value. No hierarchal stock corporation could do it. No nation-state could do it. No known organization could do it. But what if a fraction of the resources of all the financial institutions in the world and a fraction of the ingenuity of all people who worked for them could be applied? Jointly they might do it, but how?

It was beyond the power of the imagination to understand the complexity of such an organization and the diversity it must embrace, let alone the variables it would encounter. It was equally beyond the power of reason to design such an organization, even if the diversity and conditions could be imagined. It was impossible to perceive the rate and extent of change it would encounter. Yet, lying there, Old Monkey Mind kept poking me in the ribs, reminding me how evolution effortlessly tossed off countless varieties of much more complex organisms and organizations—rain forests, marine systems, cheetahs, whales, weather systems, bodies, brains, immune systems—with seeming ease. The puzzle gradually dissolved my brain, and I fell into deep sleep.

With the dawn, half-awake while surfing the shores of consciousness, came a fascinating question. Could such an organization be patterned on biological concepts and methods? The question seemed to contain its own answer. Such an organization would have to evolve; to organize and invent itself. It was not enough to reconceive the nature of the business, we must try to reconceive the very nature of organization itself.

More questions came tumbling one after the other. What if we quit arguing about the structure of a new institution and tried to think of it as having some sort of genetic code? How does genetic code in individual cells *create* recognizable patterns—platypus and people—palm tree and pine—minnow and mouse—yet never *duplicate* a single creature, leaf, blade of grass, or even snowflake? How does nature create infinite diversity within infinite patterns of infinite complexity?

If institutions have no reality save in the mind, might their genetic code have something to do with beliefs—with purpose and principles? What's the nature of a principle? Does "Honor thy father and mother," tell us how to do anything, or just what *ought to be* done? Does it prescribe behavior, or merely describe it? Aren't there infinite ways to honor a father or mother? Does a principle educe behavior or compel it? **Whoa Nellie!** Back up a minute. What was that word? *Ought? Ought to be?* Do pure principles deal with *how things ought to be done?* What if we set aside all discussion of the BankAmericard system as it was, as it is, as it might become and immersed ourselves in how it ought to be. What if—what if?

***

I raced into the fourth day of meeting with no recollection of showering, shaving, or dressing. Nor do I have recollection of the details of the following three days. Only that we decided to abandon our previous discussions and explore the principles, the institutional genetic code, that would allow such an institution to emerge; in effect, to create and develop itself. In that deeper level of thought and discussion about purpose and principles we began to discover that we shared many fundamental beliefs, although we had never experienced an organization in which we could act in accordance with them. Nor did we believe that there ever might be such an organization. But we were beyond the rational mind, scratching at heart and soul, and it was exhilarating. Slowly, painfully, a dozen or so principles emerged, at first in the form of questions; more than enough for a beginning; questions such as:

What if ownership was in the form of irrevocable right of participation, rather than stock: rights that could not be raided, traded, bought, or sold, but only acquired by application and acceptance of membership?

What if it were self-organizing, with participants having the right to self-organize at any time, for any reason, at any scale with irrevocable rights of participation in governance at any greater scale?

What if power and function were distributive, with no power vested in or function performed by any part that could reasonably be exercised by any more peripheral part?

What if governance was distributive, with no individual, institution, or combination of either or both, particularly management, able to dominate deliberations or control decisions at any scale?

What if it could seamlessly blend cooperation and competition, with all parts free to compete in unique, independent ways, yet able to yield self-interest and cooperate when necessary to the good of the whole?

What if it were infinitely malleable, yet extremely durable, with all parts capable of constant, self-generated, modification of form or function without sacrificing its essential purpose, nature, or embodied principle, thus releasing human ingenuity and spirit?

It took months to develop and gain acceptance among licensees of the principles. Once accepted, they were the foundation of every discussion. They were accepted, in part, because no one, self included, thought it likely that such an organization could be brought into being. We could not change the banking laws of a single state, let alone laws of nations. We could not change the structure or management of a single bank, let alone thousands in the United

States and tens of thousands throughout the world.

We had no money with which to purchase the system from the Bank of America, no money to hire consultants, advisors, or other "experts," no money to engage in research or hire employees. We had no power to influence regulators, legislators, or others in political power. Traditional means of approaching the problem were closed to us. But we were enamored of the emerging concepts, for there seemed no better alternative. I was more than enamored. As one of the participants put it twelve years later in a Harvard case study, "He had a passionate commitment to the ideas that bordered on zealotry."

Only in hindsight does it becomes clear as the dawn that the need to rely entirely on the power of purpose, principles, and people was what brought Visa into being. It was no stroke of genius. It was plain old necessity. Had we power, capital, position, or influence, we would undoubtedly have used them in the command-and-control style in which we had been so admirably indoctrinated. Without them, we were forced to a change of consciousness; to conceiving larger, better ideas that could transcend and enfold existing institutions and practices. Four vice presidents of four modest banks could not dominate or compel anyone. They could only explain and educe. And so they did.

Bit by bit, though we could not know it at the time, we were building a foundation on which an extraordinary enterprise would self-organize and evolve, unfinished to this day. In retrospect it seems extraordinary. What was taking shape in our minds and hearts ran contrary to conventional wisdom. At the time, there was no complexity theory, there was no Internet, there was no World Wide Web, there were no alliances, there was no information society. The Soviet Union was the evil empire to the U.S., and the U.S. was the devil incarnate to the Soviet Union. Both professed to have all the answers.

IBM, General Motors, ITT, and other such hierarchal giants were the epitome of management and the shining path to a bright economic future. Science and technology, with a few tens of billions more dollars, would see us to the promised land where we would be able to control everything. A bigger, more powerful, central government would solve all our problems. The world was an ideological battleground contesting which kind of massive, centralized power and wealth best solves societal problems. Only a handful of people questioned whether they ever could, ever would, or ever should.

***

During the next year and a half, the effort grew steadily as hundreds of minds and dozens of disciplines became intrigued and were applied to it. In the beginning, none of the licensees thought that the Bank of America would surrender ownership of a trademark and licensing system that assured them a quarter percent or more of the revenues of every participant in perpetuity. No one thought that banks would voluntarily surrender a portion of their autonomy to an external entity in order to act together for a common purpose. No one believed that such a horizontal grouping of competitors could exist within the spirit and constraints of antitrust laws. And no one dreamed the emerging ideas would bring together in common ownership and enterprise people and institutions of every race, language, custom, and culture—every economic, legal, philosophical, and religious persuasion in the world.

In the beginning, few paid the effort much attention. As it advanced and gained attention, it was subjected to much ridicule. As it approached success, bitter opposition emerged from many sources. Many times, the best abilities and worst behavior of command-and-control organizations and powerful disciples devoted to that way of thinking were brought to bear against it. Yet, each time, it had enough vitality to survive. As it advanced, the purpose, principles, and people, tempered by the fire of each ordeal, grew stronger.

There were dozens of times when I longed to quit. What prevented me is not entirely clear. All that is clear was stubborn conviction that the ideas that had been forming over the years were sound. They had to be tried. The possibility of that which has never occurred cannot be determined by opinion—only by an attempt. Attempting the impossible is not rational, though reason may play some part in it. It is beyond reason. It is a matter of hope, faith, and determination.

Each time I fell into despair and wanted to give up, and it happened often, something softly whispered, "Not now. Not while you still believe and cannot know. If you can see the next step, go on, go on!" It really wasn't courage. It wasn't compulsion to succeed. It wasn't fear of failure. More than enough failure had come my way to create healthy respect for it, along with strong aversion. Failure hurts worse than a rotten tooth, but it's not fatal. What kept me going remains a mystery. It doesn't really matter, for there was an inexpressible sense that in some profound, nonphysical way, existence would lose meaning if I did not persist. It may have had something to do with another mantra that has supported me through the years. *If you think you can't, why think.*

Jack, Fred, and Sam were dear friends and stalwarts through the next year and a half of trial and trauma. They received nothing for all their commitment and labor except the joy and satisfaction it brought. Long after life led them in other directions, we met once again in Sausalito to honor them as progenitors of Visa. Our paths then drifted apart and I do not know where they are today, but one thing I do know. Without Jack, Fred, and Sam, there would be no story to tell. Bless them one and all.

Chapter Nine

The Next to the Last Word

Trust thyself; every heart vibrates to that iron string!
—Ralph Waldo Emerson

The weeks after the Sausalito meeting were filled night and day by work with lawyers, accountants, and members of the various committees as we struggled to translate the principles into a conceptual structure. Dozens of working groups formed, dissolved, or combined as question after question was posed. No ultimate answers emerged, only better questions. If this institution were to self-organize, in effect, to design itself, it would require continual consensus. Not consensus in the modern meaning of unanimous agreement, but in the original, deeper sense of solidarity. A position where all could stand comfortably together to act in accordance with purpose and principle, learn from the acts, reflect upon the learning and formulate the next step. It required valuing innovation more than engineering—synthesis more than analysis—understanding more than knowing. Another insight was slowly forming, although I could not articulate it then. In lighter moments, I now refer to it as *the theology of chaordic organization writ simple. Heaven is purpose, principle, and people. Purgatory is paper and procedure. Hell is rule and regulation.*

In an early meeting with Bank of America officers, we had gained assurance that they would neither oppose nor endorse the intent of the committees to explore alternatives to the licensing program. They would participate in those efforts, reserving the right to act unilaterally as events unfolded. Top management of the bank would not be directly involved. Jack Dillon would continue to work with the committees on a day-to-day basis, along with a representative of the licensing corporation. Policy decisions would rest with Kenneth Larkin, Senior Vice President of the bank, who would seek approval from higher authority as required.

Larkin was a man not easily overlooked. A former football lineman, over six feet tall and massively built, he was a good many years and a great many pounds past his playing days. But there was nothing ponderous about his intellect. Casual acquaintances were inclined to describe him as a giant, temperate, teddy bear of a man, and so he usually was. But there were hidden depths to him not often displayed. Come hard up against his desire to win and "temperate teddy bear" are not words you would use. Come hard up against his temper and "giant" would do fine.

On June 24, 1969, the national licensee executive committee met in San Francisco for two days of intense work shaping the concept. Fred, Sam, Jack, and I met with Ken the third day to review our work, since an early response from the Bank of America was important to continuation of it. Although casually acquainted with Ken, none but Jack had ever dealt with him on substantive matters. It was not an auspicious beginning. Larkin rose, greeting us with what he no doubt thought was humor, but which we took as derision.

"Well, well, well. Here they are—the leaders of the revolution!"

Licensees believed that the condition of the system was largely the result of failure on the part of the Bank of America. They did not see themselves as revolutionaries, but as people with programs at risk volunteering to clean a stable fouled by Bank of America horses. It was an incendiary situation, to say the least.

I could literally hear the hair rising on the back of Sam's and Fred's necks. Mine was certainly bristling. Jack, who had worked with Larkin for years, merely grinned. Fortunately, no one responded in kind as we began to explain in considerable detail the work already done, the emerging conclusions and the direction in which the effort appeared to be heading. Near the end of the discussion, Fred James, in his polite, southern way, put a point he was making without equivocation. Ken rose bolt upright in his chair. His face grew red. His neck swelled. Veins in his forehead stood out. His anger fed on itself as he bellowed,

"We invented the *#~*'d system! We own it! We produce 40 percent of the system volume! *#*d if we will be pushed around!"

Shocked and embarrassed into silence, Sam, Fred, and I watched the performance. Jack said nothing, a touch of a grin teasing the corner of his mouth. In the silence that followed, the explosion vanished as swiftly as it came. In an impressive exhibition of self-control, Ken settled back in his chair, took a deep breath and, without apology or comment, resumed as though nothing had happened. He assured us the bank would give careful consideration to our recommendations and formulate a prompt response.

After the meeting we separated. Jack, noncommittal, returned to his duties at the bank, while Sam, Fred, and I shared a cab to the airport. Fred was furious and Sam was girded for battle. They thought the bank had little understanding, appreciation, or sympathy for what was being attempted; that they were merely creating a façade of cooperation, waiting to see what benefit might accrue, while looking for an opportunity to put the upstarts in their place. No less angry, I nevertheless felt it would be foolish to allow emotions to distract us from our objective.

For a month, we heard nothing one way or the other, only that the matter was under consideration at the highest levels of the bank, presumably, the board of directors. Near the end of July, the reply came. "The bank is in sympathy with the avowed aims of your executive committee, namely to form a national association responsive to the collective needs and desires of the licensees but..." The bank then laid out its position.

They must have representation on the board equal to their percentage of the sales volume. That would violate our fundamental principle of governance not dominated by any institution or interest. They must be retained as managing partner of the association for a minimum of five years. This violated nearly all of the principles and would leave the system subject to the same management that was responsible for the current situation. The bank, as managing partner, must retain ownership and control of all trademarks and remain as exclusive licensing agent, which it would exercise with dispassion and objectivity (presumably, an equitably elected board of a new organization could not do so). Again, it was contrary to all our principles. They must retain ownership of the goodwill, trademarks, and properties. Again, contrary to all principles.

The letter continued at some length in the same vein. It appeared to be a complete impasse. A call to Larkin revealed it was the best the bank would do. The decision had been carefully considered at the highest levels and would not be changed.

The licensee executive committee assembled to consider whether to proceed with the reorganization in view of the bank's position. We thought such an imposition by BofA would ensure the failure of the organization. Everything the new organization did would be suspect. Forming a new organization subject to the bank's conditions might be somewhat better than the present situation, but far short of our intent. It was abysmally short of my dreams. It put us in the same position as the prominent politician who received an excoriating letter from Tom Paine shortly after the American revolution. I shared the final line with the committee.

> As to you, sir, history will be hard put to decide whether you abandoned principle, or ever had any.

Were we to abandon principle? Did we really have any? It was a tough question. Some were inclined to stand on principle and abandon the effort. Others thought the bank's position was better than the present situation and should be accepted. BofA hadn't exactly slammed the front door in our face, but they had certainly told us to use the servants' entrance. Would they answer the front door bell if we rang again?

With the committee's consent, I called Ken Larkin, informing him that the committee was in session and before making a decision would like to go over the bank's position to be certain it was not based on misunderstanding of our work, or our misunderstanding of the bank's intent. We went over each point in the bank's letter. He was adamant.

"The decision has been made after careful consideration at the highest levels of the bank ... it is generous, proper, and fair ... it should be accepted ... there is nothing further to negotiate." We had no reason to doubt his word. Another defining moment. Each member of the committee would have to decide in accordance with his personal convictions. If the committee capitulated, I must step aside, for my convictions were unshakable. But were the bank's? Only one way to find out. During my years of college debate, I had held fast to the notion that until someone has repeatedly said "no!" and adamantly refuses another word on the subject, they are in process of saying "yes" and don't know it.

"Ken, let me repeat the position of the Bank of America so that I can get it down precisely." My voice gradually slowed to writing speed as I improvised a word here and there for effect.

"Ken Larkin, senior vice president, said, 'the Bank of America will not agree to an organization ... equitably ... owned ... by ... all ... banks ... unless ... it ... can ... unilaterally ... control ... management ... for—" He abruptly interrupted.

"What are you doing?"

"Ken, I understand and respect the bank's position. I can't speak for the committee, and don't know what decision they will make. However, my strong recommendation will be to abandon the effort. If the committee agrees, we have no choice but to immediately inform all licensees and the media of our decision, along with the reason. It is essential we convey the bank's position fairly and accurately. I want to quote you with precision." The silence is long and profound before his voice comes back over the line.

"Before you do that, perhaps you should come to San Francisco and meet with Sam Stewart, vice chairman of the board." *So, it wasn't their last word on the subject.*

In San Francisco, I crossed the cold, wind-swept plaza adjoining the towering

Bank of America highrise, pausing momentarily to glance at a huge, polished blob of black granite sculpture. It was fondly known by half the city's cab drivers as "the banker's heart" and by the other half as "the last deposit." After ascending the express elevator to the executive offices near the top, I was promptly ushered through a palatial executive floor to shake hands with an impressive man with a booming, bass voice so deep it seemed amplified. It emerged from a barrel chest below a generous smile and an engaging face.

Lawyer, litigator, general counsel, and now number two officer in the largest bank in the world, he had it all: polished hardwood floor—antique oriental carpet—cases of rare books—fine art—breathtaking views of city, bay, and hills. An aircraft carrier moved imperceptibly down the bay, a child's toy under a bridge crawling with eight lanes of metal ants.

After a gracious few moments, he began to set forth the position of the bank. It was apparent I was there for correction, not conversation. I sat quietly, listening intently.

The bank had pioneered the bank card business, they had created BankAmericard—they had suffered through huge losses to make it profitable—they had created the licensing structure—major problems were normal in such an expansion—banks had taken licenses in reliance on the Bank of America's experience and expertise—the name BankAmericard, the name of the bank, and the goodwill of both were at stake—they had been cooperative throughout the organizational effort—they had made many concessions—it was unreasonable to expect them to subject themselves to a new, untested concept with unknown management—it was unreasonable to abandon the effort and blame the bank—we should accept their proposal and work in good faith to resolve system difficulties." He fell silent, waiting for a reply. It was all true. There was nothing with which to argue. Everything was accurate and true—*from his perspective.*

I instinctively liked this man. He seemed without guile. What he said was honest, to the point, and articulated with all the logic and force of a powerful man of strong conviction. I was not being manipulated, and yet, and yet—something was missing. What he said was about how things were, how they are, and how they might become. He had said nothing *about how they ought to be.* The future is not about logic and reason. It's about imagination, hope, and belief. I did not believe his perception was right. It was skewed by his perspective. His candor and sincerity deserved no less in return. With a deep breath and great trepidation, the sheep went off the high dive.

"Mr. Stewart, it's not politic or sensible for a vice president of a modest bank in Seattle to tell the vice chairman of the largest bank in the world that he is mistaken, but I believe you are." The silence was deafening. I plunged on.

"What you propose is not in the best interests of the Bank of America, the licensees, or the industry." He stared at me intently, soberly, over his half-lens reading glasses for a very, very, *very* long moment, while I got loose in my chair. This meeting was about to end abruptly. His voice was measured.

"You really believe that, don't you?"

"Yes, sir, I really do."

"Then tell me why." He tipped his chair back, folded his hands across his stomach, stared into my eyes, and said not a word as I loosed conviction and belief.

"Control of management would ensure the failure of a new organization—it was contrary to all the principles we had worked so assiduously to develop, in which we deeply believed—the new organization would have no heart, no spirit if they were abandoned—truly honest people would not work under such controlled conditions—the licensing structure could never compel cooperative behavior—licensees would never surrender autonomy to an organization controlled by one bank—reconceiving product and organization could expand the market for cards far beyond anything now imagined—the Bank of America would benefit far more from its share of that market than it ever could from royalties in the present market—the bank should be the leader of a movement, not the commander of a structure." It was certainly not a performance up to Stewart's level, but it was not bad for a bloody sheep. He asked a few questions for clarification, then boomed, "Will you put your thoughts in writing and send them to me? Can you come again in two weeks?"

"Yes, sir."

Two days later, a three-page letter was in the mail to Sam. Two weeks later I returned to San Francisco. He met me at the door with a warm smile, settled us in comfortable chairs, and in that magnificent bass voice I grew to respect, then to love, bowled me over in ten seconds.

"We've thought very carefully about what you said and have come to the conclusion that, in the main, it is right. There are many things to be better understood and some to be negotiated, but you'll have our full support in the attempt to form a new organization in accordance with your principles, and our good faith in negotiating terms and conditions for transfer of ownership." Although there were a great many differences to be overcome in the months ahead, although a few people within the bank never quite got the message, from that day forward the support of Sam Stewart and the Bank of America never wavered.

To this day, the explosion of Ken Larkin remains a mystery. It was not the last conflict we would have over the years, but out of it all came great admiration and trust. Ken became a long-time director of Visa, an honest critic, a staunch supporter, and a wonderful friend.

It was a mammoth undertaking. After the purpose, principles, and concepts were clear and general consent obtained, laws had to be analyzed, a corporate charter and constitution quite unlike any that had ever existed had to be crafted, initial operating procedures written, a jurisdiction found where such an entity could be brought into legal existence, consent from the Federal Department of Justice obtained, contracts with the Bank of America for licensing of the service marks constructed, compensation negotiated, money for organization expenses obtained, and hundreds of other complexities analyzed and understood. Over the months that followed, one after the other seemingly insurmountable obstacles were encountered and overcome.

Understanding of the opportunities and excitement about the concepts were soon contagious. Hundreds of talented, dedicated people from more than a hundred banks volunteered their time, self-organized, and worked assiduously to understand and anticipate legal, marketing, operating, financial, and technological problems and opportunities. Virtually everyone had full-time jobs in their card centers as well. It had to be done with no assurance the organization could ever be brought into being, for no one could be certain what would emerge. Commitment was only to the process. Commitment to the eventual result could not be asked from any bank, not even Bank of America, until the final result was fully known and carefully documented.

Early in 1970, it appeared everything was falling in place and the greatest obstacle of all could no longer be ignored. There were more than 200 full-licensee card-issuing banks. Each had the right to sublicense other banks as agents to help them enroll merchants and solicit consumers for cards. Nearly 2,500 agent banks had been sublicensed. Meanwhile, the bank card frenzy had not subsided. Banks continued to flood into the business, fearing their traditional banking business would be eroded. More banks were being licensed every month. Problems throughout the systems continued to accelerate.

More than three thousand banks must somehow be induced to surrender their license for cancellation to Bank of America and simultaneously bind themselves to membership in a new organization quite unlike any that had existed before. It was to be called National BankAmericard Incorporated (NBI). An initial meeting must be organized to elect the first governing board, but no one could know which banks might be eligible to attend and vote until the actual membership agreements were signed.

All banks would sign an identical membership agreement. In a couple of paragraphs, each would acknowledge receipt of the NBI certificate of incorporation, bylaws, operating procedures, and agree to abide by them "as they now exist or are hereafter modified." It was a surrender of autonomy to their collective selves, since they would be the owners, members, and governors of the new organization. Never before had banks voluntarily surrendered autonomy to any organization. It may have been taken from them by government or regulatory authorities, but voluntarily surrendered?—never! Inducing three thousand banks to surrender their licenses and become owner/members of a new, untested concept of organization was no job for a sheep.

***

In the comfortable sitting room near his desk, Max Carlson, as always, settles into his chair, hooks both thumbs in the small pockets of his vest, winds one leg around the other and looks down, listening intently to an explanation of the problem. His reply is concise.

"Go directly to the top, young man, or the decision will become hopelessly mired in middle management. Such a decision will not be made in any bank without approval of the chief executive officer and, quite likely, the board. Start with ten or fifteen of the most influential, highly respected chief executive officers whose lead will be followed. Gain their consent, and ask their help in persuading others." He mentions several names. They might as well be Jesus and the twelve Apostles for all the influence I would have.

"Mr. Carlson, would you help form such a group?"

"Young man, that would be a mistake. The National Bank of Commerce is not a large, money-center bank, nor do I have the personal influence you need. If asked, we will be pleased to participate, however, it would do you and the effort a disservice if we were to take the lead. The man who could do this without difficulty is

Tom Clausen, president of the Bank of America. You should speak with him."

"But, I've only said hello to him once in passing. If I should try to speak with him he may refer the whole thing to someone who knows nothing about the situation. I don't want to start over."

"You seem to have gained the confidence of Sam Stewart. He might do as well as Clausen. Why don't you start with him?" He rises, smiling, to bid me farewell.

"Did the meeting serve your purpose?"

"Yes, sir."

***

A day later, it was a lucky sheep who flew from one statesman and wonderful human being to another. Sam had graciously crowded me into his schedule. He listened carefully, thought it a good approach, and agreed to take the lead. We drew up a list of twenty or thirty chief executive officers from which we selected thirteen, making certain there was one from each of the regions in which committees had been formed. Sam felt it would be unlikely we would get all CEOs on short notice. If not, he would ask that another top officer with full authority to act for the bank be designated to participate.

Each would be asked to become a member of an executive officers' organizing committee. They would meet for a half day in New York and listen to an exposition of problems, opportunities, and essential elements of the new organization. Each would receive complete documentation in its present stage of development, return to their bank, and have it analyzed by appropriate people. They could then suggest improvements for consideration by the working committees, which would accept only those which met the test of purpose and principle.

Thirty days after their first meeting, the CEO committee would meet again for a final discussion. Each would then either commit to support the reconception of the system or decline to participate. If two-thirds or more agreed to the program, each would continue to serve for six months and support an effort to bring NBI into being. Sam agreed to make calls to induce them to participate. If all agreed, he would arrange the meetings.

Sam was a powerful persuader. Within the week he called to say all had agreed. We would meet a week hence in New York. Sam would open the meeting, indicate that the Bank of America thought the proposals had merit, and thereafter act only as one member of the committee. The rest was my responsibility. Frightening, but fair enough.

***

It was an impressive group that met February 8, 1970, in New York in an awesome board room near the top of another towering bank headquarters. They greeted one another as old friends, comparing private jet flights, golf scores, and banking deals made. It was an intimidated sheep who sat silently, wondering if they were the kind of corporate people that bloodied the hides of obstreperous sheep. Nothing had prepared me for this, save a few conversations with Sam Stewart and Max Carlson. I'd never before been in a corporate board room. Little more than a year before, I had been sorting trash in the basement of a bank branch.

I silently repeated a small mantra devised years before. It was the only human equation that has ever made sense to me. Whenever approaching someone with greater wealth, power, and position, I silently repeat, *"I am as great to me as you are to you, therefore, we are equal."* When approached by those with less power, wealth, or position, I silently repeat, *"You are as great to you as I am to me, therefore, we are equal."* It doesn't always work, but it never fails to help.

Sam opened the meeting and made it clear the Bank of America was receptive to the concepts but would act only as one of the group. Thereafter, he seemed content to sit quietly listening to others and observing their reaction, forcing me to handle the discussion and respond to concerns.

It was clear the bank wanted freedom to act as it thought best after knowing the reaction of others. While he made no effort at persuasion, his mere presence and leadership in calling the meeting was enough to ensure a fair hearing from everyone. They were uniformly courteous, interested, perceptive—but noncommittal. Questions were to the point, and discussion centered on substantive issues rather than detail. My tension melted as I got out of myself and into the ideas that meant so much to me.

They left with the package in hand, committed only to meet thirty days later in Chicago. Meanwhile, they would receive a final package of proposals and documentation. In Chicago, after another half day of discussion, they would be asked to commit their bank or withdraw. If committed, they would agree to serve for another six months, and sponsor meetings of CEOs of full-licensee banks in their area at which the same presentation would be made. The proposal would live or die on its merits. Momentum was building.

***

March 11, 1970 is a raw, windy day in Chicago when the executive officers organizing committee gathers for the second time. Another towering bank building, another awesome board room, another splendid lunch. It's hard to imagine these folks ever meeting in a stockroom to sit on a box and laugh together over a sandwich. They are really comfortable in such posh places. I'm sure as hell not. But this is where life has led and there's nothing to be done about it except endure.

The meeting begins with sharp, penetrating questions. No one appears to have taken the proposal lightly. I have no time to coddle my discomfort.

"What happens if a bank decides not to join?"

"The organizing principles require they not be left in a lesser position. Their license with Bank of America will remain in full force and effect. Members of the new organization will be obliged to interchange with them on the same basis as they would with other members. The Bank of America will apply all regulations adopted by NBI to the licensees. However, they will have no voice in the new organization."

"What if a bank decides not to join and does not wish to continue in the system?"

"They will be free to surrender their license, have ample time to discontinue operations, sell their program to another licensee, or convert their BankAmericards to a competitive program of their choice."

"What if a bank wants to enter the program with a license from Bank of America rather than through the new organization?"

"NBI will have an exclusive, perpetual license covering the United States. There will be no further licensing by Bank of America and none by NBI. Participation will require becoming an owner-member with equitable rights and obligations."

"What about banks in other countries?"

"Creating such an organization in the U.S. is difficult enough. If it can't be done in one country, it can never be done at greater scale. Attempting to create such an organization among nations with different cultures, languages, laws, currencies, and economic systems could jeopardize the U.S. effort. The Bank of America will continue the licensing program overseas, and NBI will act on behalf of its members in relations with foreign licensees."

"How can NBI ensure equity and fairness between hundreds of U.S. banks operating under different laws in different markets?"

"If you conceive of NBI as nothing but its core board and employees, it can't. But that's a misperception. There will be no negotiated contracts. Each member will sign an identical agreement acknowledging that they have received a copy of the certificate of incorporation, bylaws, and operating procedures and agree to abide by them as they now exist or are hereafter modified. Modification can be made only by governance bodies and methods that ensure that all views will be heard and decisions are not dominated by anyone. Think of it as a reverse holding company. The regulations to which each party must submit are created by them. Any time a member does not like what has been created, they are free to walk away without obligation. It is an open, enabling, self-governing organization."

"Will NBI be formed if only a small percentage of banks agree to join?"

"No. If two-thirds commit it will become operational. We believe NBI is important enough to risk losing participants that produce a third of the volume of the system, but not more. If members producing two-thirds of the volume do not join, the effort will be abandoned."

"What if the owner-members want to make major changes, such as selecting a new name and abandoning the name 'BankAmericard'?"

"There will be no restrictions on the power of the board to act in any manner within the constraints of law. However, the constitution of the new organization requires higher percentages of approval on such critical matters. The name can be changed if 80 percent of the banks approve."

"Doesn't the antitrust law forbid the formation of an organization composed of competitors?"

"Normally, yes. But there is a provision that allows such formation if it can be demonstrated that the service or product is impossible to provide without joint action. The Justice Department will then issue a letter that does not release the organization from its obligations under the antitrust laws, but gives assurance the Department will not act against it unless anti-competitive effects are observed. We have had extensive advice from antitrust lawyers, as well as many discussions with the Department of Justice, and have received such assurance."

"What assurance do we have that NBI can resolve present problems and create the kind of markets you envision?"

"None! It's a matter of judgment and trust."

The questions continue fast and intense, hour after hour, through the morning and into the afternoon. These people are being asked to put their reputations on the line for a concept that bears little resemblance to organizational concepts with which they are familiar. It is one thing for card-center managers who are being torn apart by present problems and have little to lose by supporting the concept. It is quite another for the people who hold power and responsibility and are asked to surrender a portion of it, no matter how small.

In the middle of the afternoon, the questions dwindle and come to an end. Finally, the moment of truth. Will they commit their bank? Will they put their individual power and prestige behind the effort? They hesitate, then, surprisingly, ask if I will leave the room so they can have a half hour in private. There is no choice but to accede to their wishes. It is a half hour of torment.

The door finally opens and the reason is revealed. They have one condition without which none is prepared to make a commitment. There must be no change of leadership at this critical juncture. Will I commit to continue to lead the effort? It is puzzling. Why in the world would that require private discussion?

"Yes, of course. There is no way I will walk away until the job is done and the organization formed, even if it takes a year or more." One of the more outspoken interjects.

"I don't think you understand. We want a commitment that you are prepared to move to San Francisco and head NBI. You've led the effort since the beginning and brought it this far. We don't want to risk a change of leadership during the remainder of the process, or for several years thereafter. If you are willing, Sam will negotiate terms and conditions. Only the board of the new organization can appoint officers of NBI, but if they select you, we want to be certain you will accept. If you will make that commitment, you will have our commitment."

"All of you? Everyone?"

"Yes."

Thoughts race through my mind as I fall silent. Had I wanted to be asked to lead the new organization if it came into being? Yes, of course. I would have cursed them if they had not. Had I expected them to? No! I didn't fit the mold—had no credentials—was not a member of the club—carried no recommendation from previous employers—had been savaged often enough to expect no better.

Had I any intention of accepting if asked? None! I was exhausted. The work had taken every moment of my waking hours for a year and a half. Both sons were to graduate high school in four months. Both had been accepted at University of Washington. Our daughter was a freshman in high school. Ferol was a year out of university and well established as a speech and hearing therapist. I loved the mountains, forests, and lakes of the Pacific Northwest. There was a great sense of obligation to Maxwell Carlson. What I desperately wanted was my life back: to bring this dream into being, return to the Northwest, and perfect my retirement on the job.

I explained my position and desires. It made no difference. They would like a decision within the week. It was unreasonable. They were asking me for commitment to a job they could not offer, working for a company not yet fully structured, for owners yet to be determined, and governed by an unknown board. They were adamant. No commitment, no commitment! As simple as that. I was gibbeted, swinging in the wind.

Chapter Ten

The Corporation or the Cane

Man is not born evil. Why then are some of them infected with this plague of malevolence? It's because those who are at their head have the malady and communicate it to the rest of mankind.
—Voltaire

It is a ridiculous thing for a man not to fly from his own badness, which is indeed possible, but to fly from other men's badness which is impossible.
—Marcus Aurelius Antonius

The days after returning from Chicago to Seattle were miserable as I alternated between the multitude of things necessary to keep the organizational effort alive and a search for equanimity and clarity about what I should do. Near the end of the second day, notebook and pocket knife in my jacket, I slipped away for a long walk in woods filled with slanting shafts of light from a spring sun sinking slowly in the western sky. A few yellowed pages of notes survive from that day, resurrected from an old file where they remained unseen and forgotten these past thirty-five years. The flood of feeling they evoke is impossible to describe.

    I walked to the hill, sat on a fallen tree in the edge of a thicket and leisurely whittled a maple walking stick. It came to me that forming and building NBI, or anything of worth, is much the same. It requires sound material, a good tool, a capable hand and, most important, a vision of things to come. It requires patience and persistence to pursue the vision chip, by chip, by chip, and willingness to change the vision as the nature of the material is revealed.

    What foolish logic would rationalize becoming president of NBI? It means giving up grass, rain, trees, birds, insects—all the natural living things. It means dirty air, city jungles, confinement in steel and concrete boxes, conniving people and fussing, futile work. It means living where I do not live, liking what I do not like, and working how I work not. Perhaps I can hang onto reality if I remember the things I love best and simply write off the next three years for education of the children and my desire to provide Ferol with freedom and some of the finer things she so richly deserves. Will I come to prefer the corporation to whittling a cane? Somehow, I doubt it.

> As Old Monkey Mind and I struggled with our personal dilemma, we could not avoid then, or even now, our endless effort to understand the nature of organizations, particularly corporations. They have become so ubiquitous, so much a part of us from the moment of birth, that we accept them with as little thought as the air we breathe and the water we drink. Corporations are not natural phenomena. They are creations of man. Old Monkey and I knew we could never understand corporations unless we followed our customary practice and examined them *as they*

were, as they are, as they might become, and as they ought to be. NBI would certainly be incorporated in one legal jurisdiction or another. If it was to be truly different, we must peel the corporate onion to its essence.

We began with the dry skeletons in the dusty closets of dictionary and encyclopedia. *Black's Law Dictionary* tells us that a corporation is "an artificial person or legal entity created by or under the authority of the laws of a state or nation ... ordinarily consisting of an association of numerous individuals. Such entity ... is regarded in law as having a personality and existence distinct from that of its several members ... vested with the capacity of continuous succession irrespective of changes in its membership, either in perpetuity or for a limited term of years"—et cetera. Mr. Black was obviously struggling, along with the rest of us, to make something understandable out of the mental abstraction called "corporation."

Corporations *as they were* bear little resemblance to corporations *as they now are.* The original concept of corporation was a collective entity intended to attract people and resources needed to realize a desired social objective beyond the ability or resources of a single individual. It was created through the power of government and authorized to exist as an entity with limited, carefully prescribed rights and obligations. It was to be chartered for a limited time, to realize a limited public purpose, in a limited area. It was to be open to rigorous social and governmental surveillance. Its "natural" death in time was specified in the charter. Actions in excess of, or inadequate to the purpose, would be punished by revocation of the charter.

The proliferation of the corporate concept of organization was given great impetus in the sixteenth and seventeenth centuries by the huge, imperialist expansion of Western nation-states through subjugation of people on other continents. The increase in geographic scale, attendant risk, and capital that imperialist expansion required fueled the desire for limited personal liability, limited responsibility for risk, and unlimited opportunity for gain. The corporate form of organization became a useful instrument for government plunder. It is not to be wondered that it soon had a tendency to become an instrument for private plunder as well. Pursuit of limitations on personal liability and unrestrained opportunity for personal gain became a conflagration burning ever hotter within corporations from the seventeenth century to the present day.

In the United States, the first general corporation-for-profit statute was enacted by New York State in 1811, with other states gradually following its lead. The corporation as a business mechanism came into prominence during and after the Civil War, again as an instrument of government for achieving its purpose in a time of great civil strife and expense. The statutes governing such entities have been liberalized, broadened, and made more detailed in their provisions ever since, gradually moving away from the interests of government and society to the interests of monetary shareholders and management.

A critical moment in the evolution of the corporate form of organization passed virtually unnoticed in 1885, when the Supreme Court, in a case involving the Southern Pacific Railroad, ruled without comment that a corporation is a person within the meaning of the Bill of Rights.

What then happened was noted succinctly in 1938 by Supreme Court Justice Hugo Black in a dissent in a case involving an insurance company demanding rights of a human being, when he wrote, "Of the cases in this court in which the 14th amendment was applied during the first fifty years after its adoption, less than one half of one percent involved the protection of the Negro race, and more than fifty percent asked that its benefits be extended to corporations." Little has changed since Black expressed his outrage.

In the beginning, no one dreamed that small aggregations of wealth and power legalized in the form of corporations to achieve social purposes would persistently grind away social and legislative mandates that controlled corporate purpose, restricted its territory, confined its growth, and curbed its behavior. But they did. No one dreamed that, in addition to other rights and power, they would demand and receive the rights of human beings, but they did.

The for-profit, monetized, shareholder form of corporation has demanded and received perpetual life. It has demanded and received the right to define its own purpose and act solely for self-interest. It has demanded and received release from the revocation of its charter for inept or antisocial acts. It has demanded and received ever more protection and privilege from government. The roles of giant, transnational corporations and government have slowly reversed. For all practical purposes, government is now more an instrument of monetized corporatism than such corporatism is an instrument of government.

They are no longer, not even indirectly, an instrument of the societies they affect, but an instrument of the few who control the ever-increasing power and wealth they command. The purpose of wealth is to acquire power. The purpose of power is to protect wealth. The purpose of wealth and power combined is to acquire more wealth and power. The use of the commercial corporate form for the purpose of social good has become incidental.

The monetized, commercial form of corporation has steadily become an instrument of those with surplus money (capital) and those with surplus power (management) to reward themselves at the expense of the community, the biosphere, and the many without surplus wealth or power, commonly called "consumers" and "human resources." (Demeaning but revealing phrases.) Thus, "human resources" are smelted, shaped, made into products, worn out, and discarded with little more consideration on the part of monetary stockholders and management than they might give to a load of ore or a pile of lumber.

Nor is corporate power restricted to power over the employed. Global corporations now have implicit sovereignty over people throughout the world, since they are beyond the reach of any nation-state. They hold government and its instrumentalities to ransom for use of land, for reprieve from taxation, for access to natural resources far below cost, for direct monetary subsidization, and for use of land, air, and water as a repository for refuse. They do so by the simple expedient of bargaining one government against another for the claimed economic benefit of their presence.

Under the guise of free markets, they are now able to move their money, their operations, their

> products, and their management at will worldwide. No government can do so. No community can do so. Few individuals can do so. Global corporations are steadily creating a market for government in which they are the sole buyers. It is hard to imagine a more ubiquitous, finely honed instrument for the simultaneous accumulation of power and evasion of responsibility than monetized, commercial corporations.

As Old Monkey and I walked out of the woods with the maple cane and the journal, the choice was extremely difficult, yet simple. Either say no, abandon the dream or say yes and wholeheartedly accept the consequences, whatever they might be. With a heavy heart, but convinced it was the right decision, I returned to write a letter to Sam Stewart, mentioning but two needs: a salary small in relation to the responsibility and difficulty of the job ahead, but a bit more than our present income, and three years salary guaranteed should they wish me to step aside, or move the headquarters east of the Rocky Mountains.

The modest salary was suggested to make it clear this was a labor of love, not a matter of money. I fully expected that Sam and the committee would insist on more generous terms. The three years was based on conviction that if I faced without equivocations the decisions and acts necessary to restore stability to the system I would so alienate members that continuance beyond three years would be impossible. Remaining west of the Rocky Mountains was pure personal indulgence. Western bred and born, I could not imagine living elsewhere.

A week later, I met with Sam to discuss the letter. Sam was a lifelong employee and an integral part of the culture of the Bank of America. A.P. Giannini, the founder of Bank of America, gained fame by living in the same modest, suburban house throughout his life and paying himself a small salary. Salary scales in the bank went down from there. Whether he did so from conviction, or as a means of keeping costs low, was never known.

At the very least, it was disingenuous, for he enjoyed vast wealth from his shares in the bank and a host of amenities from organizations and foundations he controlled, while few employees had any. Whatever A.P.'s motives, as the growth of California in the first half of the century pushed the bank to prominence as the largest, most profitable in the world, it was equally prominent for abysmally low salaries. Sam is blunt.

"Dee, as President and CEO of NBI, your salary will be public information. There are only a half dozen people in the Bank of America who make as much as the salary you suggest. If NBI pays that salary it will become known in the bank, causing considerable discontent, and personal difficulty for me. We would be comfortable with a salary of $44,000 a year, beginning with the formation of NBI. We are also prepared to make a one-time payment of $10,000 in recognition of all that you have done in the past year and a half and must do in the months ahead to persuade the banks to join NBI and bring it into being."

He can't be serious! Forty-four thousand dollars, no benefits and no equity to straighten out a $2 billion dollar mess? Ten thousand dollars for two years of innovation and grinding work against impossible odds? Only a half dozen people in the Bank of America who make $60,000 a year? Even if true, what of stock options, other benefits, perquisites, and lifetime security? But Sam is serious. He senses my distress and tries to ease the situation.

"Dee, these things take time. There was a period, earlier in my career with the Bank of America, when I went for years without a raise. It wasn't easy, but it worked out in the end."

"Sam, if that is true, the Bank was undoubtedly in error the second year, the third year, and every year thereafter. Have you discussed this with other members of the CEO organizing committee?"

"No. They authorized me to handle the matter. It should be settled here and now if we want their commitment."

Had I misjudged this man? What possible motive could underlie this absurdity? Even if what he says is true, why should my compensation be determined by the bias of a single man in a single bank? I refuse to believe this man dishonest or insincere. Mistaken, yes! Deceitful, no! I had not expected unpleasant circumstances to arrive so quickly or my convictions to be so rudely tested, but my decision had been made without equivocation, and so it would remain.

"Sam, I'll do as you wish. But don't ask me to agree with you. You're wrong again, but this time it only compromises my pocketbook, and I can live with that. Tell the committee yes and accept their commitment. I'll be back in a week with a plan." As I left for Seattle, his pleasure seemed genuine and immediate.

> Old Monkey and I have continued to search the dark side of giant, monetized, shareholder corporations for many years. Not only are they creating a global market for government in which they are the sole buyers, they have become a superb instrument for the capitalization of

gain and socialization of cost. When a corporation rips from the Earth irreplaceable energy or resources, no matter how much it pays for them; when it uses any resources more rapidly than they can be replaced, or at less than full replacement cost, it has socialized the cost (spread it to society as a whole; the people at large) and capitalized the resultant gain.

When a corporation "downsizes" workers, abandons a community, or pays less than a living wage; when it creates and dumps waste in the process of manufacturing or marketing a product, or at the end of its useful life; when it receives a subsidy, guarantee, or relief from taxation by government, it has socialized a cost and capitalized the gain.

When a corporation utilizes highways, railroads, airlines, postal departments or other public infrastructure at less than their full cost; when it uses the military, the CIA, or any other government instrumentality to protect its interests;

when it diminishes topsoil, depletes the water table, or pollutes and poisons any biological system on which life depends, it has socialized a loss and capitalized the gain.

When a corporation engages in unsound lending, or currency speculation and looks to government, the World Bank, or the International Monetary Fund to bail out its customers, public or private, in order that they may repay their debt; when a corporation is awarded scarce portions of the electromagnetic spectrum to market its ideology and wares, it has socialized a cost and capitalized the gain.

The possibilities for socializing cost and capitalizing gain are endless, as those who hold power or wealth within monetized corporations have discovered to their endless benefit.

This effect of this vast corporate socialization of cost and capitalization of gain is no longer limited to the current generation. Liability for the socialized loss is transferred to the unlived life of the young and to generations yet unborn through countless government guarantees and instruments of long-term debt, and through depletion of natural resources that require centuries for regeneration. Interest is added to such debt and, when collected, paid to the same people who hold most shares in corporations, for it is their surplus wealth that is borrowed to fund government debt that future generations must pay.

Round and round the merry-go-round, as fewer and fewer get richer and richer and more powerful, while more and more people fall into poverty and despair, and generations unborn are placed deeper in bondage to voracious appetites of the moment for ever more power and wealth. The fascinating thing about the whole of it is that there are no evil people who wish it so, or who have conspired to make it happen. All are victimized by a false metaphor; a wrong concept of organization, an internal model of reality that is no longer relevant, a consciousness of reality neither whole nor wholesome.

The rationalizations they use and we too often accept ring hollow. "That some have, is evidence that all may get." "Power and wealth result from superior intelligence, effort, and ability." "Poverty results from lack of determination and character." "That some rise to the top is proof that all others could if they had sufficient intelligence and will." "Unlimited pursuit of self-interest (the 'invisible hand') will result in the greatest good for all." "A rising tide lifts all boats."

When we trumpet the glories of monetary capitalism and praise the fiction of free markets while decrying the evils of socialism we are engaging in cant and hypocrisy. Clearly, we make love to socialism in the balance-sheet bedroom called cost, and make love to capitalism in the bedroom called gain. It is tearing the physical world apart, and most people as well.

If the purpose of each corporation is not primarily the health and well-being of the Earth and all life thereon, if its principles are not based on equitable distribution of power and wealth, if it avoids responsibility for the sustenance of family, community, and place, if it has no belief system, or one devoid of ethical and moral content, it is difficult to see why it should have the sanction and protection of society through the arm of government.

We know how monetized corporations were. We know how they are. We know what they are becoming, and it is not a happy prospect for the vast majority of people. It is far past time to examine how such corporations ought to be and find ways in which they can evolve into a more constructive order of things. There can be no doubt that the people at the head of such corporations should be foremost in such transformation. *If they profess to be leaders; if they care at all how they ought to be, they should "go before and show the way."*

With an extremely heavy heart and troubled conscience I entered the sitting room in which I had spent three of the best moments of my life, once again to be greeted by Maxwell Carlson in his gentle, kindly manner.

"What can I do for you, young man?"

"Mr. Carlson, what I have to say is extremely difficult. You know how deeply I believe in the formation of NBI. The executive officers organizing committee, which you suggested, has unanimously agreed to support the formation of NBI and committed their banks to membership. They have one condition. They insist I continue to lead the effort through the organizational phase and for the first three years of operation. I don't want to leave the National Bank of Commerce or the Northwest. The travel, notoriety, and stress of the job are not pleasant to contemplate. The pay is poor. Yet, it's a concept in which I deeply believe and desperately want to succeed. A host of people have worked hard to bring it about and are depending on its success. It is not a happy choice, but I must leave the bank and can't make return for all that you have done." There is the usual, thoughtful moment of silence as he looks down; the inevitable gentle smile as he raises his head to reply.

"Well, young man, I rather thought this might happen. Put your mind at rest. We have been amply repaid by doing as we thought we should. If the new venture succeeds, we will be repaid time and again, both in material and more important ways. If it doesn't, there will always be a place for you at the National Bank of Commerce. Good luck, and if I can ever be of assistance, please let me know. Did the meeting serve your purpose?"

Let there be no doubt about it! If Maxwell Carlson had been a lesser human being, Visa would never have come to be.

Chapter Eleven

And Then There Was One

This spreading radiance of a true human being.
Has great importance.
Look carefully around you and recognize
The luminosity of souls.
Sit beside those who draw you to that.

—Jalal Uddin Rumi

When I returned a week later with the promised plan, Sam did not like it. "Dee, it's impossible. There is absolutely no way three thousand banks can be persuaded to surrender their licenses, become members of NBI, hold an annual meeting of members, elect a board, and have the whole thing in operation in ninety days. It can't be done."

"Sam, we can't know that without making the attempt. We have the support of thirteen powerful people. We have the interest and participation of dozens of others who have worked on it for a year and a half. The concepts are sound. The need is compelling. Momentum is building. If we link people in the right relationships, challenge them, and free them, they'll perform miracles. I've seen it happen before. Never on this scale, but we've got to try. If we drag it out it may never happen." Sam begins to waver.

"What would you need from the bank?"

"Six or eight dedicated people for sixty days to process the surrender and cancellation of all licenses."

"It would not be easy but it might be done. What else?"

"A management agreement under which NBI can borrow up to a dozen experienced, willing people from your card, legal, marketing, and systems departments, for six to eight months, to work solely in the interests of NBI and its prospective members. They will need the kind of independence I've had from the National Bank of Commerce. NBI to pay the bank 150 percent of all salaries and benefits. The people must be assured they can return to the bank at comparable jobs."

"That would be difficult, but it might be arranged."

I plunged ahead. "We'll need a $200, 000 line of credit at market rates for organizational expense, to be repaid from service fees of members once NBI is operational. If the effort fails, it should be divided among the banks represented by the executive officers organizing committee and written off as expense."

"We could look into that. What else would you need from BofA?"

"Assistance from your personnel department in recruiting, investigating, and hiring a small initial staff should the effort succeed."

"That would be possible."

"Temporary space in the vacant part of your old building across the street at reasonable month-to-month rent, and the loan of some old desks, files, and typewriters."

"We can look into that as well. Anything else?" Do I know him well enough? Can I take the risk? It's irresistible. I rephrase his words from our salary discussion and give them back to him.

"Sam, there's no time to 'look into' these things. The operating committees authorized me to handle the matter. It should be settled here and now if we want their commitment." He laughs, paraphrases my words, and makes return.

"OK, we'll do as you wish. I'll accept and never say more— but don't ask me to agree with you. You're wrong. There is no way this will be done in ninety days. Tell your operating committees 'yes' and accept their commitment. I'll be back with a plan for the bank's part in a week."

***

Within a day after meeting with Sam, I called each member of the executive officers organizing committee with a brash request. Would each arrange a half-day, morning meeting with senior executive officers of each full-licensee bank in his region? Would each attend the meeting he had arranged, explain the work of the committee, and its commitment to the concept? The chairmen of the regional working committees and I would attend each meeting and present the proposal. Would each accept an equal share of the organizational expense if the effort failed? It caught their fancy and all agreed.

They were as good as their word. Within ten days, they had coordinated with one another and twelve meetings were arranged, each on consecutive days at locations less than two hours flight time apart on well-traveled air routes. Those same ten days produced offices and employees borrowed from BofA. Every prospective attendee had been sent a complete package of material. Every member of every working committee had been briefed and was in touch with the executive officer from their bank who was scheduled to attend the regional meeting.

There was no one with authority to command or control anyone else. What needed to be done was discussed and agreed, each person to take responsibility for any part was to coordinate with others, decide how best to proceed, and get it done. There was excellent communication and growing trust. Order, coherence, and cohesion emerged.

In another ten days, I lifted off from the Seattle airport on the first leg of an impossible schedule. It's all a blur now—meeting after meeting—intense questions, skepticism, enthusiasm, criticism, confusion, persuasion—mad dashes to airports—catch-as-catch-can sleep—no time, no time—twelve days, twelve cities, two hundred banks, hundreds of people.

The executive officers of the licensee banks were to take their copy of the certificate of incorporation, bylaws, license cancellation agreement, membership agreement, and operating material, review it with anyone they wanted, then send suggestions, if any, for improvement to the executive working committee, which would make final decisions for incorporation of essential changes. A final owner/member charter package would then be created and simultaneously sent to each bank, each containing a provision for acceptance within a charter period of thirty days after receipt. Not a sentence, not a word, not a comma of the final charter package would be changed. Accept or reject—no other alternative, although membership would be open to any qualified bank at any time thereafter should the organization come into being.

Every bank electing to join would sign an identical, brief agreement in duplicate original, acknowledging receipt of the material and committing to abide by all provisions of the documents *"as they now exist and are hereafter modified."* A threshold of acceptance was specified. If reached, all charter member agreements and all contracts between NBI and the Bank of America would immediately be in full force and effect. If the threshold was not reached, all membership agreements and contracts would be null and void. A first meeting of owner/members was scheduled shortly after the deadline, at which the governing board would be elected and officers appointed, providing the effort was successful.

Each member would have one vote for every thousand dollars of sales volume transacted by their BankAmericard customers in the preceding year. Service fees would be one-quarter of 1 percent of that same sales volume. Thus, taxation and representation would be linked. Dividends or distributions, if any, would be on the basis of that fraction of the service fees paid by any member to that paid by the total membership. There would be no need for endless negotiating, endless contracting, endless disputes, and legal battles. *Essential rights and obligations, as well as the structure itself, would be self-organizing and self-governing in perpetuity.*

Memberships would be nontransferable and disconnected from cards and receivables. Portfolios of business could be bought and sold, but not owner/membership in the organization or rights to use of service marks or other properties. Those rights could only be acquired by eligibility, application, and acceptance to membership. However, it would be no closed club. Directors could determine general eligibility for membership but would have no power to decline any applicant meeting those requirements, or any power to accept an applicant who did not.

Although voting rights would be related to size of the program, there would be a one-bank, one-director rule. No matter how many votes a member acquired as a result of sales volume, once an employee of that bank was elected to the board, votes could not be used to elect another. Once elected, each director would have legal and fiduciary responsibility to the whole of the system, not to their bank or to the constituency from which elected. Each director would have a single vote with respect to board decisions.

There would be different types of directors. The country was divided into regions, each of which would elect a director. Only members headquartered in that region could vote for that region's directors. Five directors at large would be elected by the entire membership under cumulative voting procedures. One director would be elected by the smallest banks. Any bank having more than 15 percent of the sales volume could appoint a director.

Every director must be reelected every year. The board could appoint a nominating committee to suggest candidates for election. However, if any other individual was nominated by a member and seconded by another, the person must be put on the ballot and given equal treatment with board nominees. Elections for regional directors could be by mail, but if a single member requested a meeting for purposes of election *it must* be held. Nominations could be made from the floor by any member at any meeting.

The president, appointed by the board, would be the chief executive officer and a member of the board by right of that appointment, but could not hold the chairmanship. The chairman would be elected by the board, but would have no executive or operating authority. The president would be responsible for preparing the agenda for board meetings. Any matter could be put on the agenda by any director. The chairman would preside at all board meetings, make certain all views were openly, equitably heard, and that decisions were in accordance with all provisions of the bylaws and policies of the organization, and relevant laws and regulations. The chairman would be free of any responsibility to support the views of management, and would have no right to suppress them.

Once the organization came into being, the board could amend the bylaws, but they were carefully crafted to require votes as high as 80 percent to prevent gerrymandering of provisions essential to the organizational principles on which the bylaws were based. Critical provisions required approval by 80 percent of the board *and* 80 percent of the membership.

Over and over again I explained the purpose, principles, concept, and structure, and repeated my mantra: "You will not like everything about the organization and you will not like everything it does. But one thing on which you may depend is that it can be trusted. No member of any class will have greater or lesser rights than any other. No director will have a greater or lesser voice. Management will have no control over composition of the board. The minimal autonomy necessary to the common good will be surrendered by each member to yourselves as a cooperative whole. You the participants, and you alone, will make all decisions through the most open and equitable structure that hundreds of participants could devise. Deliberation and debate will be open to all and controlled by none, particularly management."

Many were skeptical, but as the days wore on they could find nothing in the charter documents to the contrary. Suggestions of all kinds flowed in. Some reflected misunderstanding. Some were self-serving, couched in terms of "we will only join if you change this or that." Some were clearly improvements. Every suggestion was carefully examined by a legal committee composed of counsel for a representative group of banks and by the operational committees. Final decisions for inclusion were made by the licensee executive committee.

The immense pressures of trying to bring into being a new form of organization to deal with the credit card mess did not deter Old Monkey and me from our incessant search for answers to the three questions with which we were obsessed. It led to an attempt to understand the phenomenon of accounting, a profession and practice that plays a dominant role in our present societal structures. In the deepest sense, there is no such thing as "accounting." Accountants are merely a modern version of the tribal storyteller, whose role was to accurately portray the tribe as it was, as it is, as it might become, and as it ought to be, thus informing its evolution and future.

That the tribes are now called corporation, nation, university, church, county, partnership, or any other appellation is irrelevant. That the primary language used to inform those tribes is now mathematics and accounting is relevant only to the degree they help explain how the tribe was, how it is, how it might become, and how it ought to be.

An article in the *Journal of Cost Management* by H. Thomas Johnson, an economic historian, CPA, and former president of the Academy of Accounting Historians put it well. He wrote:

The Cartesian/Newtonian world view has influenced thought far beyond the physical sciences, and accounting is no exception. Double-entry bookkeeping and the systems of income and wealth measurement that evolved from it since the 16th century are eminently Cartesian and Newtonian. They are predicated on ideas such as the whole being equal to the sum of the parts and effects being the result of infinitely divisible, linear causes.... Quantum physicists and evolutionary biologists, among others, now believe that it is best to describe reality as a web of interconnected relationships that give rise to an ever-changing and evolving universe of objects that we perceive only partially with our limited senses. In that "systemic" view of the world, nothing is merely the sum of the parts; parts have meaning only in reference to a greater whole in which everything is related to everything else.... Why should accountants continue to believe that human organizations behave like machines if the scientists from whom they borrowed that mechanistic world view now see the universe from a very different perspective?...

The language of financial accounting merely asserts answers, it does not invite inquiry. In particular it leaves unchallenged the world view that underlies [the way] organizations operate. Thus, management accounting has served as a barrier to genuine organizational learning.... *Never again should management accounting be seen as a tool to drive people with measures. Its purpose must be to promote inquiry into the relationships, patterns and processes that give rise to accounting measures.*

In more precise terms, in the years ahead we must get beyond numbers and the language of mathematics to understand, evaluate, and account for such intangibles as learning, intellectual capital, community, beliefs, and principles, *or the stories we tell of our tribe's value and prospects will be increasingly false.*

We must understand, evaluate, and account for wholly new, nonmonetary forms of ownership, assets, and liabilities that have no tangible market price or mathematical means of measurement, such as participatory rights, alliances, systemic interdependence, and defined relationships, *or the stories we tell of our tribe will be increasingly archaic and misleading.*

We must understand, evaluate, and account for the full cost of everything removed from or returned to the Earth, the biosphere, or the atmosphere, including reversion to natural elements in the original proportions and balance, *or our stories will result in increasing environmental catastrophe.*

We must conceive of and help implement wholly new forms of ownership, financial systems, and measurements, free of the attempt to monetize all values that binds our tribes to next quarter's bottom line, gross maldistribution of wealth and power, degradation of people, and desolation of the ecosphere, *or our stories will be increasingly immoral and destructive.*

And we must interconnect our stories with those of all other tribal storytellers in order to integrate them into a new, intelligible, larger story to inform the global community now emerging, *or our stories will continue to set tribe against tribe in ever-accelerating, economic, social, and physical combat.*

We are not helpless victims in the grasp of some supernatural force. We were active participants in the creation of our present consciousness. From that consciousness we created our present internal model of reality. From that internal model of reality we created our present concepts of

> organization and accounting. With those concepts we created our present society. We did it! All of us!
>
> We know that we must do better. We know that we must do it together. And we must come to understand that such "together" must transcend all present boundaries and allow self-organization and governance at every scale, from the smallest form of life to the living Earth itself.
>
> It will take time. It will require great respect for the past, vast understanding and tolerance of the present, and even greater belief and trust in the future. It is an odyssey that calls out to the best in us, one and all.

Two months after Sam's consent to try, a final package of charter owner/member materials was on the way to all licensee banks and the charter commitment period was under way. It was highly likely the thirteen banks represented by the executive officers organizing committee would accept the final package. Another fifteen or twenty banks had indicated strong intent to do so. An equal number had expressed reservations. A few among them were strongly opposed. The position of the remainder was unknown.

Needing undisturbed time, and every minute of it, a tiny, unused bedroom of our home was emptied, a small table moved in, and two telephones installed. On the table was a large spreadsheet with the names and telephone numbers of every bank officer who had attended any of the meetings or worked on any of the committees. There were brief notes about the interest or opinions each had previously expressed. With no commute, it was possible to be on the telephone to east coast bankers by five A.M.

"Did you receive the charter member package of materials? Do you have any questions? When might you have time to finish your review? When would it be convenient to call again to discuss any matters that might arise in the process?"

"You can't locate the material? Another package will be sent by courier immediately. We'll call in two days to make certain it's been received."

"She's gone for two weeks? Would you put me through to whoever is handling the matter in her absence?"

"He's away from his desk? Please ask if he can call me back; anytime from five in the morning until ten at night."

Hour after hour, day after day, bank after bank, person after person, over and over, cajoling, sympathizing, explaining, appealing, and thanking, all the while making a careful record of the needs, desires, and position of each. Not a day was free of demands, anger, patronization, and occasional abuse flowing back through the line. But there was even more generosity, understanding, appreciation, and trust as well.

By the middle of the second day, the small bedroom was stifling, the confinement unbearable. The table was moved to the garden and long telephone extension cords strung through the window. There, under a flowering pear tree, next to a tiny pool and waterfall surrounded by rhododendrons, the work went on into the dark of the evening, illuminated by light from the window.

The commitments began to come in, accelerating each day. If anyone had major problems and seemed on the verge of refusal, I made excuses to end the conversation and resume it another day. Committed banks who might be influential were induced to call the reluctant who became aware of respected friends who were committing to the concept. Within three weeks it appeared likely we would reach the threshold that would automatically trigger formation of the organization. A day or two later it was certain.

But certainty was not enough. Fewer than twenty banks remained uncommitted. A half dozen were adamantly opposed. But none was refusing to have another word on the subject. We had come so far, overcome so many obstacles, maybe, just maybe! Back to the telephone, this time digging to know much more about the individuals and institutions involved, trying to understand their perspective and discover something that might help them to a different conclusion. One by one, they began to waver as the deadline approached. If so many banks whose judgment they respected were committed, could they have been wrong?

As the number of uncommitted banks dwindled, realization dawned on the few remaining that refusing to join and retaining their license would be a lonely place indeed. Even though they could continue with full rights of interchange, they would have no participation in future decisions. Although they could join at any time after the charter period expired, they would have no voting rights or eligibility to serve on the board during the first year. Was it better to become an owner/member of NBI and influence its direction, or remain carping on the outside? As the mass of committed banks had grown, so had enthusiasm for what the new organization might be able to achieve. It was infectious.

Two days before the deadline, I made the call I had dreamed of. It was to a senior officer of a responsible, capable bank. I liked him a great deal, for he was open, honest, and intelligent. He was convinced that such an unusual organization would not succeed, and had the courage of his convictions.

"Nolan, we greatly appreciate the time you've given this matter and truly understand your position. We have too much respect for your decision to make another appeal. On the other hand, the present situation is so unusual, I felt you should be aware of it."

"Dee, I'm aware that we're in a minority and that the organization will be formed. What is the situation that concerns you?"

"It's difficult to know how to put it, but you should know that every licensee card-issuing bank, save one, has committed to the new organization." There was a long moment before he replied.

"You're not joking with me? We're the only licensee who will not be a member?"

"I'm not happy to say as much, but, yes. You will be the only one." Another moment of silence before his reply.

"No, we will not. We may have been the only one this morning, but we'll not be the only one tonight. Count us in."

"Nolan, there are moments when great gifts arrive and you have just given us one. We're deeply grateful."

"Thank you for letting us know. We're grateful as well."

***

As I wrote in the Introduction, even today I can hold a Visa card overhead before any audience in the world and ask, "How many of you recognize this?" Every hand in the room will go up. When I ask, "How many of you can tell me who owns it, where it's headquartered, how it is governed, or where to buy shares?" a dead silence comes over the room. The audience realizes something extraordinary has occurred, and they have no idea what or how. Nor, in my judgment, should they. The results of chaordic organizations are apparent, but the structure, leadership, and process are not.

Thirty-five years ago, the Visa community was no more than a set of beliefs and a vague concept. Today, its products are created by 21, 000 owner/member financial institutions. More than a billion people use Visa products to purchase $3.2 trillion of goods and services from 20 million merchant locations in more than 150 countries—the single largest block of consumer purchasing power in the global economy. Visa has grown a minimum of 15 percent and as much as 50 percent compounded annually for more than three decades, through the best and the worst of times, with no end in sight.

But numbers reveal nothing about the nature of organizations. What Visa was, I knew well. What it is now, I no longer know. What it may become is no longer my affair. But what it ought to be is entirely another matter. So I shall write about it as I experienced it then, and believe it ought to be.

Visa was a quasi-governmental, quasi-for-profit, quasi-not-for-profit, quasi-consulting, quasi-franchising, quasi-educational, quasisocial, quasi-commercial, quasi-political alliance.

It was none of them, yet it was all of them. It was chaordic.

In the strict legal sense, Visa was a nonstock, for-profit, membership corporation. In another sense, it was an inside-out holding company in that it did not hold, but was held by its functioning parts. The financial institutions that create its products were, at one and the same time, its owners, its members, its customers, its subjects, and its superiors. It existed as an integral part of the most highly regulated of industries, yet the core of the organization was not subject to regulatory authority, since it made no loans, had no stock, and engaged in no external business. The core was an enabling organization that existed for the sole purpose of assisting owner/members to engage in providing devices for the exchange of value with greater capacity, more effectively, and at less cost.

Visa could not be bought, raided, traded or sold, since ownership was in the form of perpetual, nontransferable, rights of participation. However, that portion of the business created by each member was owned solely by that company, was reflected in its stock prices, and could be sold to any other member or entity eligible for membership—an extremely broad, active market.

Visa espoused no political, economic, social, or legal theory, thus transcending language, race, custom, and culture to successfully bring together people and institutions of every political, economic, social, and religious persuasion. It went through a number of wars and revolutions, the belligerents continuing to share common ownership and never ceasing reciprocal acceptance of products, even though, from time to time, they went to war and killed one another.

In less than five years, it transformed a troubled product with a minority market share into the most profitable consumer service in the financial services industry. At the same time, it reduced by more than half the cost of unsecured credit to individuals and the cost to merchants of handling payment transactions. Through this new concept of ownership, banks distributed a substantial amount of their expense at the cost of a minuscule amount of income. It spawned new industries and new ventures in the tens of thousands, creating conditions by which members could connect with them without permission or limitation. With no interest in controlling or owning technology or participants, the unlimited ingenuity and creativity of thousands of external entities was freely brought to bear on the needs and opportunities of the system.

Any member could retain full rights of membership in perpetuity if it issued a single Visa product to a single customer. However, the right to issue any and all products at any time, in any amount, in any area in accordance with complete freedom to determine services, prices, terms, conditions, and marketing, is subject only to minimum standards necessary for reciprocal acceptance of all cards.

The system became enormously robust, since virtually all innovation occurred in individual banks that formed the periphery of the system. Mistakes died quickly without affecting more than a single bank, while successes were swiftly emulated and improved upon as they spread throughout the system. While the core of the organization could develop products and services to be offered by members, it had no power to require that any member issue or promote any of them. Thus, central mistakes died as quickly and harmlessly as peripheral ones.

Its products were among the most universally used and recognized in the world, yet the organization was so transparent its ultimate customers, most if its affiliates, and some of its members did not know it existed or how it functioned. At the same time, the core of the enterprise had no knowledge of, information about or authority over a vast number of the constituent parts. Visa had multiple boards of directors within a single legal entity, none of which could be considered superior or inferior, as each had irrevocable authority and autonomy over geographic or functional areas.

No part knew the whole, the whole did not know all the parts, and none had any need to. The entirety, like millions of other chaordic organizations, including those we call body, brain, forest, ocean, and biosphere, was self-regulating.

A staff of less than five hundred scattered in more than a dozen countries on four continents coordinated this system as it skyrocketed past a hundred billion dollars on a trajectory to the present $3.2 trillion, providing product and systems development, global advertising, and around-the-clock operation of two global electronic communication systems with thousands of data centers communicating through millions of miles of communications lines. Today, those systems clear more electronic financial transactions in a week than the U.S. Federal Reserve System does in a year—in excess of 6,200 a second.

Its employees received mediocre salaries by commercial standards, and could never be compensated with equity or acquire wealth for their services. Yet, those people selected the Visa name and completed the largest, global trademark conversion in commercial history in a third the time anticipated.

They built the archetype of the present electronic system in ninety days for less than 30 thousand dollars.

Time and time again, they demonstrated a simple truth we have somehow lost sight of in our mechanistic, industrial age, command-and-control organizations. *The truth is, that given the right circumstances, from no more than dreams, determination, and the liberty to try, quite ordinary people consistently do extraordinary things.*

***

The chaordic concept of organization for societal institutions is immensely more powerful than even the success of Visa might suggest. There were many weaknesses in the Visa version of the concept. Certain external conditions could not be overcome. Commercial law did not anticipate, thus could not prevent, but did not fit the concept. Like a dead tree lying on a sapling, the law continually warped and constricted the natural evolution of the concepts in ways beyond correction. Today, the law is beginning to understand and accept such concepts.

Although the core and concept of Visa were chaordic, most members remained mechanistic and linear. They did not fully understand and exploit the concept. Many continually tried to reimpose on it old structure and management practices with which they were comfortable. As its growth exploded, managers hired into the organization did not properly understand or practice the beliefs and concepts on which it was based. Consciously and unconsciously, they brought their archaic mental furniture and installed it in the new organization. I did not realize the immense cultural change required of each person if they were to fully understand, develop, and implement the concepts. Today, such cultural change is slowly emerging throughout the world.

I could think of no way to fully realize the concept by including merchants and cardholders as owner/members. The slightest hint in that direction raised a storm of opposition. We should have included them. Perhaps, with more time, tenacity, and ingenuity we could have. But that can never be known.

I had neither the experience nor strength of character to hold my convictions inviolable or develop them fully. I never ceased to try, but failed to properly keep at bay the four beasts that inevitably devour their keeper: ego, envy, avarice, and ambition. Today, as I continue to struggle with those same beasts, hundreds of thousands, perhaps millions of other people have done, and will do better.

Had such constraints not existed, it is impossible to know what the Visa community might have become. In the decades ahead, constraints will diminish and the opportunity for new forms of chaordic, enabling, organizations will expand enormously.

But we're getting ahead of the story, for the formation of National BankAmericard Incorporated was only the first of a great many scarcely believable events that led to Visa International and what it came to be.

***

The end of the beginning was drawing to a close. The first annual meeting of members of National BankAmericard Incorporated was at an end. All business on the agenda had been covered. Relieved to have survived the ordeal, I asked the rhetorical question, "Is there any other business to come before the meeting?"

Sam Stewart rose to his feet, stern and unsmiling. His booming voice filled the auditorium.

"Yes, there is. I have some unfinished business."

Oh my God, what now, I thought, as Sam faced the audience and began.

"When the Bank of America agreed to support the attempt to form NBI, we were convinced a quarter of the licensees would drop out. When Dee insisted we must perfect the new organization and convert the entire system in ninety days, I told him there was absolutely no way it could be done." He paused for effect and with great emphasis boomed, "I just want you to know I haven't changed my mind one bit!" The meeting dissolved in laughter and ended. You have to love a man like that.

The newly elected board met, elected Sam chairman, and appointed me president and chief executive officer. Thus began what I expected would be a three-year commitment before I could regain a measure of freedom and return to a more private life in the Northwest. Had I an inkling those three years would become fourteen, or of the trials and trauma that lay ahead, I would have walked away on the spot.

Chapter Twelve

Quite Ordinary People

> *If you have built castles in the air your work need not be lost: that is where they should be. Now put the foundation under them.*
> —Henry David Thoreau

The evening before the first annual meeting of members, lawyers from the Bank of America had asked for a meeting, saying they had something they wished to discuss, insisting it must be held in strict confidence until it could be made public. I was astonished at what they had to say.

The bank had been in secret discussions with American Express for months. They had jointly developed a plan for the two companies to build a nationwide credit card authorization system, to be owned and controlled by the two of them. At the time, American Express, by a huge margin, was the largest travel and entertainment card issuer in the world. Bank of America, by a similar margin, was the largest bank card issuer. Other credit card issuers would be invited to become participants in the new system, each paying a substantial sum at the time of commitment, which would provide most of the capital for development of the authorization system. However, they would have no ownership. The plan would be announced within days.

I felt completely betrayed. It was contrary to the spirit of the effort to form NBI and could materially affect its success. Throughout the effort to form NBI, all participants, including those from Bank of America, had agreed that one of the principal reasons for its formation was to create an effective means of authorizing credit card transactions. The joint venture, from my perspective, was nothing but an attempt by the two credit card giants to make tenant farmers of the remainder of the industry. In fairness, their effort may have been underway before it was certain NBI could be brought into being.

I could say nothing without breaching their confidence. There was nothing to do but swallow my feelings and move ahead with the NBI organizational meeting, trusting that the new NBI concept was weak indeed if it could not survive storms of deceit and opposition.

The announcement was made with great fanfare. The two organizations swept the country with salesmen. They found no more than a handful of takers. Nearly all NBI members found the new concept of organization compelling enough to wait and see what it could achieve. Within months, the joint venture died a quiet death—well, almost.

During the years that NBI had been in process of formation, the American Bankers' Association had organized an effort to examine growing problems of the paper check-clearing system. A nationwide money and payment system committee (MAPS) of bank executives had been formed, along with a plethora of subcommittees. Its charge was to examine in depth the problems of the check-clearing system, which was owned and operated by the Federal Reserve banks. Law permitted only commercial banks to enter transactions into the clearing system.

Prevailing wisdom at the time held not only that the check-clearing system must be converted from paper to electronics, but that competitive electronic authorization and check-clearing systems for financial transactions were not economically feasible. Any such system should be a monopoly of the Federal Reserve System.

The MAPS committee was in the final phases of its work when NBI came into being. NBI was asked to participate. On occasion, I shared with the committee my conviction that the real message of electronic technology was not gadgets, but radical social and institutional change. Some listened politely, but none were interested. Preaching institutional change in this venue was like preaching Protestant theology in a medieval Catholic church. The committee report, which predicted disaster ahead if something was not done, was widely distributed, discussed, filed, and forgotten. It died a quiet death—well almost.

Out of the ashes of the Bank of America-American Express joint venture and the MAPS committee, a more ominous form arose. A new committee was formed composed of representatives from the two companies, other large bank card issuers, travel-and-entertainment card issuers, major retail merchants, and MAPS committee members. NBI and MasterCharge were invited to participate. The intent was to investigate formation of a single, electronic, authorization system as a monopolistic joint venture of all credit card issuers.

From my perspective, neither the institutional nor technical thinking made sense. It was just another attempt to centralize power and control. It had always seemed to me that one of the principal tricks of evolution was to preserve the substance of the past by clothing it in the forms of the future. Creating a single, monopolistic, electronic payment system seemed precisely the opposite—an attempt to warp the substance of the future in order to perpetuate past forms. It was contrary to all my beliefs about the nature of organizations and the possibilities inherent in electronic communications. Exchanging authorization information and monetary value in the form of electronic particles ought to be a highly decentralized, competitive business. Trying to design and impose a single, monolithic system on such an essential flow of information seemed absurd.

> Old Monkey and I had spent countless hours trying to understand information and its relevance to organizations by asking our endless questions. What is the significance of the "in-form" part of the word "information"? What is the nature of that which is received from external sources and "forms us" within? What is the nature of that which "forms within us" which we then feel compelled to transmit to others, and how does it form others within when it is received? What allows formation of information, permits it to endure unaltered, yet be available at any time

for use and transformation in infinite ways?

Why and from where came the universal, perpetual urge to receive and transmit information—the incessant desire to communicate? Is it an urge at all, or is it an unavoidable necessity—an integral component essential to life itself? Indeed, is it the essence of life itself? Or is it a principle beyond life itself? Could information be the raw material of some *dispersed form of intelligence; some fundamental, formative essence* that calls dispersed energy to condense into physical form, shape, and distinction; some fundamental part of an inseparably whole universe that calls all things into being?

It helps to think what information is not. Certainly information is far more than digits and data. They may be components of it—the shape it sometimes takes. They may be of it, but they are not it. Certainly, it is not just another "thing": one more finite, physical entity. Gregory Bateson, in a rare insight, proposed that "information is a difference that makes a difference." If something is received that cannot be differentiated or, if once differentiated, it makes no difference, he asserts it is just noise.

Bateson's perspective is fascinating but limited, for it implies only mind-to-mind communication. If you are hiking alone in the wilderness and a rock comes bounding down the mountain and crushes your knee, that is certainly a difference that makes a difference. The same can be said of running barefoot through the house and breaking a toe on a chair leg. Is that information? Both are certainly a difference that makes a difference. Both certainly convey meaning. If your crushed knee and broken toe are a difference that makes a difference, then, by Bateson's definition, condensed, inanimate matter and gravitational force clearly have the ability to communicate. Locked in our box of self-awareness, we think of it as one-way communication—rock to leg, or chair leg to toe, but we truly have no way of knowing what information, if any, flows the opposite way.

The more questions Old Monkey and I asked, the more we came to agree with Bateson's perception. But we wanted to understand even more, to see beyond to what information might become and ought to be. More characteristics began to emerge.

Unlike finite physical resources, information multiplies by transfer. It is not depleted by use. Information transferred is not lost to the source, yet is gain to the recipient. Information can be utilized by everyone without loss to anyone. As far as we know, the supply of information is infinite, therefore, it does not obey any of our industrial age concepts and laws of scarcity. It obeys only concepts and principles of infinite abundance, infinite utilization, infinite recombination. We have only dim perceptions of what those principles might be, or if they exist at all.

Projecting onto information our old notions of property, thus turning it into a method by which one person can extract wealth from another, neither reveals nor changes the extraordinary nature of information. It reveals only the limited nature of humans and our reluctance to change our internal model of reality and behavior based upon it.

Information is a miser of energy. It can endlessly replicate, move ubiquitously at the speed of light, and massively condense in minute space, all at minuscule expense of energy, in other words, cost. In countless ways, it is becoming a replacement for our present enormously wasteful use of matter. To the extent that we increase the value of the mental content of goods and services, we can reduce the value of the physical content. We can make them lighter, more durable, more recyclable, more versatile, and more transportable.

Information breeds. When one bit of information is combined with another, the result is new information.

Information knows no boundaries. It cannot be contained. No matter what constraints we try to put on information, it will become the slave and property of no one. Efforts to make information conform to archaic notions of scarcity, ownership and finite physical quantity—concepts that grew out of the agricultural and industrial age—merely lock us into old mental boxes of constraint and exploitation.

Information is ethically neutral. Its immense power is as applicable to destructive, inequitable, violent ends as it is to constructive, equitable, peaceful ends. The history of modern science has been an effort to divorce the ethical dimensions of life from the physical, to divorce subjective values from objective observations; to divorce spirituality from rationality. The effect has been the deification of the rational, physical, objective perspective as ultimate truth, and demonization of the subjective, ethical, and spiritual perspective as superstition, delusion, and ignorance.

Thinking about a society based on information and one based on physicality requires radically different perspective and consciousness. However, we too often prefer to ignore the fundamental differences and carry over into the age of managing information (more accurately thought of as the age of mind-crafting) ideas, values, concepts, and assumptions that proved useful in the mechanized industrial age: concepts such as ownership, finite supply, obsolescence, loss by conveyance, containment, scarcity, separability, quantifiable measurement, and command-and-control management.

Products, services, and organizations in which the value of the mental content begins to dwarf the value of the physical content require wise people of deep understanding. To endlessly add to the quantity of mechanistic information, knowledge, and technology without similar evolution of values and wisdom is not only foolish, it is dangerous. To massively develop means and act in accordance with what those means permit, without careful consideration of ends in the context of values is a grossly foolish, very dangerous misuse of information.

The emergence of this new age based on information, whatever we choose to label it, calls into question virtually every concept of societal organization, management, and conduct on which we have come to rely. Clinging too rigorously to old concepts, dismissing new concepts too lightly, protecting old forms that resulted from those concepts too fiercely, imposing those forms on a changing society too resolutely, are a certain path to failure. As Sir Francis Bacon put it precisely centuries ago in admonishing those who opposed the scientific revolution and the industrial age,

They that reverence too much the old times are but a scorn to the new.

The new concepts he so ably defended with that assertion are excruciatingly old today. They have become the concepts we now revere too much.

We were not going to revere too much the old times at NBI. We would pay them due respect and try to preserve their substance, but we would challenge their forms at every opportunity. We began quietly to collect information and explore the feasibility of building our own proprietary electronic system. If we could build an efficient, cost-effective, proprietary system, it would shatter conventional wisdom and the natural monopoly argument forever. We had little experience building such systems. We had few employees with the requisite skills.

Years of iconoclastic management, of watching ordinary people consistently do extraordinary things when their spirit was challenged and their ingenuity released, had given me confidence in the infinite capacity of every individual. One need not know and be able to prove in advance what could be accomplished. One need not have a precise plan about how to get there. In a complex, rapidly changing world, a clear sense of direction, a compelling purpose and powerful beliefs about conduct in pursuit of it, seemed to me infinitely more sensible and robust than mechanical plans, detailed objectives, and predetermined outcomes. Yet, my confidence remained scarred by years of conflict and rejection.

The unanswered questions were legion. What degree of innovation could members and the board accept? How much risk and uncertainty could such a new organization tolerate? Could extraordinary results be delivered by ordinary people on a large scale? Could an innovative, unorthodox organization survive and prosper embedded in an extremely conservative industry? Much of what we ought to do seemed impossible. Yet I had strong belief that possibility cannot be determined by opinion, only by attempt. And we were determined to make the attempt.

The NBI board was composed of senior bank officers, many of whom had participated in the miracle of the formation of NBI and its early accomplishments. Pleased with the swift success of the organization and the benefits it had brought to their troubled card programs, they had become less apprehensive about iconoclastic thinking.

The board meeting at which the decision was taken was unforgettable. We proposed that NBI break with the industry, withdraw from the joint effort, and announce intent to build a proprietary, competitive system for the electronic authorization of sales and the clearance of transactions and payments. There followed intense discussion among twenty-two powerful directors with diverse, strongly held opinions. It was far more important than any decision we had yet made. Failure meant risking the reputation of the new company, its ability to attract new members, its opportunity to undertake major ventures, and its financial stability. Near the end, when there was little left to say, one of the more dubious directors asked bluntly,

"Precisely how will you proceed, and what if you fail?" There was only one honest answer.

"We have no precise plan, only a clear sense of direction. If we make an all out attempt and fail, that will teach us what to do next. However, failure is not really an option. If you approve the attempt, we will get it done, whatever that requires." There was a momentary silence as he pondered my answer, heaved a sigh, and said:

"I move that we approve the effort. How many of you want to join me and vote for this shot in the dark?" They did, every last one of them, bless their souls.

The next day we shocked the industry with an announcement that NBI was withdrawing from the industry-wide effort and would build its own competitive, proprietary system. We were off the high dive. There was no way back. The only question was how we would hit the water.

It was a horrendous belly flop. Fail is exactly what we did. With very little experience among the staff, we had agreed it would be prudent to hire a systems development expert from outside the company. Within days, our expert persuaded us to follow tradition, write a request for proposal and put it out to bid with leading development companies. It seemed sensible enough. As the weeks went by, I became a little nervous. The "expert" leading the effort continually assured me all was well, but seemed reluctant to share much information, claiming he wanted to be certain of his facts before making a final recommendation. Well, trust is not negotiable. One either trusts or one does not. I prefer trust.

Eventually, the day came. The best bid from a responsible vendor was several times the anticipated amount approved by the board. The system would take twice as long as expected to build. No vendor was willing to warrant the performance of the system that might result. It was not a problem in the mind of the expert or the vendors. We should go back to the board and ask for more money and time. It was customary in the computer industry. Well, it was not going to become a custom at NBI. Some lessons must be learned over and over again before they sink to the bone. Emerson said it best. "Trust thyself; every heart vibrates to that iron string."

The people involved in the effort were brought together, everyone, inside and outside the company, at every level. There was little that needed to be said.

"We're told the system can't be built within the time and with the money we expected, some of which we have already wasted. If it can, it's clearly up to us. There is no answer out there. If there is an answer, it's in here. It's in us. We can go back to the board for more money and time, or we can believe that there is more than enough intelligence, ability, and ingenuity in this room to do the job. If there are enough of us with sufficient desire and trust in one another, we can close the door and not come out until we have decided how to meet our commitment within the promised time and with the money remaining."

Intense, innovative discussion erupted. There were more than enough excited, committed people, but the "expert" was not among them. He quietly went his way. Several exceptional people working for vendors leaped at the challenge and joined the company. We shut ourselves in a room and didn't come out until we had an approach to which we were totally committed. We called it Bank Authorization System Experimental (BASE 1).

***

The following months were among the most exciting in the early history of the company. We were determined that the needs of our members and cardholders would be served, not the needs of technology or vendors. That required internal responsibility. We decided to become our own prime contractor, farming out selected tasks to a variety of software developers, then coordinating and implementing results. Conventional wisdom held it to be one of the worst possible ways to build computerized communications systems.

We rented cheap space in a suburban building and dispensed with leasehold improvements in favor of medical curtains on rolling frames for limited spatial separation when required. IBM, then the infallible behemoth of the computer industry, was the supplier of computers to 80 percent of our members. Early in the process, as we had prepared the proposal to the board,

IBM had promised a quarter million dollars of support in connecting members to the system. Now they waffled, saying only that they would see what they could do when the time arrived. We threw them out, telling them not a single piece of IBM equipment would come through our doors in the future, not even a typewriter. We selected a relatively new, innovative company, Digital Equipment, to provide the computers, thinking they would be more responsive to the spirit of our people.

Swiftly, self-organization emerged. An entire wall became a pin board with every remaining day calendared across the top. Someone grabbed an unwashed coffee cup and suspended it on a long piece of string pinned to the current date. Every element of work to be done was listed on scraps of paper with the required completion date and name of the person who had accepted the work. Anyone could revise the elements, adding tasks or revising dates, providing they coordinated with others affected. Everyone, any time, could see the picture emerge and evolve. They could see how the whole depended on their work, and how their work was connected to every other part of the effort. Groups constantly assembled in front of the board as need and inclination arose, discussing, deciding, and forming work groups in continuous flow, then dissolving as needs were met. As each task was completed, its scrap of paper would be removed. Each day, the cup and string moved inexorably ahead.

Every day, every scrap of paper that fell behind the grimy string would find an eager group of volunteers to undertake the work required to remove it. To be able to get one's own work done and help another became a sought-after privilege. Nor did anyone feel beggared by accepting help. Such Herculean effort meant that at any time, anyone's task could fall behind and emerge on the wrong side of the string.

Leaders spontaneously emerged and reemerged, none in control, but all in order. Ingenuity exploded. People astonished themselves at what they could accomplish and were amazed at the suppressed talents emerging in others. Position became meaningless. Power over others became meaningless. Time became meaningless. Excitement about doing the impossible increased, and a community based on purpose, principle, and people arose. Individuality, self-worth, ingenuity, and creativity flourished; and as they did, so did the sense of belonging to something larger than self, something beyond immediate gain and monetary gratification.

No one ever forgot the joy of bringing to work the wholeness of mind, body, and spirit; discovering in the process that such wholeness is impossible without inseparable connection with others in the larger purpose of community effort.

Money was a small part of what happened. The effort was fueled by a spontaneous expansion of the nonmonetary exchange of value—things done for one another without measurement or prescribed return—the heart and soul of all community. The people gave of themselves without expectation and received in ways beyond calculation. A few who could not adjust to the diversity, complexity, and uncertainty wandered away. Dozens volunteered to take their place. No one articulated what was happening. No one recorded it. No one measured it. But everyone felt it, understood it, and loved it.

The dirty string was never replaced and no one washed the cup. "The Dirty Coffee Cup System" became legendary—a metaphor within the company for years to come. The BASE 1 system came up on time, under budget, and exceeded all operating objectives. It forced the industry to abandon notions of natural monopoly, innovate, and create other systems. It was a foundation of commitment and practice from which the global Visa communication systems evolved. Out of initial failure, grew a magnificent success.

> Long before, during, and after the BASE 1 year, Old Monkey and I continued to explore the significance of information in the form of arranged particles of energy, trying endlessly to get at the essence of its meaning. By then, peeling such a mental onion

by asking hundreds of layered questions was not only habit, it was recreation.

In time, a new perception gradually emerged, based upon trying to understand the history and effect of a single, fascinating capacity: **The Capacity to Receive, Utilize, Store, Transform, and Transmit Information (CRUSTTI).**

Not information from the common misperception of alphanumeric data but from Gregory Bateson's perspective that *"information is a difference that makes a difference."* If something perceived cannot be distinguished from its surroundings in a relevant way, it's just noise. If it can be differentiated and truly makes a difference, then it becomes information. It then becomes capable of informing us, forming us within, and allowing us to formulate differences that can make a difference to others.

To understand CRUSTTI, it is essential to begin at the beginning. If we examine early examples of single-celled life, it is apparent they possess the capacity to receive, utilize, store, transform and transmit information. In fact, CRUSTTI precedes even such simple forms, for to do so is the very essence of DNA. CRUSTTI even precedes DNA, for when physicists attempt to examine the smallest known particles of matter, the particles change their behavior. And when they do, the physicists change their behavior in response. Particle and physicist find themselves in a fascinating, quantum cosmic dance. Clearly each is perceiving a "difference that makes a difference." They are exchanging information.

In ways we don't begin to understand, information escapes particles, transcends them, and binds them together into more complex systems in which all particles constantly exchange information. It seems a principle of evolution, perhaps *the fundamental principle, that the greater the capacity to receive, utilize, store, transform, and transmit information, the more diverse and complex the entity.* It holds true from neutrino, to nucleus, to atom, to amino acids, to proteins, to molecules, to cells, to organs, to organisms. From bacteria, to bees, to bats, to birds, to buffalo, right on through to baseball players.

CRUSTTI didn't stop there. In time, information transcended the boundaries of organisms and led to communication between them. Whether the dance of the bees, the pheromone of ants, the sonar of bats, the song of birds, or the language of people, once that capacity transcended organisms, there was immediate evolution of complex *communities* of organisms—hives, flocks, packs, colonies, herds, and tribes.

Let's follow that capacity with respect to our species. Throughout history, many of our finest minds have argued that the two characteristics that most distinguish the human species are memory and language. Memory, but the ability to store and recall images. Language, but the means to share those images.

Over the centuries, we have ascended a ladder of diversity and complexity. With language, information escaped the boundaries of a single mind and experience became shared. Immediately, there was a corresponding leap in societal diversity and complexity. With written language, came expansion to that which could be manually recorded and personally transported. Another leap in capacity, another leap in societal diversity and complexity.

Leap followed leap, each exponentially greater and more frequent. With mathematics came expansion to that which could be commonly understood by means of a global language. With the printing press, came expansion to that which could be mechanically recorded and transported. A library, after all, is nothing more than a collective memory of the species.

With the telegraph came electronic alphanumeric capacity. With the telephone came phonic capacity. With television came visual capacity, followed by multimedia capacity. Leap followed leap, each exponentially greater and more frequent. Each was immediately followed by an even greater leap in societal diversity and complexity.

One could paraphrase Einstein's most famous equation as follows: Where **I** equals the capacity to receive, utilize, store, transform, and transmit information, **D** equals societal diversity, and **C** equals societal complexity, the equation is:

$$I=DC^{\wedge}$$

The capacity to receive, utilize, store, transform, and transmit information equals societal diversity times societal complexity squared.

Then it happened! Suddenly, with the revolution in microelectronic technology, in less than twenty-five short years, we have on the order of a thousand times better algorithms, a million times more computing capacity per individual, and a billion times more mobility of information. The entire collective memory of the species will soon be no more than a few keystrokes away. Software to efficiently navigate that immensity of information is rapidly emerging. We don't begin to understand the significance of all this, let alone the societal change it has unleashed, or the institutional change it requires.

But that is nothing compared to what lies ahead. Around the corner are other revolutions of enormously greater significance, such as nano- and biotechnology. Simply stated, nanotechnology is the engineering of self-replicating assemblers and computers so tiny they can manipulate atoms, the basic building blocks of nature, as though they were bricks. The necessary science has already been discovered. What remains to be done is the engineering of tools at the atomic scale. In his book, *Engines of Creation,* K. Eric Drexler, a pioneer in the field, writes: "When biochemists need complex molecular machines, they have to borrow them from cells ... advanced molecular technology will eventually let them build nanocircuits and nanomachines as easily as engineers now build microcircuits or washing machines."

In answer to the question, "What could we build with these atom-stacking mechanisms?" Marvin Minsky, Professor of Science at MIT, writes: "...could manufacture assembly machines much smaller even than living cells ... make materials stronger and lighter than any available today, hence, better spacecraft, hence, tiny devices that can travel along capillaries to enter and repair living cells."

The possibilities are profound. Efficient solar collectors durable enough to repave highways and parking lots or to surface buildings. The ability to create large structures on site swiftly at little cost from material as common as dirt and air by arranging atoms into a desired object. Even more important, the deconstruction into atoms of garbage, industrial waste, and atmospheric pollutants, thus, turning them into abundant, cheap, raw material.

There is nothing new in all this. Nature has used this fundamental technique to create everything since the beginning of time, whether trees, monkeys to climb in them, or people who cut them down. Information in the form of DNA is endlessly replicated at no cost and distributed in seeds. A process of replication driven by the power of the sun begins. Molecules and cells assemble on the spot into known patterns from atoms of surrounding air, soil, and water. In the case of animals, it happens not only on the spot, but on the move.

When such creations are no longer viable, nature breaks them down into atoms once again for re-creation into something new and useful—a never-ending, effective, nonpolluting chain of events of ever-evolving diversity and complexity. No factories, no waste, no despoiled resources, no pollution, no mechanistic organization, and no command and control. Nature does it all with a complex, diverse flow of information that mobilizes energy into physical material, then into both animate and inanimate forms.

How soon and how likely are such things? One need only remember that a few decades ago the atomic bomb was scarcely a theory, travel to the moon a fantasy, television the dream of a few odd engineers, a plastic card for the global exchange of value unthinkable, and genetic engineering securely locked up in the secrets of DNA. Yet none had a better theoretical or scientific foundation then, than nanotechnology or biotechnology have today, and none was being driven by the incredible forces of change now common throughout the world.

As microtechnology builds down and nanotechnology and molecular biology build up, they will come together. Within two or three decades, for better or worse, we will be constructing products and services from the atom up and *the capacity to receive, utilize, store, transform, and transmit information will be at the heart of it.* And we're going to manage such a society with the same old seventeenth-century, mechanistic, industrial age concepts of organization and management? Not the chance of a snowball in that proverbial hot place. The message is simple.

Fasten your seat belts, the turbulence has scarcely begun. Unless evolution has radically changed its ways, we must face an explosion of societal diversity and complexity much greater than we now experience or can yet imagine. If you think to perpetuate the old ways, try to recall the last time evolution rang your number to ask consent.

Chapter Thirteen

The Victims of Success

There is nothing more difficult to take in hand, more perilous to conduct or more uncertain in its success, than to take the lead in the introduction of a new order of things.
—Niccolò Di Bernardo Machiavelli

Hand in hand with NBI's early success went equal failure. The issue of duality was the greatest example. On no issue were we more right. On none did we fail more ignominiously. On none did our failure have a greater effect on the future of payment systems, or a greater outward appearance of success.

At its inception, NBI inherited a two-tiered system created by the Bank of America licensing program. Banks were divided into two classes, A and B. The A class was composed of two hundred card-issuing, merchant-servicing banks that became full owner/members of NBI. The remainder were class B members—participants sponsored by A members. They enrolled merchants, bought merchant transactions, entered them into the system, and assisted A members in developing cardholders. Naturally, the class B members wanted to be members of both Visa and its principal competitor, MasterCharge (now MasterCard), in order to offer merchants a single point of deposit for all card transactions. This, in turn, placed pressure on A members to also become owner/members of both systems in order to offer merchants the same services. A few had already done so before NBI was formed. NBI placed a moratorium on such duality until the board could thoroughly look into the matter and try to determine what was most likely to produce maximum competition.

    Having come from a relatively poor family, I knew that the economic power of ordinary people arises from freedom of choice and sufficient resources to pursue them. It led me to strong belief that they would be best served if there were many competing card systems, and many competing card issuers within each system. I was deeply convinced that there could and should be many card systems within the consumer banking industry, and that there was ample opportunity for others to emerge in the retail, travel, and communications industries. I was equally convinced that complete freedom of banks to become owner/members of both the MasterCharge and BankAmericard systems would foreclose the emergence of new systems, and severely limit consumer choice.

There were compelling arguments on both sides of the issue. Banks that wished to join both systems argued that an NBI prohibition of dual owner/membership would infringe on their freedom to offer any products they wished to consumers and merchants, thus restraining bank-to-bank competition. No one denied that prohibition of dual membership would place some constraint on bank behavior. But was that a necessary restraint in order to ensure the emergence of new systems and foster even greater competition? I, along with many others, thought that it was.

Banks would not band together, incur the expense and take the risk of forming a new system if their competitors were free to join and reap the benefits the moment the new system became more effective. Nor would groups of institutions in any other industry take such a pointless risk. I was equally convinced that interlocking ownership of MasterCharge and BankAmericard would inevitably result in diminishment of competitive vigor between the two, eventual dominance of one or the other, and merger of the two, in substance if not in form.

Was prohibiting institutions from becoming owner/members in competing systems an essential restraint to foster the emergence of many systems and ensure maximum competition between them, as well as between banks? I thought that it was. Would unlimited dual owner-membership in competing systems allow rapidly consolidating giant banks to dominate all systems? I thought that it might. Would unlimited duality lead owner/members to close ownership to new participants, thus restricting system deliberations, decisions, and power to a self-selected group? I thought that it could.

The NBI board was divided. So was management. If we decided on a complete prohibition and no new systems developed, evidence might someday emerge that competition had suffered. The possibility of class-action lawsuits alleging violation of antitrust laws with treble-damage liabilities could not be discounted. If we took no action at all, the same anticompetitive consequences might emerge, but the chance of damages would be minimal, for it would be the acts of countless banks that led to the eventual result, not the act of the NBI board. If the Department of Justice took no action to prevent duality, the NBI board could hardly be blamed for not acting to do so.

There were signs that the same division of opinion existed within the Department of Justice. At the time, the antitrust division was headed by a knowledgeable lawyer, Donald Baker, who had a good grasp of the issues and deep interest in them. It was without question the most complex, difficult issue we faced and the subject of intense investigation and debate. The system was growing rapidly. Pressures were mounting. A decision could not be delayed.

In the midst of our efforts to find our way through the legal, operating, and competitive complexities of dual ownership, one of our smaller class A members, the Worthen Bank of Little Rock, Arkansas, which had also become a member of MasterCharge, threatened to sue NBI if it adopted a proposed bylaw prohibiting duality. I flew to Little Rock to meet with the president and other senior officers of the Worthen Bank in an effort to persuade them that the issue was larger than a single bank and obtain their support. I was greeted with the graciousness, charm, and hospitality for which the South is justly famous, and discovered the steely, stubborn determination so often attributed to it. There was conviction on both sides. We could not agree.

Near the end of 1971, the NBI board adopted a bylaw prohibiting duality in competing systems by class A members, but allowing class B members to continue to accept both BankAmericard and MasterCharge sales drafts from merchants. The Worthen bank promptly filed a lawsuit alleging violation of the antitrust laws and asking for an injunction to prevent enforcement of the bylaw. We were served with the usual interrogatories, part of pretrial discovery allowed by law. The plaintiff demanded we produce copies of every possible record that could have any bearing on the issues at hand and make available for extensive depositions all people who may have had anything to do with the decision.

We were a small staff with limited resources in the midst of incredible industry problems and insatiable demands on our time. Since the beginning of the company, I had insisted that the nature of the company and its beliefs required that we do nothing we would be reluctant to see on the front page of any newspaper. The need to deserve the respect and trust of all participants demanded no less.

The burden of searching our files was punitive for such a small staff. We swiftly decided on a course of action without precedent. We filed a petition with the court stating we had neither time nor resources to produce the requested documents, offering instead to provide office space, copy facilities, and other amenities to the plaintiff's lawyers. *All records* of the corporation and *all employees* would be available for examination by them. For weeks on end and lawyers on end, they bent over file drawers combing our records in vain for evidence of a conspiracy to violate the antitrust laws.

Depositions were long and wearing. To a sheep never before involved in a lawsuit, the plaintiff's lawyers seemed unduly antagonistic and not above lawyerly tactics to try to induce testimony that might appear contradictory. In the midst of such pressure came another of those dark periods of the soul, so much a part of attempting anything new.

***

In the mail delivered to our home one morning was an envelope containing a sheet of paper on which an anonymous message was pasted composed of words, letters, and partial sentences cut from newspapers and magazines. It was extremely abusive and warned of dire things to come. It appeared to be from a deeply disturbed person.

The former FBI agent who headed our security and fraud activities agreed to look into the matter and advised me to try to put it from my mind. That became impossible when I entered my office two weeks later to discover a huge cross slashed on the back of my chair. Nothing appeared missing, and no message was left. Questions flooded my mind. Had the cross been there some time unnoticed? Not likely, or, at least, not for more than a few days. Were the two incidents connected, or were they pure coincidence? One would be foolish to assume the latter. If connected, it meant this was not the act of some unknown crank, but the deliberate act of someone who not only knew me, but had access to my office.

Meanwhile, the incredible demands of the burgeoning system, disruption of our offices by plaintiff's lawyers, and the pressure of personal depositions ground on. Within the week, concern became deep distress. A package arrived at my home. Carefully prepared to conceal its origins, it contained an unusual, out-of-print, small volume of *Gracian's Maxims,* unmistakably stolen from my library. Driven through the book from cover to cover was a huge screw. Another cut-and-pasted abusive message warned of catastrophe ahead.

It was not uncommon to move my books between home and office libraries. The questions became frantic and incessant. Had the book been stolen from my home or from my office? Did the person responsible have access to one or both? Was it someone intending only to terrify, or someone with serious intent to harm? Why was this happening now? Each day, I had to rise and deal with countless problems, for the business went on and responsibilities could not be shoved aside. I began to slide into depression, that dark, dismal swamp that robs one of ability to think or function normally.

We consulted local police, the FBI, and other law enforcement agencies. They would do nothing without specific death or bomb threats. Ferol and I discussed the matter and could think of nothing to be done. She is much braver than I—more inclined to deal with problems as they occur, rather than invite them by excess worry. Yet she was concerned that I might not be able to bear up under the strain. It was not my courage that brought us through, it was hers. She reminded me of all the difficulties in our past and the comfort we had taken in the parental homily, "This, too, shall pass." She insisted we must go about our affairs in accordance with our beliefs, taking what precautions we could, but not allowing circumstances to dictate our lives, trusting in The Essence That Is to set things right.

Throughout the affair, nothing was said to anyone but NBI security people, counsel, and law enforcement officials. We did not want to disturb others, cause rumors to emerge, or give any indication to the person responsible that their efforts had an effect. Twenty years making and collecting loans had taught me that anger, blame, condemnation, and other negative emotions are fueled by like response. They are least able to be sustained when met with calm indifference. It has always been my inclination to quietly suffer through adversity while attempting to find a constructive solution. That was slim comfort now.

During dark times, long walks in the woods have always sustained me. This time, I broke the law to do it. The closest open space was the San Francisco watershed—miles of forested hills bordering Crystal Springs Reservoir near where we lived. It was posted everywhere with "no trespassing" signs. I would walk along the bordering road until there was no sign visible in either direction, pretend they did not exist, excuse myself on the basis of dire need, slip through the fence, and lose myself deep in the woods. There I would climb for hours, licking my wounds in the hope a solution would appear. A sense that in the great picture of things my trials and tribulations were of no consequence would slowly seep into my bones and allow me to face the next week.

When and how the answer appeared I did not know then and do not know now. Somewhere, somehow, at a level beyond conscious thought, I knew who had done the deed, and why. I knew the person was capable of worse, but also capable of reversing course and taking his dirty, little secret quietly to the grave. How to give him that opportunity to do so was the question. If the threats continued, we would have no alternative but to make every effort to identify beyond question and prosecute the person responsible. We would prefer not to do so, hoping the situation would end without damage to anyone.

That message was selectively conveyed to others in ways we were confident would get back to the source of the problem. The threats and intrusions vanished as mysteriously as they appeared. Whether they were indirectly connected with the lawsuit can never be known. It was many months before the depression gradually faded, and years before the memory became less painful.

> Turmoil, stress, and depression notwithstanding, Old Monkey Mind and I could not free ourselves of our obsession with information and its effect on institutions. We began to puzzle over words and concepts that are thrown about interchangeably with little thought of their relationship or meaning when the subjects of cognition and learning arise—knowledge, data, wisdom, information, understanding. All such words are integral to *the capacity to receive, utilize, store, transform, and transmit information.* We began to examine the essential nature and distinguishing characteristics of each and relate them in order of quantity and quality, knowing that such distinction, while useful, can never extinguish the essential wholeness of that which they compose.
> Noise, in its broadest sense, is any undifferentiated thing that assaults the senses. It is pervasive and ubiquitous,

whether auditory, visual, or textural. The supply of noise is infinite.

Noise becomes data when it transcends the purely sensual and has cognitive pattern; when it can be discerned and differentiated by the mind.

Data, in turn, becomes information when it is assembled into a coherent whole that can be related to other information in a way that adds meaning (Bateson's difference that makes a difference).

Information becomes knowledge when it is integrated with other information in a form useful for deciding, acting, or composing new knowledge.

Knowledge becomes understanding when related to other knowledge in a manner useful in conceiving, anticipating, valuing, and judging.

Understanding becomes wisdom when informed by purpose, ethics, principle, memory of the past, and projection into the future.

The fundamental characteristics of the opposite ends of this spectrum are very different. Data, on one end of the spectrum, is separable, objective, linear, mechanistic, and abundant. Wisdom, on the other end of the spectrum, is holistic, subjective, spiritual, conceptual, creative, and scarce.

The fundamental characteristics of the opposite ends of this spectrum are very different. Data, on one end of the spectrum, is separable, objective, linear, mechanistic, and abundant. Wisdom, on the other end of the spectrum, is holistic, subjective, spiritual, conceptual, creative, and scarce.

Science has traditionally operated in the provinces of data, information, and knowledge, where measurement, particularity, specialization, and rationality are most useful. It has often blithely ignored the provinces of understanding and wisdom.

Theology, philosophy, literature, and art have traditionally operated in the provinces of understanding and wisdom, where subjectivity, spirituality, and values are most useful. It has often blindly opposed the scientific way of knowing. When there is an explosion in the ability to receive, utilize, store, transform, and transmit data and information (the lower cognitive forms), then the higher forms (understanding and wisdom) are inundated. Today we are drowning in a raging flood of new data and information and the raft of wisdom to which we desperately cling is breaking up beneath us.

In time, the data may gradually become information, the information may gradually become knowledge, the knowledge may gradually become understanding, and the understanding may gradually become wisdom. Such transformation takes time. Unfortunately, with the collapse of "float," time is a luxury we no longer have.

Native societies, which endured for centuries with little increase in the capacity to receive, utilize, store, transform, and transmit information, had time to develop a very high ratio of understanding and wisdom to data and information. They may not have *known* a great deal by today's standards, but they *understood* a very great deal about what they did know. They were enormously wise in relation to the extent to which they were informed, and their information was conditioned by a high ratio of social, economic, and spiritual value.

In contrast, our society understands very little about what it knows. It has ever less understanding of the information at its command. It has ever less wisdom about the knowledge it develops. The immensity of data and information that assaults our lives is conditioned by an ever-declining ratio of social, economic, and spiritual value. Vast scientific, technological, and economic power is thus unleashed with inadequate understanding of its systemic propensity for destruction, or sufficient wisdom to creatively, constructively guide its evolution.

Thus, we remain confined within our archaic seventeenth-century concepts of organization and leadership, and our isolated specialities with their ever-narrowing perspectives, while in millions of rational, insular acts we pour billions of tons of 70,000 man-made chemicals into the biosphere that it cannot recycle—allow them to accumulate with little perception of how they are systemically combining to affect all living things—punch holes in the ozone layer of the atmosphere—dissipate and alter genetic material—destroy species by the thousands—denude the land of tens of millions of acres of trees and plants essential to maintenance of the chemical balance of the atmosphere—destroy topsoil at thousands of times the rate at which it can be replaced—create countless tons of virulent poisons, some with a half-life of twenty-four thousand years—and starve twenty-four thousand people to death every day.

Who could have imagined that such a wealth of information, science, and technology could have resulted in collective madness, but so it has. *Indeed, if life depends on wolf or*

> *man, it would seem prudent for nature to take the wolf every time.*

Things did not stand still while Old Monkey and I asked our questions and indulged our love of philosophy. The problem of dual ownership grew more acute as the Worthen lawsuit dragged through the labyrinths of the judicial system. It was not until February 1974, that the appeals process was exhausted, the injunction denied, and we were free to enforce the bylaw. Duality had spread rapidly among class B banks, and gradually among class A owner/members. Creative sponsoring contracts between class A and class B banks blurred the operational distinction between the two. It no longer seemed feasible to try to enforce a prohibition of duality in one class and not the other.

The only alternative appeared to be a complete prohibition of dual membership at all levels. A bylaw to that effect was adopted. However, it would not be enforced until after asking the Department of Justice for a "railroad letter," a term used for a process whereby the Department of Justice would neither approve nor disapprove the proposed policy, but would give written assurance it would take no immediate action but would retain its freedom to act when and how it chose when the effects were known. We assumed that the issues and pressures were well understood by the antitrust division of the Department of Justice and a prompt reply could be expected. We were wrong.

The Department put itself above reproach and announced it would launch a full-scale investigation, putting staff in the field to interview all parties and investigate all issues in depth. And they did, the most junior and inexperienced staff who had neither experience nor capacity to understand the full complexity of the issues. Bank after bank assured the investigators they would never become dual issuers because of duplicate cost and lack of consumer demand. Senior people in the Department of Justice appeared to share some of our concerns about the possible anticompetitive effects of unlimited duality, but they were obviously influenced by consistent denial by banks that they would ever become dual issuers.

The investigation crept along month after month for a year, then into a second year. Pressure for a decision continued to build. At the critical stage, in one of those political brouhahas that periodically sweep the nation's capital, it was suddenly announced that Donald Baker was stepping down as head of the antitrust division to be replaced by an academic lawyer from a Midwestern university. The investigation slowed to a crawl. It was the better part of two years after our request for a "railroad" letter before we were informed that a decision was imminent. We asked for an opportunity to plead our case before the head of the antitrust division and full panel of investigators. It was granted. Our corporate counsel, antitrust counsel from our outside law firm, and I flew to Washington, D.C.

***

The staff of the Department sat as solemn as a flock of crows on one side of the room, we on the other. They said little as we passionately argued our convictions. The senior investigator informed us that the vast preponderance of banks had assured them they would never go dual. He reminded us that MasterCharge, our principal competitor, then larger than NBI, had publicly announced that they did not share our views and had no intention of adopting a similar prohibition. What proof did we have for our conclusions?

"Look," I argued, "there is never a way to prove a prospective situation. It's not a matter of evidence, it's a matter of judgment. I've spent the last seven years intensely involved in this business, working at the heart of how banks act and react. If we withdraw or fail to enforce a prohibition against duality, within two years you will find it difficult to discover a half dozen banks that are not dual owner/members of both systems. They will be aggressively issuing both cards and, within a year or two more, questioning why they should support two systems and urging management of both to coordinate their activities. If you refuse us the letter, it is unlikely we can sustain enough support from our board and membership to enforce the prohibition. We can't fight the Department of Justice and intense pressure from many of our own members at the same time, no matter how strong our convictions." They sat, impassive, listening intently, hearing nothing. I plunged on.

"If you take a neutral position and issue the letter, we have a decent chance to roll back duality. If we're successful, we'll see the emergence of a third and fourth, perhaps fifth and sixth bank card system, for no bank in a given market will then want to issue the same products as a direct competitor. There will be real economic benefit for each bank in a given market to belong to and help develop a separate system. If that happens, retailers and others with ample ability and resources will form their own systems, for they will have no justification to demand entry and owner/member participation in bank systems." They continued to sit impassive, unresponsive, as I continued.

"If we do not prevent duality now, there will never be more than two bank card systems. Pressure to diminish their competitive vigor, perhaps even to merge the two will never end. The precedent will roll over into debit cards and other payment systems. It's not a matter of proof, it's a matter of common sense." There was no response but polite thanks. They were lawyers. Disbelief was in every pair of eyes. On the way out our antitrust counsel was hopeful.

"I think we got our point across. I think we may get the letter." My heart was in my shoes as I replied.

"You're the expert, but if I were on trial for a capital crime and that was the jury, I'd be thinking about my last meal."

The labyrinthine Department of Justice, like all mechanistic, Newtonian, industrial-age organizations, was fat on data and information and starved for understanding and wisdom. The letter was denied. If we attempted to enforce the bylaw, we could expect to be sued. Strong convictions notwithstanding, subjecting the new organization and its members to treble-damage antitrust penalties in the face of such a divided industry and in defiance of the Department of Justice seemed impossible. I gave up. After four years of extraordinary expense, effort and trauma, I recommended to the board that we accept our destiny, withdraw our prohibition on duality, and turn our attention to everything we could do to enhance bank-to-bank competition and minimize erosion of competition between the systems.

***

What I told the hanging jury at the Department of Justice proved wrong. The banks didn't take two years to go dual. They did it in six months. Today there is no third, fourth, or fifth bank card system. Diners Club and Carte Blanche are wholly-owned subsidiaries of Citicorp. Eurocard system has emerged in central Europe but is interlocked with MasterCard. The JCB card system emerged in Japan. Both have achieved limited regional acceptance, but neither has prospects of becoming a global presence. Visa and

MasterCard are swiftly emerging as dominant debit card systems. Although there is now some effort to prohibit banks from issuing competing debit card brands, it may prove more form than substance.

Visa and MasterCard have been enjoined by the courts from preventing banks from affiliating with the Discover Card and American Express. Both Discover Card and American Express have filed antitrust lawsuits against Visa and MasterCard claiming billions of dollars of damages for their prior restraints against banks who wished to affiliate with Discover and Amex.

Visa has 60 percent of the global bank card business and continues its exponential growth. Within Visa, card issuance is rapidly consolidating in the hands of giant card issuers. The vast majority of all bank card business in the United States is now in the hands of less than a dozen giant banks. Processing of merchant transactions is rapidly consolidating in the hands of a few banks and joint stock companies. It is conceivable that two, at most three payment system behemoths may straddle the Earth and that a handful of member financial institutions will control boards and management of all three. It need not have been so in the past. It should not be so now. It might become worse in the future. *It ought not to be so, ever.*

To this day I often have regret I did not screw my courage to the sticking point and fight on: go down then and there, unbowed and unrepentant. To this day I wonder if the implied death threats affected my courage and judgment. Whether removing the prohibition of duality was a prudent act or a failure of courage and judgment I shall never know. What the eventual end of it will be I shall never see. Robert Frost, in one of his most loved poems, immortalized such choices:

> I shall be telling this with a sigh
> Somewhere ages and ages hence:
> Two roads diverged in a wood, and I—
> I took the one less traveled by,
> And that has made all the difference.

Chapter Fourteen

The Golden Links

What was the scenery of this beautiful universe which we inhabit; what were our consolations on this side of the grave—and what were our aspirations beyond it, if poetry did not ascend to bring light and fire from those eternal regions where the owl-winged faculty of calculation dare not ever soar.
—Percy Bysshe Shelley

As NBI struggled with duality, communications systems, marketing, security, and other major efforts required to turn the BankAmericard system around in the United States, the Bank of America Service Corporation continued to license banks in the remainder of the world. Each license was different, leading to a morass of different marketing, computer systems, operations, and names. The blue, white, and gold card known as BankAmericard in the United States was known as

Sumitomo Card in Japan, Barclaycard in the United Kingdom, Chargex in Canada, Bancomer in Mexico, and a multitude of other names in different countries. The situation quickly led to even greater and more complex problems than those experienced earlier in the United States, partially due to the diversity of language, currency, culture, and legal systems.

Influenced by the formation of NBI, international licensees formed a committee and made an effort to create an international organization. The effort failed. Late in 1972, the international licensee committee requested that the management of NBI lead a second effort to form a worldwide organization. We were not averse to the idea, although it raised complex issues. How could NBI take the lead without extending the perceptions and experience of one culture into many others? That would be anathema to the remainder of the world, and properly so. How could we reconcile our clear obligation to act in the best interests of NBI members with an obligation to act in the best interests of banks outside the United States?

Could we afford to divert time and energy from the many difficult problems in the United States? On the other hand, could we afford not to, since our success was irrevocably intertwined with the success of the program overseas? *How could the ultimate dream of creating the world's premier system for the exchange of value be realized without an effective global organization?*

The effort would be immensely more complex than NBI. A global organization would need to transcend diverse languages, cultures, currencies, customs, legal systems, political traditions, and technologies. It would involve thousands of banks scattered around the world, as well as national consortiums of banks in France, Canada, Scandinavia, Japan, the United States and other countries. It must anticipate that tens of thousands of diverse financial institutions in more than 200 countries and territories might wish to participate. It could easily take several years of effort with no assurance of success. Yet such an organization, if it could be created, would have a huge advantage in the U.S. market as well as the rest of the world. Clearly, the experience gained and trust developed in the formation of NBI would be invaluable. It was time for NBI to be a good global citizen.

I approached the NBI board in the spirit of Maxwell Carlson, pointing out that management could not undertake the effort unless released from its obligation to represent the interests of NBI. Nor could the effort succeed if we were without position, income, and ability to continue to lead NBI. Many of the NBI directors, including the chairman of the board, Sam Stewart, had been on the NBI executive officer organizing committee. They understood how important my independence from the National Bank of Commerce had been to the success of that effort. They knew how fiercely I had defended that independence, and the right of the various committees to act openly, in the best interests of all.

By board resolution, they authorized the management of NBI to act as organizing agent with freedom and obligation to act in the best interests of all parties worldwide. We were released from any obligation to act in the express interests of NBI in connection with the international organizing effort. The executive committee of the board was charged with representing NBI in the event of conflict of interest. It was an extraordinary act on the part of the NBI board of directors.

***

Thus began two years of simultaneous service as the president and chief executive officer of NBI, and as independent organizing agent on behalf of the international licensees. It was fascinating beyond description, filled with support, betrayal, and surprises beyond anything I could have imagined.

It was once again necessary to organize regional committees with representatives from every licensee—in Europe-Mid-east-Africa, Asia-Pacific, Latin America, and North America. Each multinational, regional committee was, to some degree, composed of subcommittees within countries or areas of common interest, such as Scandinavia and East Asia. Each regional committee contained representatives from countries with long histories of bitter commercial, ethnic, and cultural conflict, including open warfare and periodic subjugation of one another. Differences in language, culture, religion, economics, and law made communication difficult and possibilities for misunderstanding legion.

Fascinating patterns emerged. After hours of intense discussion, one or another of the participants would inevitably draw me to one side for a bit of private persuasion or complaint. When speaking of others, rarely was a person referred to by name. The language suggested object or thing, not person. There was classification of individuals by nationality, race, or religious origination, and generalizations about each class. There was reluctance to deal with others as individual human beings. There was even greater reluctance to be revealed as one, with all attendant weaknesses, hopes, and dreams. There was the usual, penguin-like business dress and the stiff behavioral dance by which we demonstrate mastery of the role of "sensible, practical businessman."

Casually, bit by bit, without suggesting that anything was amiss, I disciplined myself to respond by using the name of the person complained about, while gently questioning the characterization. Imperceptibly, meeting by meeting, the tenor of the language changed. Minds began to open, mine foremost among them. Trying to understand others is a reflective mirror. It teaches far more about self than about others. I could not bring about change without becoming the change I wanted to bring about. It was unwelcome, often unpleasant, always difficult. No matter how constant my effort, I could never fully get entirely beyond that which I *was* and *might become,* and fully embrace that which I *ought to be.*

Nine months into the effort, progress slowed considerably. Something not readily apparent was awry. Actions by some of the international committee members were inconsistent with what they professed. I began to watch patterns of behavior much more closely and make discreet inquiries that might illuminate whether we were merely frustrated by lack of progress, or had a correct intuition that things were not as professed. The more I observed and reflected, the greater my concern.

At a meeting of the international organizing committee in Mexico City, things came to a head in a way no one expected. The two of us from NBI were convinced that some members of the committee, for reasons unknown, had decided to circumvent the formation of an international organization. But who, and why? Did it reflect the views of their institutions or was it self-interest? Was it sincere conviction that the present system was superior to anything that might be proposed? Was it misunderstanding? Was it fear of change? Was it weakness in our performance as organizing agent?

Even if we knew identities and reasons, confrontation would bring denial, polarize the situation, and make agreement impossible. It was a perplexing problem that I thought about long into the night before the last day of the meeting, trying to understand what might lie beneath the surface of so many contradictory words and acts, and what might be done about it.

> During our sixteen years of conflict with industrial age, command-and-control organizations and the extraordinary experiences forming NBI, Old Monkey and I had encountered more than our share of the extraordinary, often bizarre behavior that radical change often incites. Nor were we strangers to the fact that innovative change is never accompanied by sufficient information and knowledge; it often requires acting wisely and prudently on the basis of very little formation.
> Making good judgments and acting wisely when one has complete data, facts, and information is not leadership. It's not even management. It's bookkeeping. Leadership requires ability to make wise decisions and act responsibly upon them when one has little more than a clear sense of direction, proper values, and some understanding of the forces driving change.

Old Monkey Mind and I spent many years trying to understand why, in the midst of an abundance of information, we find it so difficult to act with wisdom, foresight, or compassion. One way to understand the situation is to examine the means by which we create understanding and wisdom. Every individual is embedded in an increasingly complex, diverse number of communities—cities, states, nations, governments, churches, corporations, schools, neighborhoods, and countless other institutions, entities, to say nothing of the natural world.

Within those communities, at the superficial, sensory level, we continually act, experience the results of those acts, learn from the experience, make decisions based on that learning, and act again. This does not happen in a linear, singular manner but in a continuous, integrated flow of countless events, second by second, minute by minute, and hour by hour. Nor can this flow of acting, experiencing, learning, and deciding be either completely voluntary or controlled, since countless other people and organizations are doing the same. We are affected by their acts, experiences, and judgments, and must respond. Myriad living entities and physical things composing the natural world are continually acting and reacting. We must respond to them as well. All our acts, experience, learning, and decisions are an inseparable flow of larger wholes. They are equally an inseparable flow of smaller wholes of which each individual is composed. No one is without some autonomy, yet no one is separably autonomous.

At a deeper, partially subliminal level, we assimilate experience, relate it to other experience, attempt to understand the relevance, and make projections about the future based on that understanding. Those predictions, immediate and long-term, largely determine the decisions we make, the acts we take, and the results we experience.

At a much deeper level, usually without awareness, we inevitably construct a concept of reality, a world view, an internal model of reality against which we compare current experience in order to create meaning. It is here we make sense of the external world, our place in it, ourselves, and our actions. It is, or at least ought to be, the home of wisdom.

When there is an explosion in the capacity to receive, utilize, store, transform, and transmit information, the external world changes at a rate enormously greater than the rate at which our internal model evolves. Nothing behaves as we think it should. Nothing makes sense. At times the world appears to be staging a madhouse. It is never a madhouse. It is merely the great tide of evolution in temporary flood, moving this way and that, piling up against that which obstructs its flow, trying to break loose and sweep away that which opposes it. At such times, we experience extreme dissonance and stress.

At the heart of that dissonance and stress is paradox. The more powerful and entrenched our internal model of reality, the more difficult it is to perceive and understand the fundamental nature of the changing externalities we experience. Yet without such perception, it is extremely difficult to understand and change our internal model of reality.

This is precisely where we are today, and it is rapidly getting worse. Deep in most of us, below our awareness, indelibly implanted there by three centuries of the industrial age, is the mechanistic, separatist, cause-and-effect, command-and-control, machine model of reality. If you do not think your internal model of reality is not largely based on the machine as metaphor, carefully keep track of every thought and every expression you have or hear that is based on the machine metaphor—got a screw loose—monkey wrench in the machinery—nuts and bolts question—get down to brass tacks—sand in the gears—grease the wheels—put the pedal to the floor—stuck in low gear—hit the nail on the head—get down to brass tacks—get up a head of steam—he's bombed—jet set—built like a tank—change gears—turn this ship around—hit the brakes—rudderless ship—let's take off—locked up—in our sights—steamroller it—blast off—give it wheels—no one at the wheel—ticking like a clock—well-oiled machine—running on empty—crank it out—gone ballistic—shoot the works—you can easily list thousands.

When our internal model of reality is in conflict with rapidly changing external realities, there are three fundamental ways to respond:

First: We can cling to our old internal model and attempt to impose it on external conditions in a futile attempt to make them conform to our expectations. That is what most institutions compel us to attempt, and what we continually dissipate our ingenuity and ability trying to achieve. It is futile.

Second: We can engage in denial. We can refuse to accept the new external reality. We can pretend that external changes are not as profound as they really are, deny that we have an internal model, or that it bears examination. When the world about us appears to be irrational, erratic, and irresponsible, it is all too easy to blame others for the unpleasant, destructive things we experience. It is equally easy to abandon meaning, embrace fantasy, and engage in erratic behavior. Denial is also futile.

Third: We can attempt to understand and change our internal model of reality. That is the least common alternative, and for good reason. Changing an internal model of reality is extremely difficult, often terrifying, and always complex. It requires a meticulous, painful examination of beliefs. It requires fundamental understanding of consciousness and how it must change. It destroys our sense of time and place. It calls into question our very identity. We can never be sure of our place or our value in a new order of things. Changing our internal model of reality requires an enormous act of faith, for it requires time to develop, and we require time to grow into it. Yet it is the only workable solution.

Those with the greatest power and wealth and the most prominent place in the old order of things have the most to lose. It is, therefore, understandable that so many of them close their minds to different possibilities and cling tenaciously to the old order of things. It is understandable that they engage in cosmetic change to palliate their discomfort and placate critics. It is understandable that they seek one another and merge the institutions they control to amass more and more power and wealth in order to perpetuate that to which they cling. It is understandable that they blind themselves to the fact that they are attempting to preserve the form of things long after form no longer serves function, a certain formula for failure, since the closest thing to a law of nature in the organizational world is that form has an affinity for expense, while function has an affinity for income.

Those in positions of power, wealth, and prestige who tenaciously cling to the present order of things deserve understanding, not condemnation, for they intuitively sense what Machiavelli discovered five centuries ago when he wrote: "Nothing is more difficult to take in hand, more perilous to conduct or more uncertain of success, than to take the lead in the introduction of a new order of things."

No one should be condemned for failure to welcome change. This pervasive problem plagues us all. Dostoyevsky put it into perspective in the last century when he wrote: "Taking a new step, uttering a new word is what people fear most."

The undeniable fact is that we have created the greatest explosion of capacity to receive, utilize, store, transform, and transmit information in history. There is no way to turn back. Whether we recognize it or not, whether we will it or not, whether we welcome it or not, whether it is constructive or not, we are caught up together, all of us and the Earth as well, in the most sudden, the most profound, the most diverse and complex change in the history of civilization. Perhaps in the history of Earth itself.

But, what if those with the greatest power, wealth, and position were to open their minds to new possibilities, loosen their tenacious grasp on the old order of things, abandon the palliative of cosmetic change, open their eyes to new forms of organization, *seriously question and change their internal model of reality?* What if they were to cage the four beasts that devour their keeper—ego, envy, avarice, and ambition—and take the lead in a new order of things? What if they were to go before and show the way? Now there's a

> challenge worthy of both the best among them and the best within them. I know that they can. And I will never give up that belief, or hope, that in time, enough of them will.

As the two of us from NBI talked long into the night in Mexico City, we could find no way to be certain of who was involved in the effort to subvert formation of a new international organization. It was not really important. The struggle to form the organization on the basis of complete openness and trust had been breached. The meeting of international licensee banks was but six weeks away. Licensees would want to know the prospects for formation of the new international organization. It was another of those circumstances when one must act on conviction and principle, openly and honestly, trusting that constructive events will emerge.

The next morning I announced that the management of NBI could no longer act as organizing agent. We were willing to be part of the committee but would no longer lead the effort. There was immediate consternation. Those honestly supporting the effort demanded to know the reason for our sudden withdrawal. Our explanation was simple:

"We're convinced that the process is not as open and honest as it ought to be. Our conviction may be in error, but we're compelled to step aside as organizing agent, since we no longer sense the commitment or trust that the process requires." There were immediate demands for a detailed explanation. We refused to say more.

"We're not here to accuse or condemn. We're here to help create an equitable, transnational organization if conditions are such that it is possible. At the moment, they are not." There was intense discussion about what should be reported to the annual meeting. We maintained the committee ought to report the facts; we were withdrawing as organizing agent because we no longer felt everyone was acting in good faith. Under the circumstances, we did not feel the organizing effort was something we could continue to lead. It was as simple as that.

The meeting adjourned at noon, all agreeing nothing further could be done until after the annual meeting of all licensees in Spain a few weeks hence. Upon our return to San Francisco, we immediately wrote to licensee banks conveying our decision to withdraw. Telephones were soon ringing off the wall. We adamantly refused to say more.

***

The annual meeting in Spain was planned and conducted by the Bank of America Service Corporation in concert with the chairman of the international committee. Attendees had but one thing on their minds: What had happened to the effort to reconceive the international program? There was considerable surprise when the meeting began as though nothing had happened. One could feel the tension in the room mount as the meeting droned on with presentations about plans to seek more licensees and make adjustments to some of the operating regulations.

Three hours into the morning, an agenda for the remainder of the three-day meeting was proposed. It contained nothing about the failed effort at reorganization other than a brief report at the end of the final day. An annoyed murmur swept the room. A member rose and angrily complained.

"We didn't travel halfway around the world to spend three days on this agenda. We came to find out what happened to the effort to reconceive the system and create an equitable, international organization. I, for one, have no intention of waiting until the end of the last day to find out." A chorus of "Hear, hear," "Absolutely," "Right on," immediately arose. An officer of the Bank of America Service Corporation tried to paper over the difficulty with generalities. The hum of discontent grew louder.

The chairman of the international committee rose to offer his version of the situation and induce the members to accept the proposed agenda, as did another member of the committee. No one admitted that they were opposed to the effort. But it was becoming obvious who wanted to discuss the organizational derailment in depth and who didn't. We sat quietly and said nothing. The murmur of discontent grew louder. Another member rose.

"We came expecting to hear from the organizing agent. Why are they not on the program? What is going on here?" Another crescendo of "Yes," "Hear, hear," "Absolutely." All eyes were now looking at us, leaving nothing for the meeting chairman to do but ask if we had anything to say. I rose to speak briefly.

"We're here to participate as one licensee among many. We believe deeply in the effort to create an equitable international structure. Some may honestly feel that the present system is preferable. That would be understandable and welcome, however, we believe that some may not be acting openly in that regard. No equitable organization can arise under such conditions. It is not constructive to say more, for our belief may be in error. If you wish to know more, it must come from other sources."

Efforts to continue the proposed agenda collapsed, as members demanded time to meet privately with one another and discuss the situation with their representatives on the organizing committee. Ken Larkin, the most senior representative of the Bank of America and a member of the NBI board, immediately sought me out. Although we did not always agree, mutual respect and trust had grown steadily. He was deeply concerned.

"Dee, what's going on here? This is not at all what I expected, based on what I've been told."

"Ken, some of your people may not yet understand Bank of America's commitment to the international effort. That's not for me to say. It's not my affair. You know the depth of NBI's commitment to these concepts. You know that withdrawing as organizing agent is not a decision we came to lightly. To say more would not be productive."

"What can be done to get things back on track?"

"I don't know. It may already be happening. Ken, we've worked through some difficult times together. If you were to assure the group of your personal commitment to the effort, and the commitment of the Bank of America, I would certainly accept it, and expect the others would as well. Perhaps you should give everyone space to meet and talk as they like. Perhaps the licensees themselves will lead us where we ought to go."

***

In the afternoon, Ken rose to express his personal concern and assure everyone of his personal commitment, and the commitment of the Bank of America. He asked if they would like time to discuss the situation with others and contact their institutions, if required, to determine if they wished to abandon the effort or continue and, if so, how they wished to proceed. They were confused but delighted, assembling and disassembling for short meetings and private discussions far into the night.

We participated in none. No accusations were ever made. But most licensees were digging to learn all that they could and form their own conclusions. The agenda was resumed the second day, but few paid any attention to it. Self-organizing discussions continued. By the end of the second day, several people had gracefully withdrawn from the international organizing committee with profuse thanks for their hard work. Others had been appointed. The chairman had withdrawn "to allow others an opportunity to serve."

In the late afternoon of the third day, the newly constituted committee met, firmly committed themselves to a renewed effort, and asked if we would resume our efforts as organizing agent. We agreed, providing only that henceforth all differences should be open, honest, and constructive. All agreed that was as it should be, and from then on, with minor exceptions, so it was. By the end of the meeting, no one had lost face, all those who had served were honored for their efforts, no more was said of the past, and everyone's energy turned to the future. There were extraordinary problems ahead and times when it appeared the new international organization would never come to be, but the future was not to be denied.

***

The most treasured memory came at the end of the effort. After two years of constant struggle we had resolved an incredible number of differences but three powerful disagreements remained. The conflicting positions had been adopted at the highest level of each licensee bank as a condition of their participation in the new organization. The differences seemed impossible to reconcile. The committee had agreed to a final day and a half meeting, after which the effort would be abandoned if positions had not changed. In conversations leading to the meeting, it became apparent that positions, rather than softening, had hardened. As organizing agent, we were desperate to think of a way to break the impasse. We could think of no compromise that had a chance of being accepted.

I had a life long habit of backing away from difficult situations and approaching them in a playful, unorthodox way. I gave up efforts to find a compromise and began to reflect on the exceptional effort of the past two years and the progress that had been made. I began to peel the mental onion; to get at the essential nature of that which had lifted such a complex, diverse group over seemingly insurmountable obstacles. It was hard to get at, but simple when it emerged. At critical moments, all participants had felt compelled to succeed. And at those same moments, all had been willing to compromise. They had not thought of winning or losing, but of a larger sense of purpose and concept of community that had transcended and enfolded them all.

Several members of the staff joined in and within the hour, we had a plan. We reduced our thoughts to the simplest possible expression: *The will to succeed, the grace to compromise.* Conveying those principles in the living language of any member of the group was sure to give offense to others. It must be in a dead language. A linguist was asked for a translation into Latin, which he rendered as *Studium ad prosperandum, voluntas in conveniendum.* To this day I do not know the accuracy of his translation, nor does it matter, for it has taken on a meaning larger than the language itself.

We contacted a fine, local jeweler and asked that a die be created from which to cast sets of golden cufflinks. On one would be a half round of the Earth with continents in relief; circling it in raised letters, "Studium ad prosperandum." The other cufflink would be the other half of the Earth and its continents, circled with "Voluntas in conveniendum." We had a set made for every member of the committee. We said nothing to anyone about what we had done.

The meeting convened on a splendid, warm day in San Francisco. It was polarized and cantankerous. The four large banks that composed Chargex in Canada were adamant. Unless others around the world accepted their demands they would not participate. In desperation, I looked around the group and asked,

"Well, it is obvious Canada cannot accept the position of others on this issue. Is it the sense of the group that you wish to proceed to form the new organization without our friends from Canada?" Nods all around.

"Well, then, it appears Chargex representatives will no longer be part of the process. Would it be appropriate to have them remain as observers with the understanding they will not participate in remaining discussions?" Again, nods all around. The Canadians were shocked, but did not leave.

Things got no better. There was adamant disagreement on the remaining issues. As the day ended, gloom deepened. I suggested we adjourn the meeting, since agreement appeared impossible. We could meet in the morning to disband the effort. Meanwhile, in recognition of their past extraordinary efforts, we wanted them to experience the finest that San Francisco had to offer. We boarded a private boat at Fisherman's Wharf for a trip across the bay to a fine French restaurant, Le Vivoire, in Sausalito. It was within a block of where Sam, Jack, Fred, and I met four years before to ask the impossible question, *If anything imaginable was possible, if there were no constraints whatever, what would be the nature of an ideal organization to create the world's premier system for the exchange of value?* It seemed fitting to bury the idea where it had been born.

Mother Nature could not have been more generous. As the boat departed from Fisherman's Wharf, a magnificent sun was sinking behind the Golden Gate Bridge, painting huge, cumulus clouds over spectacular shades of pink and purple, turning the colossal bridge to its famous, flaming, golden color, bringing out the marvelous pastel hues of the city, and swathing the deep blue of the bay with a path of sparkling light from the boat to the horizon. It was shirtsleeve weather as the boat circled the fortress-like buildings of the former federal prison on Alcatraz Island, then slid past the lush green of Angel Island to dock among the quaint houseboats lining the shores of Sausalito.

After a short walk to the restaurant, a few bottles of fine wine, and a splendid dinner, it was a mellow group of people who faced me when I asked for a moment to say a few words before the evening ended. After reminiscing for a few moments about the many experiences we had shared, the obstacles overcome, and the exceptional effort expended, a small gift was placed before them as I concluded.

"It is no failure to fall short of realizing such a dream. From the beginning, it was apparent that forming such a complex, global organization was unlikely. We now know it is impossible, notwithstanding two years of exceptional effort. Not knowing with certainty how today's meeting might end, we felt compelled to do something that would be appropriate no matter what happened. Would you please open the small gift on the table before you?" As they each opened a small, beautifully wrapped box and began to examine the contents, I quietly continued.

"We wanted to give you something that you could keep for the remainder of your life as a reminder of this day. On one cufflink is half of the world surrounded with the Latin phrase, 'Studium ad prosperandum'—the will to succeed. On the second cufflink is the other half of the world surrounded with 'Voluntas in conveniendum'—the grace to compromise. We meet tomorrow for the final time to disband the effort after an arduous two years. There is no possibility of agreement. As organizing agent, we have one last request. Will you please bring your cufflinks to the meeting in the morning? When it ends, each of us will take them with us as a reminder for the remainder of our lives that the world can never be united through us because we lacked the will to succeed and the grace to compromise. But if, by some miracle, our differences dissolve before morning, this gift will remind us to the day we die that the world *was* united because we *had* the will to succeed and the grace to compromise."

There was a moment of profound silence as they examined their gift. It was shattered by one of my more exuberant Canadian friends, may his soul rest in peace, who rose with a huge grin and exploded, **"You miserable bastard!"** The room filled with laughter as the dinner ended.

The next morning, no one was without their cufflinks. Many committee members had been up much of the night calling officials of their bank or members of their constituency, demanding authority to reach agreement. The chairman was greeted by silence as he opened the meeting with a quiet question,

"Is there anyone who wishes to speak of disbanding the effort?" The Canadians immediately ceded their previous position in deference to the others and announced that they were to be part of the new organization. Within the hour, as individuals quietly touched one or the other of their cufflinks, agreement was reached on every issue.

When the international organization, then called Ibanco, now Visa International came into being a few months later, *The will to succeed, the grace to compromise* became the corporate motto. As far as I know, to this day, every new director receives a set of the golden cufflinks and a parchment relating the story. Money could never compensate me for mine.

Chapter Fifteen

What's in a Name?

Either the Stars are great geometers or the eternal geometer has arranged the stars.

—Voltaire

It was perfect—perfect in its beauty—and perfect because, from the sun in the heavens to the fly with burnished wings on the hot rock, there was nothing out of harmony.

—Mark Rutherford

In 1973, it became apparent that continuing proliferation of names for the card could hinder growth of the system. At the time, the only common worldwide identity was the blue-white-gold bands design. The product had a different name in every country and in some countries, several names. In the United States, the common name was BankAmericard. In Canada, Chargex. In the remainder of the world, it was usually known by the name of the issuer, such as Sumitomocard in Japan, or Barclaycard in the United Kingdom. Once the card had been introduced in the name of one bank, others were reluctant to join. The multitude of names was confusing to merchants, seriously undermining card acceptance. Ability to conduct international marketing and ensure acceptability of cards was severely limited.

Merchant windows and counters were plastered with the name of the bank that contracted with the merchant for acceptance of cards. "Barclaycard Welcome Here." "Sumitomocard Welcome Here." Merchants resented commercialization of their premises by banks. Cardholders were often confused, thinking only cards of the named bank were acceptable, a misunderstanding some of the banks were not unhappy to perpetuate. As the system grew, so did the problem. In the United States, the name BankAmericard was limiting, as other banks were not happy promoting the identity of Bank of America. Savings and loan companies and credit unions gained legal authority to enter the business. They did not like the "bank" connotation of the name. The "American" connotation of the card was not appreciated in other countries. "Card" was out of keeping with possible new products such as travelers checks and money orders. Each year that passed made solution of the problem more difficult. With the formation in June 1974 of Ibanco, the name chosen for the new international corporation, the whole of the enterprise finally had a governance mechanism capable of approaching such a vast, complex problem.

***

At the formation of Ibanco, another extraordinary event occurred. As the international committee turned its attention to management of the new corporation they were not anxious to lose the management that had seen them through the effort. Could there be common management between two such organizations? At first, it seemed impossible. They were two entirely different legal entities: National

BankAmericard, composed of U.S. banks, and Ibanco, composed of several national consortiums such as NBI, Chargex, Carte Bleue, and hundreds of individual banks throughout the world.

On issue after issue, whether in marketing, service fees, operations, new products, or other areas, the interests of NBI members would often differ from those of other Ibanco members. Conflicts of interest would be inevitable, yet that was exactly the case during the two years we acted as organizing agent to create Ibanco. We agreed to look into the matter.

An unusual agreement was devised. Ibanco and NBI would enter into a joint management agreement in which the same staff and officers would serve both organizations. Any officer could be terminated by either board, but it would take both to appoint them. Thus, management would be promoted and rewarded by joint agreement, but could be discharged or demoted by unilateral decision of either. In the event of a conflict of interest, management would be obliged to declare it, and announce which party they intended to represent.

The other party would be represented by its board.

It would require extraordinary trust and credibility, along with exceptional standards of fairness and candor. It would mean constant scrutiny, suspicion, and criticism. What person of sound mind and body would want to work under such conditions? In ways, no one, but we had been doing it for six years, and with too much success to back away from another challenge. Conventional management wisdom held that common management reporting to such diverse, autonomous parties with divergent interests could never function effectively, but it did, surprisingly well—and quickly.

***

Soon after the formation of Ibanco we approached the board for authority to investigate adoption of a common, worldwide name. It was an awesome task for a new organization. Every card in the world would have to be reissued. Every merchant decal on every window and at every point-of-sale counter would have to be replaced. Every electronic sign would have to come down and be replaced—twenty thousand in Japan alone. Every form, every bit of stationery, and every sign in every bank would require replacement. All advertising would have to be changed. It would involve dozens of languages, cultures, and legal systems. No single center of authority or management group could ever hope to know, let alone understand, the full extent of the diversity and complexity involved.

Not only would such immense change have to occur, it could not be done in lockstep. It would have to be done by an incredibly diverse complex of thousands of independent institutions, each of which would need autonomy in making its part of the conversion. Each would need freedom to explain and market the change in competition with all others. Yet, it must happen swiftly and cooperatively, with equity and fairness. It must seamlessly blend cooperation and competition.

The situation was further complicated. Although Ibanco had obtained an exclusive license from the Bank of America for the blue-white-gold bands design, and the name BankAmericard, both were still owned by the bank. Fortunately, at the time of formation of Ibanco, we had negotiated an agreement compensating the Bank of America for surrender of ownership of the international part of the system. The agreement provided that should a new name be adopted acceptable to 80 percent of the system, ownership of the bands design would be transferred to Ibanco without additional compensation. Use of the name, BankAmericard, would be discontinued by all banks and revert to the Bank of America for its exclusive use.

Conversion to a new name under such circumstances was another of those problems for which there was no pattern and little experience. We'd had enough outside experts during our initial efforts to create electronic systems. I had great confidence in the ingenuity and ability of our modest staff. When their creativity was challenged and they had latitude to use it, their accomplishments had been extraordinary. If such a monumental change was to happen, we must be the ones to do it.

We again turned to our growing habit of looking for underlying purpose and principle as the point of beginning. The purpose part was quite simple—to create a common, worldwide name for the organization and all its products to compliment the common blue-white-gold bands design, with ownership of both cooperatively vested in the totality. With no thought to what the new name might be, we began to create principles that it must embrace. One by one they emerged.

The new name must be short, graphic, and capable of instant recognition. It must be easily pronounceable in any language. It must have no adverse connotations in any language or culture. It must be capable of worldwide trademark protection for the exchange of value and all related activities. It must have no restrictive connotations, whether related to geography, institution, service or form, such as *Ameri-, Euro-, bank, charge, credit,* or *card.* It must have implications of mobility, acceptance, and travel. Before we were done, the list contained more than fifteen principles to which any new name must conform. It was daunting. We decided to simply release human ingenuity and see what happened.

We called the entire staff together, from the newest mail handler to management. If they wished, anyone was free to participate in any way they found interesting and challenging, whether individually or in self-organized groups. A representative group would form to consider all suggestions and help formulate the best possible answer. There would be no consultants or outside experts. The employees were the experts, one and all. The person who came up with the answer would receive a munificent fifty-dollar check. Should it be a team effort that produced the result, each member of the team would have a check. The payment was purely symbolic. A large amount would produce a tendency to hoard ideas and information. Desire to have the check as a framed memento, in addition to the excitement and challenge of open participation, was compelling enough.

There was an explosion of ingenuity. The effort swiftly self-organized. Those technically inclined wrote software programs to fabricate names from letters of the alphabet. Family and friends were engaged. Dictionaries of roots and meaning in numerous languages were sifted and combed. Meetings and groups evolved and dissolved. I doubt anyone involved read, saw, or experienced anything in their daily lives without wondering if it might contain a clue to the answer. Great excitement arose each time someone thought they had solved the puzzle, only to be met with good-natured skepticism and challenge by others. Marketing people felt compelled to find the answer before someone in the mailroom beat them to it. Mailroom people felt challenged to demonstrate they were as creative as anyone in marketing, which many proved to be.

Lists of possibilities emerged, were combined in various ways, suggestions appearing and disappearing as the winnowing process continued. Hundreds of ideas emerged, failed to meet the test of purpose and principles, and were abandoned. Within months, no more than a handful remained. One, which had been discounted on the assumption it was so common it could never meet the test of trademark protection, continually reappeared and often rose to the top. *VISA.* Was it possible such a common name, used for centuries to denote an entry document to a foreign country, might be capable of trademark protection for financial services worldwide? Maybe, just maybe, it was so old and common that no one had thought of using it for financial services.

A worldwide trademark search was quietly undertaken to determine if it had ever been used in the field of financial services. One by one, the reports came in. There was a Visa car. There were Visa golf clubs. There were Visa fabrics. We held our breath. There were Visa pens. There were Visa appliances, there were Visa products of many kinds, but we could find no use of Visa for financial services, publications, or related activities of any significance. We quietly filed worldwide trademark registrations in every possible jurisdiction for the use of the name for financial and related services.

Whether or not we could gain worldwide acceptance for the change among our members was unlikely, but at least we had a beginning, a protected name to propose. But who was to get the fifty-dollar check? There were dozens of different recollections of where and how the name first appeared. No matter how hard we tried, none among us could unravel the puzzle. The name had appeared as an integral part of a self-organizing process. In a staff meeting to celebrate our success and untangle the puzzle someone wisecracked, "Maybe it suggested itself. Either make the check payable to 'everyone' or to 'no one'. It belongs to us all." Amid much laughter, the matter was settled.

***

How the largest, most complicated trademark conversion in commercial history was agreed upon, then completed in a third the time anticipated would require a book of its own. However, memories of a few critical moments remain strong. One came near the end of the approval process at an international member meeting in Hawaii. After nearly two years of intense effort, the vast majority of members had slowly become convinced of the need for the change. However, a few were strongly opposed. We were reluctant to proceed if the decision had to be imposed on anyone.

The Sumitomo Bank in Japan was very concerned. They had, at great expense, installed thousands of electronic signs at merchant locations with "Sumitomo Card Welcome Here" emblazoned in the middle of the blue-white-gold bands design. The cost of changing the signs and the thought of removing their identity from merchant premises and substituting a generic, blue-white-gold VISA was a bitter pill to swallow. On the other hand, sense of belonging to a greater whole and accepting sacrifices for the common good was a powerful tradition in Japanese culture.

It was not so in other cultures, such as Britain and France. Our only member in Britain was Barclay's Bank, one of the oldest, proudest, and largest financial institutions in Europe. With a substantial presence in countries throughout the world, they were by no means free of imperialist notions or the sense of manifest destiny. In France, our member, Carte Bleue, was a consortium of large French banks. Carte Bleue, quite rightly from their perspective, felt entitled to more consideration than any single bank. The leader of that group felt that there was insufficient awareness of the difficulties of maintaining cohesion and cooperation among diverse French banks, or of their combined power.

It was the kind of situation to which one had to adjust in such an enabling organization. Rarely was there clear right and wrong. There were only differing perspectives and perceptions. There was rarely a best. There was only better. Interests were diverse and positions often diametrically opposed. Each was legitimate, powerfully held, and ably defended. Each, from the perspective of a given culture, custom, or law, was undeniably constructive, fair, and right, yet, from the aggregate perspective, each could be destructive, selfish, and wrong.

***

It was at a meeting in Hawaii that the final decision would be taken. I was frantic to know how to bring everyone to the table in constructive agreement. The night before the meeting, as Ferol and I wandered alone along a path bordering the ocean, we noticed an enticing promontory and walked out to sit on a bench. Another couple appeared and asked if they might enjoy the sunset with us, to which we warmly agreed. We fell into pleasant conversation about the beauty of the spot and the spectacular show Mother Nature was providing as the sunlight faded and stars emerged.

The next day, as the meeting began, I discovered my acquaintance of the evening before, John Clinton, was a managing director of Barclay's bank, concerned enough to travel halfway around the world to persuade others that the name change was a wrongheaded notion. Discussions were intense, differences strong, and nothing resolved as the day progressed. In accordance with our custom, the meeting was adjourned early in the afternoon, so that people could mingle, privately share views, and enjoy the company of one another. John asked for a private word with me. We agreed to meet on the beach in an hour.

As we lay prone on the sand under a hot tropical sun, he explained with great clarity and depth why Barclay's bank simply could not accept the name change. I listened carefully, trying to put myself into his skin and see things through his eyes. Clearly, from his perspective, he was right. Were anyone in a similar situation, they would feel the same. There was no point in argument. On the other hand, had he put himself in the skin of others? Could he see with their eyes? Were other perspectives equally relevant to the interests of Barclay's bank?

I asked if he had time to listen to the perspectives of others, which I would try to convey. He readily agreed. I smoothed out a section of wet sand and began to sketch merchant decals and card layouts, illustrating the difficulties experienced worldwide and the opportunities presented by a common name. From one corner of my eye I could see a member of the NBI staff, signaling an urgent need to speak to me. I waved him away, since John was swiftly absorbing dimensions of the problem that had escaped his attention and I did not want to break the flow of conversation. My back was beginning to burn. I choked back a grin as the inevitable parental homily popped into mind: "It's no skin off my back." This may well be skin off mine. It was a small price to pay. Within the hour, John said,

"We may not have fully understood the issues. I want to think about this overnight and speak with others from Barclay's. We may be able to support the name change." I thanked him and left.

***

The staff had bad news. Bernard Sue, head of Carte Bleue, had been roughly handled by some of the proponents of the name change. He had angrily announced he was returning to France on the next flight, would no longer participate in the meeting, and stormed away. It could easily disrupt the consensus that had been building. "Where is Bernard?" I asked. "Has he left yet?" Someone extended his arm, pointing to the ocean. At first, I could see nothing. As the swells rose, Bernard appeared, far out in the ocean.

My heart sank. A dinner meeting at which I must preside was but an hour and a half away. In his younger days, Bernard had been an Olympic-class swimmer. I was a country kid, reasonably at home in ponds and canals, but the ocean was another matter. I was determined Bernard must not leave. Duty calls in strange ways. There was nothing to do but to plunge in and slowly work my way out. Fortunately, Bernard was on his way in.

We met a hundred yards offshore, treading water as we spoke. It was a stroke of good fortune, for he was relaxed and in his element. We talked for more than half an hour, he breathing easily as I struggled to stay afloat. Whether it was pity for an awkward creature in distress or the calming effect of the great mother ocean is hard to say, but he was receptive and kind, agreeing that the importance of Carte Bleue to the system was too great to be jeopardized by unintended offense, no matter how egregious. He would set the matter aside and remain.

Good and bad fortune, like bananas, often come in bunches. At dinner that evening, I sat next to the representative from Sumitomo Bank in Japan. We fell into a deep discussion about bonsai, a hobby I was then clumsily pursuing. He was an expert in the field and gently told me of a bonsai tree handed down through five generations of his family. It was now in his custody. It gave him a profound sense of the continuity of life, the importance of honoring ancestors and the obligation to respect the needs of generations yet to be. When he traveled, he had concern about remaining too long, for he felt great personal responsibility for the tree. It must be passed to the next generation, healthy and enhanced. I shared with him my deep conviction that life is not a possession. Nor is life merely a contract between the living. Life is a sacred contract between the dead, the living, and the unborn.

Without intention on either part, the conversation drifted to Ibanco, the extraordinary relationships on which it was based, the sacrifices that had been made to bring it into being, and whether it too was a living thing that should be passed from generation to generation enhanced. We lapsed into silence, realizing a profound sense of shared responsibility. Not a word was said about our differences regarding the name change. Yet, in the beautiful, subliminal way that comes so easily in Eastern cultures, I had the feeling that we were becoming as one on the work to be done.

When it came time to make a few remarks to end the dinner, I asked his permission, then quietly shared the story he had told me about his family bonsai and concern for its welfare. I reminded the group that the Sumitomo family had originated as samurai warriors four hundred years earlier, migrating into the mining of copper, eventually into banking and a great many other businesses, adding:

"We should think carefully before we drag out our discussion tomorrow, put in jeopardy the life of such a tree, or arouse the samurai spirit of one who is responsible for its life." He was smiling gently as I finished.

Indeed, people must come to things in their own time, in their own way, for their own reasons, or they never truly come at all.

One can never understand why things happen as they do. Perhaps it was no more than imagination, but discussions the next day seemed to have a different quality. They were no less intense and penetrating, yet had a subtle feel of desire for commonality rather than difference; a feel of something beyond self, nation, culture, or institution tugging at one's sleeve.

A unanimous decision emerged at that meeting to change the corporate name, Ibanco, to Visa International Services Association. The acronym, of course, was VISA. National BankAmericard became Visa USA. At the same time a unanimous decision was taken to change all products worldwide to the name Visa. Thus the corporate names and product names became one. Those decisions caused many individuals great trouble as they returned to explain to others within their institutions what had happened. It may have been detrimental to some of their careers, yet they made the decision and never turned back.

Within weeks, plans were made for a four-year phase-in of the conversion to allow time for the complex work to be done. General objectives were established that allowed every institution complete freedom to make the conversion in any way it chose. There were no commandments, threats, or penalties. No member was told how to do anything. Instead, dates were agreed on by which they would be expected to reach certain objectives. Cardholders and merchants responded with enthusiasm, the conversion self-organized, and a year and a half later, there were few old cards, decals, or forms to be found. It was done in a third the time anticipated. Within another three years, Visa had surpassed all its rivals by a substantial margin.

> Whether in the middle of trauma or triumph (there seemed little else in those early years), Old Monkey and I could not stop playing with the future, with how things might become and how they ought to be. It seemed to us that we are emerging from a society based upon industrial production, for more than a century dominated by the separatist, mechanistic concepts of corporation and nation-state, into an extraordinarily complex, diverse, global technocracy, wherein it is increasingly possible to produce at any point on the globe a unique product or service for a single individual located at any other point.
>
> The very foundation of such a society, its economic neural system, is the intricately webbed, global data communication systems now rapidly emerging. Just as the human body is organized around biological neural systems so complex as to defy description, so too are increasingly

complex, electronic neural networks evolving and interconnecting around which the world's political, social, and commercial bodies will be forced to reconceive themselves, and wholly new ones will be formed.

The production of goods and services has progressed from the age of "hand-crafting," through the industrial age, more accurately thought of as the age of "machine-crafting," into the so-called information age, which can best be understood as the age of "mind-crafting," since information is nothing but the raw material of that incredible processor we call mind and the pseudo-mind we call computer. Software, the tool with which we shape information, can be best understood as "thought-ware" since it is clearly a product of the mind. The industrial age (the age of machine-crafting) was primarily an extension of muscle power. The information age (the age of mind-crafting) is primarily an extension of mental power. Whether it will eventually lead to yet another age characterized by an extension of ethical and spiritual power is a much more compelling question. We can always hope.

In the age of hand-crafting, the dominant forms of organization were the all-powerful churches, kingdoms, and hand-craftsmen guilds. Just as the age of machine-crafting led to the emergence of today's organizations, ending the dominance of guilds, kingdoms, and churches, so too will the age of mind-crafting give rise to new, more chaordic concepts of organization that will end the dominance of today's organizational structures.

Changes in existing organizations and the evolution of wholly new ones will have many characteristics in common. Just as the human body is not a vertical hierarchy with each part superior to another in ascending, linear order, organizations of the future will not be so structured. Great pyramids of superiors and subordinates will yield to affiliations of semi-independent equals, whether they be individuals within an organization, or organizations within a larger whole. This is not to say that all present industrial organizations are doomed. Evolution is rarely so cruel. It is patient, though inexorable. Most organizations will evolve, however slowly and painfully, into a form in which power, wealth, and information are more widely dispersed and commonly shared.

The concept of organizations composed of semi-autonomous equals affiliated for common purpose, such as Visa, the Internet, and Linux software, has intensified the endless debate as to whether competition or cooperation should rule the day. Each has passionate messiahs to preach its virtue. Both are wrong.

Competition and cooperation are not contraries. They have no opposite meaning. They are complimentary. In every aspect of life, we do both. Schools are highly cooperative endeavors within which scholars vigorously compete. The Olympic Games combine immense cooperation in structure and rules with intense competition in events. As the runners leap from the blocks, competition and cooperation are occurring in a single, indistinguishable blur. Every cell in our bodies vigorously competes for every atom of nutrient we swallow and every atom of oxygen we breathe, yet every cell can sense when the good of the whole requires they cooperate by relinquishing their demands when the need of other cells is greater. Life cannot reach its highest potential, in fact, cannot exist without a harmonious blend of competition and cooperation.

No societal, commercial, or governmental endeavor has ever existed without combining the two. Human history has always been a race without a victor between combat and compromise, between concepts of power and concepts of service. Cooperation gone mad results in the mindless pursuit of equality, use of centralized force to achieve uniformity, ever-increasing coercion to sustain it, and eventual slavery. Competition gone mad results in the mindless pursuit of self-interest, abuse of others, retaliation, accelerating anarchy, and eventual chaos. Only in a harmonious, oscillating dance of both competition and cooperation can the extremes of control and chaos be avoided and peaceful, constructive societal order be found.

In organizations of the future, it will be much more important to have a clear sense of purpose and sound principles within which many specific, short-term objectives can be quickly achieved, than a long-range plan with fixed, measurable objectives. Such plans often lead to futile attempts to control events to make them fit the plan, rather than understanding events so as to advance by all means in the desired direction. In time of rapid, radical change, long-term plans are often so generally stated as to require endless interpretation, in which case they are no plan at all, or they become so rigid that they diminish thought, obscure vision, and muffle advocacy of other, more innovative views.

In organizations of the future the centuries-old effort to eliminate judgment and intuition, art if you will, from the conduct of institutions will change. Organizations have too long aped the traditional mechanistic, military model wherein obedience to orders is paramount and individual behavior or independent thinking frowned upon, if not altogether forbidden. In organizations of the future it will be necessary to have people in every position capable of discernment, of making fine judgments and acting sensibly upon them. The industrial age trend toward stultifying, degrading, rote work that gradually reduces people to the compliant, subordinate behavior one expects from a well-trained horse will not continue.

It extends far beyond a factory worker on an assembly line. Vast white-collar bureaucracies exist everywhere, with mountains of procedures manuals depressing minds, avalanches of directives burying

> judgment, forests of reports obscuring perception, floods of studies inundating initiative, oceans of committees submerging responsibility and drowning decisions. You know what I mean. You have endlessly suffered through it and, worse yet, may be inflicting it on others. It has created a society of people alienated from their work and from the organizations in which they are enmeshed. Far too much ingenuity, effort, and intelligence go into circumventing the mindless, sticky web of rules and regulations by which people are needlessly bound.

Adoption of the global name, Visa, was not the end of such changes. In time, the system was so successful management thought it would be wise to reduce the size of the Visa name and logo from the face of the entire card to a much smaller logo in the center of the card, opening up space for greater bank identification, and co-branding with nonmember bank customers. It was the same old story. The customary had become sacred. Reasons why it should not be done came fast and furious—bank identification will dwarf and degrade the Visa name and service marks—merchant clerks won't recognize the reduced logo—consumers will see the product as inferior and turn to competitive cards with more powerful identification—it's foolish to diminish a dominant brand. Powerful directors from some of the largest card-issuing banks were opposed. There was a hue and cry for exhaustive market research and ample documentation.

As a management group, we were not persuaded of the efficacy of supposedly objective research, for it seemed to result in catastrophic mistakes as often as success. Nor, after constant pioneering in incredibly short time frames, were we inclined to drawn-out processes. We enjoyed approaching problems in a playful, innovative way, with raucous laughter, freewheeling discussions, and nothing off-limits or too unusual to be heard. I had often reminded them that *wool is meant to be grown on the hide, not in the head.* Yet the discussions were serious, for decisions had to be made, the consequences were huge, and agreement must be educed from an incredible complex of members.

We returned to our old habit of peeling such a complex mental onion with constant questions. What is the ultimate test of the acceptability of a card? What is the most difficult, most risky card to present and have accepted? Who does it? How is it done? An idea emerged that was compelling. The most difficult card to create and have accepted was a counterfeit card. Our wallets and purses emerged as we examined the cards we each carried. There were at least two or three issued by each of the most reluctant banks. What if we were to design cards with a reduced logo identical to what we were proposing, emboss them with the bank identification and card numbers of each of our legitimate cards, and simply present them to merchants in the normal way as we went about our affairs, recording transaction-by-transaction what we experienced and what the merchant said and did? *What if we counterfeited our own cards?* Now that was a fiendishly intriguing idea.

It had a major flaw. Our experience would be suspect, for we were recommending the change. But what if we enlisted the employees of our accounting and law firms, asking them to allow us to counterfeit their cards, as well. What if they were to help design an impeccable process to tabulate and verify the results? Within a day, we had all the elements figured out and individuals designated to conduct confidential discussions with card suppliers, accountants, and lawyers.

We could say nothing to directors or members without compromising the validity of the counterfeiting market research. It was beautiful. Not a procedure to change, not a customer to disturb, not a questionnaire to create, not an expert to hire. Just a simple booklet in which everyone would record exactly what happened when they presented their counterfeit card to merchants. We were the only ones to be discomfited if our cards were questioned. Each of us could carry a properly issued card in our wallets for backup in the event that happened.

It was with considerable trepidation that I pulled into a gas station and, for the first time, removed my counterfeit card from my wallet and nonchalantly hung it out the window while the attendant pumped the gas. (Yes, there were attendants still pumping gas in those days.) He looked at the card, did a double take and asked, "Is that a new Visa card?"

"I guess it must be," I replied, "I just got it." He took the card without hesitation.

In the weeks that followed, the booklets began to fill. Not a card was rejected because of the new design. There were no significant negative reactions. Most cards were accepted without comment. Many responses were positive, usually from merchant employees wondering when they would get their new Visa card. It was as though the public had come to expect innovation from Visa. They assumed that the new model was somehow superior to the old. The results of our counterfeiting exceeded all expectation.

***

On the eve of the next board meeting, I decided on the ultimate test, inviting Ken Larkin, executive vice president of the Bank of America, and three other directors who opposed the change to dinner at The Banker's Club, a private luncheon club during the day and fancy restaurant open to the public at night. They had a fascinating discussion about all the problems that were certain to occur if we were to adopt a new design. I said as little as possible in order to avoid biasing the discussion.

In time, I signaled for the bill, which the waiter brought on a tray. I produced my counterfeit card, and laid it on top of the bill in full view of everyone. No one noticed as the discussion continued. The waiter approached, picked up the tray, and walked away, returning shortly with a sales draft for signature. With the card in full view, I looked the draft over and signed it. The waiter picked it up and walked away without a word.

No one noticed. I left the card on the table, casually edging it toward the center, as talk about the problems we would encounter with the new design continued. No one noticed. I picked up the card and began to fiddle with it in full view. No one noticed. The suspense was excruciating. The card was practically in front of Ken Larkin's nose. A former football lineman, he was not unacquainted with locker-room language when excited. Finally, it came.

"What the hell is that?"

With what I am certain must have been a devilish grin I softly replied, "I think it's the new Visa card from Bank of America."

"The hell it is!"

He scrutinized the numbers. He had everyone's attention, including people at surrounding tables.

"That's our bank number, where did you get this?"

The other directors were grabbing at the card as I chuckled in delight, "Well, Ken, to be honest, it's counterfeit, but I certainly hope that at the board meeting tomorrow the directors will carefully examine the results of our research and approve the new design so that you can send me a legitimate one."

At the board meeting we confessed our sins and revealed the results of our "market research." We asked all the directors if they would like a counterfeit card of their own to validate the data. They did not. The decision was taken and the results are history.

At times, it was pure fun to "work" at Visa.

Chapter Sixteen

Breaking the Mold

> *The true strength of rulers and empires lies ... in the belief of men that they are inflexibly open, truthful, and legal. As soon as government departs from that standard, it ceases to be anything more than "the gang in possession" and its days are numbered.*
> —H.G. Wells

> *They that reverence too much the old times are but a scorn to the new.*
> —Sir Francis Bacon

How could you treat people who performed a miracle of communications with a piece of string and a dirty coffee cup and proved the validity of a new design by counterfeiting their own cards as though they were no more than "human resources?" You couldn't and we didn't.

The greatest delight from all my days leading Visa were open staff meetings, from which we never wavered. Within a day after every board meeting, staff meetings were held to include every employee of the company at every level including the newest. They were conducted by the most senior person present. At the meeting, every decision of the board was fully disclosed. Every employee was free to ask any question about the decisions, or anything else of concern to them. Their questions were answered fully. "That's confidential" was not considered an answer. "I don't know but I will find out and tell you at the next meeting" was permissible, but only if the promise was faithfully kept. All I ever said to them of a cautionary nature was, "You realize that some things you will learn could be detrimental to our purpose if they were bandied about publicly or prematurely leaked to the press. However, until we are consistently proved wrong, we will do our best to behave in accordance with the belief that mutual respect and trust is the strongest bond among people, and can be relied upon. I hope to earn your trust and respect and you shall certainly have mine."

It was often put to the test by skeptical employees. Near the end of one meeting, after reminding the people that nothing was off-limits and asking if there were more questions, a secretary rose, fixed her eyes on mine, and said, "Yes, I would like to know what you are paid, all the other benefits and perquisites you enjoy, and why you think they're justified." There was absolute, ominous silence as I stood before three hundred intent faces, collected my wits, consulted conviction, swallowed hard and answered—fully and in detail.

On another occasion, a woman new to the company, rose and in a somewhat abrasive manner said, "No company tells the truth to its employees and I don't believe that this one is different. There is no way you tell us everything." In your teeth, Mr. President, you're a liar, was the unspoken message. Her comment did not rise from desire to create trouble, but from conviction she was being lied to, and resentment at that perception. What could I say that would not result in confrontation, yet reassure her that we did our very best to live up to our beliefs?

It was taken out of my hands. Rising, with an accusatory finger pointing like a dagger at the questioner, one of our senior secretaries, in a voice shaking with outrage, said "You don't know what you're talking about! I've typed the board minutes for ten years and you're told everything! Everything!"

The tension in the room was palpable, but there was no need to do more than to say, "When we act from our deepest convictions it is impossible to reach perfection. The question was sincere. So was the reply. And so is our effort to live in accordance with our beliefs about an open company. If we can all accept that, there is nothing more to be said,:" and nothing more was.

***

In time, a custom emerged which I dearly loved. When everyone had their questions answered and the meeting was nearing an end, it would be my turn.

"What is the juiciest, most titillating rumor circulating the halls and circling the water cooler?" With great laughter, they would be obliged to tell the truth. It was marvelous fun to speculate where the rumors may have originated and how—whether from fear, suspicion, anxiety, or just plain old human love of juicy stories to tell. I have always suspected that some people concocted harmless rumors and planted them for the fun of having them revealed at the meetings. They knew that you can't tickle yourself, it's a social act. I may have planted one or two myself, but if so, no one will ever know.

In the darkest times, and there were many, I could never look out at so many wonderful people, engage them in laughter and give-and-take, without walking from the room filled with wonder at the human spirit. They could do anything! Anything! And so can everyone, everywhere, if our minds are open enough, our hearts warm enough, and our spirits strong enough to conceive of institutions that enable us to do so.

***

Something even more surprising arose from the tradition of open staff meetings. When Visa International came into being, it was impractical to convene a board composed of people from a dozen countries more than quarterly. Each meeting was held in a different country to familiarize directors with other cultures. One of the four meetings was held in conjunction with the annual meeting of members, attended by hundreds of officers of member banks from dozens of countries. Meetings required simultaneous translation in four languages.

In the beginning, the annual meeting followed a typical pattern: business meetings for representatives and a separate program for spouses and guests. In an effort to broaden the perspective of members, we began inviting world-class speakers and entertainers from a variety of cultures to address the business meetings in order to stretch imagination beyond the limited, traditional world of banking.

Accustomed to the openness of Visa staff meetings and our policy of inviting families to all management retreats, several spouses of Visa officers and directors approached me at one of the annual meetings to ask why they were expected to attend tours and other such events when they thought the business meetings might be much more interesting.

"Would it be possible for us to attend?" they asked. It had not occurred to me that they would have more interest in business meetings than programs arranged for their entertainment. There was no plausible reason why they should be excluded. An invitation was issued. The attendance was overwhelming and interest high, swiftly putting an end to separate programs. Thereafter, member events and sessions were open to everyone, whether representatives, spouses, or guests.

At the end of one such meeting, I was again approached by a half-dozen wives of directors. They were quick to the point. For years, they had listened to stories of board meetings and how decisions were made. They were fascinated by what they had experienced at the annual business meeting of members. Was there any possibility they could be invited to a board meeting? Whoa, Nellie! This was a horse of a different color. I bit off an emphatic "no," thinking to engage them in a bit of clever dissuasion. It was an error in judgment.

"There is an immense amount of work at each meeting that could not possibly be done if there were audience participation, "I argued. *Of course, but why did I think they would not honor that need and remain silent? All they wanted was to observe and be informed.*

"Confidential matters are discussed that must not be carried from the room." *Yes, but why did I think they would be any less conscious of confidentiality or any less responsible than a director or a member of the staff?*

"It would make the directors ill at ease and self-conscious." *Yes, but isn't that just the result of custom? Would they not become accustomed to an open meeting?*

"We could not invite spouses of Visa officers and directors without inviting all members, spouses, and guests." *Of course not. Why should we?*

"It would require a large room with circular seating in order for several hundred people to observe and hear." *Yes, but facilities for that are available at hotels able to accommodate the annual meeting. Why couldn't annual meeting locations be selected with that in mind?* Pride at being a powerful persuader began to take a terrible beating, but I pressed on.

"It just isn't done in the business community." *Well, why not? Isn't innovation what Visa is all about?*

"The board would never accept such an arrangement." *Perhaps, but we've heard you say many times that possibility is not determined by opinion, only by attempt. How can you know without making the attempt.* Ouch! Desperate, I called on Sir Isaac Newton for a little command-and-control.

"There is no way it can be done! The answer is no!" Withering looks. *That's not a reason. That's just another version of 'because I said so.' It just means you refuse to consider it.* I limped off in defeat with a lame, "Well, if that's the way you want to put it." A group of people I genuinely liked and respected walked away, denied and disappointed.

***

It gnawed at me for months, as Old Monkey and I replayed past board meetings as though they had been conducted in front of members and spouses. We could think of nothing that had been said or done that would be a compelling reason against making the attempt. There was the risk of premature disclosure of confidential matters, but we were not a shareholder company where that could have an effect on the price of stock.

And why was secrecy such a fetish in our institutions anyway? Might it be doing more harm than good? Might observing their elected board in action not reassure members about the extent of the discussion and intense effort made to act for the good of the whole? Why should I assume they would be any less inclined to hold sensitive matters in confidence than directors and officers? Had I not argued since the beginning that the true capital of Visa was credibility, not money? Would such a step increase or decrease our credibility?

Three months before the next annual meeting of members, I screwed my courage to the sticking point and asked the board for permission to conduct each board meeting that was contiguous with the annual meeting of members in open forum, with the board surrounded by the people they were elected to serve. You shall be spared details of that discussion. There are some things said that are best left to the silence of the past. Yet, in time, they agreed to try.

Months later, in just such a setting, I rose to welcome an audience of four hundred, asking only that they respect the process and refrain from audible response to what occurred—no comments, cheering, jeering, or applauding, please! They were superb. So were the directors. Within half an hour, we were so involved in discussion that no director seemed conscious of the audience. I could detect no lack of intensity, candor, or involvement. There was, however, one small difference, which I pointed out to the audience as the meeting ended and I thanked them for their interest and courtesy.

"Never have we as directors been more to the point, more gracious to one another, or more willing to understand a different point of view. For that, I must thank you, the audience, most kindly." After the meeting, my former interrogators crowded around.

"Fascinating." "Better than any play I ever attended." "Now I understand what board meetings are all about." "Will we be able to come again next year?" And, of course, they did, year after year.

In all those years there was but one breach of confidentiality. News of an important new Visa service was bandied about in the press before we had an opportunity to make a full public announcement. The next day, before we had any opportunity to investigate, one of the senior Visa officers instrumental in creating the new service asked to see me. He said that the news had leaked because of a careless comment he had made in a public setting. He wanted to be certain that I did not think that the leak resulted from any employee due to our policy of open meetings at which we confided everything to the entire staff. He insisted on making an apology to everyone at the next meeting, and so he did.

During the seventeen years forming and leading the Visa family, for so we often called it, there were many such customs that saw us through difficult times. From the beginning, we were determined that we would neither seek nor offer favor of any kind. During those years, we never parted with a penny to a politician, to any regulatory body for approval, or to anyone for entry into a country. It was a price we would not pay for success, regardless of the sum. We never gave or accepted gifts of any kind, except for small tokens in cultures where to arrive without one would give offense.

Nor were we interested in the business entertainment syndrome. During all those years, I assiduously declined all invitations to rocket launchings, Super Bowls, golf tournaments, and other extravaganzas. Even complimentary subscriptions of magazines in which we bought substantial advertising were returned with a gracious declination. In retrospect, it seems almost absurd, but then as now, to do otherwise seemed demeaning.

For more than a decade, until I left in 1984, I worked in the midst of such increasing complexity, testing its strengths and weaknesses, learning from both joyous and bitter experience the demands of leading such systemic diversity, discovering the richness of diffusion of power and wealth, exploring the limits of individual capacity for change, and studying how to increase it. It was nothing but learning, learning, learning as we struggled to escape the mechanistic, separatist, linear mind-set that insists we bifurcate everything into quantifiable, combative opposites; as we walked the knife's edge of order that spontaneously emerges between control and chaos, between cooperation and competition, between compelled and anarchic behavior.

At the end, after Visa had created separate, autonomous regions, I was reporting to more than a hundred directors from dozens of countries, comprising six boards, meeting on every continent, as the sales volume rocketed past one hundred billion dollars, with virtual certainty it would increase eightfold each decade well into the next century.

But success was only part of the story, as you shall soon discover.

Chapter Seventeen

The Successful Business Failure

I cannot praise a fugitive and cloistered virtue, unexercised and unbreathed, that never sallies out and sees her adversary, but slinks out of the race, where that immortal garland is to be run for, not without dust and heat ... that which purifies us is trial, and trial is by what is contrary.
—John Milton

It is painful to think about weakness and failure. It is even more painful to write about it, but it is an essential part of the story.

At times our failures were highly visible. I have already written about one in Chapter Thirteen, the fight to prevent duality. Another of the more visible was immense. After a number of early successes in building an electronic system for authorization, BASE 1, and another for clearing transactions, BASE 2, we were approached by several members who professed to have common needs (mistake one, they did not), asking if we would undertake the creation of cardholder and merchant-processing software for member banks to use, BASE 3.

By pooling money and effort, it was thought that much more sophisticated software could be developed at reduced cost. The members having immediate need would underwrite development of the product. It would then be available to all other members who would, if they elected to use it, pay a proportionate share of the development cost, to be distributed back to the initial funders.

A group of Visa staff interested in the project assembled, along with representatives of interested banks. A decision was reached to purchase previously developed software that could be adapted (mistake two, it could not) to build the new system. Mistakes pyramided. Costs soared above the original estimate and we went to the board for more money (mistake three, inability to recognize and admit failure).

A vendor with marginal worth underbid a major part of the job and we were blinded by price. Members could not agree on specifications. The scope of the project expanded without careful analysis of time or resources required (mistake four, ignorance is expensive).

The people handling the project were blinded by desire to succeed and determination not to let the company down. We made a second trip to the well for more money and time, thinking it would surely see the project to even greater success than originally planned. It did not. The lesson finally sank in. We had never gone back to our purpose and principles to ask what card-processing software for bank use had to do with "creating the world's premier system for the exchange of value." It had nothing to do with our purpose, or our belief about decentralization of function in pursuit of it.

It was not a mistake of the people, it was a mistake of leadership. We were extremely good at some things, we were very good at many things, but we were not good at everything. One of the principal arts of leadership is to make such distinctions and we had failed to do so.

I called each director to take full responsibility for the failure and advised them that unless they had compelling reasons to the contrary (they did not), we would immediately cancel the project, return all money paid by the participant banks, and assist them in any way possible to pursue other alternatives. We would announce publicly the failure of the project and absorb a three million dollar loss from the general revenues of the company. It was a bitter pill to swallow, for the third attempt may well have been successful. But that was precisely the problem. Such a success would lead us even farther away from our purpose and principles.

***

The failures that remain most bitter are those that were less visible. One of the first came early when establishing permanent NBI quarters. Something about confinement in private quarters had always annoyed me. To a lover of woods and fields, restraint in a building for the better part of every day was depressing, smacking of the prisons of school and church. Yet, in the world of institutions, physical separation from others had become a hallmark of success, power, and prestige. It was the heyday of gigantic corporate headquarters with palatial executive offices, and warrens of compartments and cubicles for the lesser folks. Something about such corporate "show-and-tell" quarters offended me, probably because I was normally excluded from them and when I was not, often had poor experiences in them.

Nevertheless, I convinced myself that banks, government officials and regulators, suppliers, and prospective employees would never accept NBI as a substantive organization if it were located in inexpensive, modest quarters. At the time, that judgment may have been correct. What is now clear, is that I lacked ability and courage to lead in the direction of natural inclination, rather than acquired behavior, regardless of the difficulty.

Our first permanent office was a compromise. We leased a half-floor high in the Bank of America building in San Francisco. Around the core of the building, which contained elevators and mechanical systems, we built a series of sitting rooms similar to those at the National Bank of Commerce. In the outer projecting corners, we built other sitting rooms with round tables and comfortable chairs so that visitors could relax while enjoying the views. Otherwise, the office was completely open, with huge bay windows framing immense vistas of the city, bay, bridges, ocean, and mountains, spreading for more than thirty miles in every direction.

Employees were at amply spaced desks with enough plants to differentiate space. That is, all employees but one, for with a constant stream of visitors, I spent far too much time in the outer conference room, which, de facto in the minds of the staff became my office. It was the purest form of leadership. I went before and showed the way. Absolutely the wrong way!

There was constant pressure from other senior people for offices, something to which they had been accustomed at their previous employers. Instead of demolishing the outer rooms and disciplining myself to behave in accordance with my better instincts, I succumbed to the pressure, and bit by bit, the magnificent space was cut into offices.

However, I insisted on one principle: No employee would be cut off from full view of the outside. Interior walls of all offices would be floor-to-ceiling glass so that every employee could see through to the outside. And so it was in every Visa office for the fourteen years, until I left. Slim consolation, for after I left, the glass came out and blind cubicles became the norm.

***

In the beginning, there were no titles at NBI. When recruiting new people accustomed to the old ways, the question of titles would inevitably come up. In my desk was a long, typed list. With a serious expression, I would explain it was our custom to have each employee select their own title, which they could change from time to time if it failed to meet their needs. On the list was a rich selection: Grand Duke, Lord, Lady, Prince, Queen, Princess, King, Duchess, Ayatollah, Bishop, etc. If employees wished to add a descriptive addition, that would be all right. They could be the Ayatollah of Advertising or the Grand Duke of Accounting. The only requirement was that the title must be used on all occasions. No one accepted.

Using the same logic, we had no job descriptions. I was often asked,

"How will people know what I do?"

"If what you do is not readily apparent to everyone, that becomes a very interesting question," I would reply.

It was great fun while it lasted. Unfortunately, we were embedded in one of the most title-conscious of industries; one with a long tradition of rewarding people with labels rather than income. In time, we bent to the pressure and accepted the need for "manager of" or "director of." Bit by bit, the old patterns reasserted themselves until a host of "Vices" arose, all bred from the simple fact that I was not farsighted enough to embed in the original bylaws something other than "President, " and thus became the first virus to infect the lot.

***

At the time NBI was formed, Bank of America cardholders produced more than a third of the volume of the system. It was neither possible nor equitable to induce the bank to surrender ownership of the system, give up the quarter percent of the sales volume they extracted from all other banks under the licensing agreement, and accept the obligation to pay a third of the service fees of the new system as well. It was agreed BofA would pay at the same rate as all other banks, but with a prescribed maximum. It was my belief that, as sales volume became more evenly distributed, the maximum would be eliminated.

Quite the opposite occurred. As the success of the system pushed the volume of other members near the maximum, they banded together to assert that the success was due to their superior efforts and insist that they were entitled to pay at a lower rate. No amount of persuasion could open their minds to another view. The board, over my opposition, decided that the maximum should apply to any bank whose volumes reached the prescribed level, no matter what percentage of system volume they enjoyed. In my mind, the inequity of larger members paying at a lower rate than the smaller members was obvious, but it made no difference. The cap remained as a sort of divine right of kings; the right of those with the largest incomes to pay the lowest taxes.

***

From the beginning, I believed in and worked for a transition from the concept of credit card to the concept of a transaction device for the exchange of value, a "debit card," to use the jargon of the day. It was my hope that issuers would evolve from marketing the card primarily as an instrument for debt, to marketing it as an instrument for the exchange of value. It was my hope that revenues of issuers would evolve from reliance on interest on cardholder debt and discount from merchants, to reliance on transaction pricing for services provided. It was my hope that this would equitably distribute cost between the most affluent and least affluent customers. Twenty-eight years later, that has not happened, and interest on debt of those who need to pay monthly supports free service to the more affluent.

***

During the formation of National BankAmericard and Ibanco, wrack my brain and twist Old Monkey's tail as I might, I could devise no way to include cardholders and merchants as owner/members of the system. They should have been, for they are certainly relevant and affected parties. The slightest hint of the subject in 1969 and those involved in the reconception of the BankAmericard system went into shock. Thoughts of including merchants and cardholders as equitable owners of the system had to be set aside, since everyone was already pushed to the limits of their ability to accept change by the formation of National BankAmericard.

***

Perhaps the greatest failure of all was to completely underestimate the degree of individual cultural change such an organization required, both in self and others. The organization was so new, success so immediate, growth so explosive, and resources so short it was necessary to hire most management from outside the company. Each person came full of the techniques, culture, and habits of the mechanistic, industrial age organizations from which they emerged. Many took the openness and liberty of Visa as applicable to them, but not in relation to those over whom they had authority.

As the company grew, time after time I would discover departments within the company where people were subjected to ridiculous rules and regulations. When I would forbid it, managers quite rightly saw my efforts to restrain their conduct as command-and-control, and so it was. I used command-and-control techniques to prevent command-and-control. Plain stupid! All too often, I was simply unable to be the change I wanted to see.

Members of the board brought to the table all the old assumptions about good management. The success of the organization created considerable tolerance of new and different management techniques. On the whole, however, each new approach was on sufferance. Each failure brought pressure to conform to the old ways. Since the board was deliberately structured so that management could not control its composition and to ensure 10 or 15 percent annual turnover, there were always new directors with a full load of old management baggage.

They had little or no idea of the concepts that had led to the success the organization now enjoyed. No matter how much success we had, they were convinced it could be much greater if done in the manner to which they were accustomed. No matter what the failure, they were persuaded it could have been prevented, had it been handled in the traditional way.

Occasionally, there was some truth in what they said. Always, there was no way to refute it.

At the time, I did not understand the depth of the hold that mechanistic, dominator concepts had on the minds and hearts of people, including my own, nor how tenaciously and powerfully they would reassert themselves. It was not then apparent how difficult it was for people to understand and sustain the concepts; how long it would take for them to sink to the bone and become habitual conduct. The pressure to revert and conform, both from within and without the organization, was intense and unceasing.

On the whole, we had poor methods and techniques and far too little of them to bring about the individual cultural change that a chaordic organization requires, nor did we have a leader who was fully alert to the need for it. Although Visa arose from thinking about organizations as living, biological systems, *I missed completely the need for an institutional immune system to thwart the viruses of old ways.*

***

Judged by orthodox methods of objective measurement—growth, size, profit, market share, and volume—Visa has been a phenomenal success. It would be a lie to deny a strong sense of privilege and substantial pride in presiding at its birth and guiding it to maturity.

But other methods of evaluation transcend measurement and objectivity. By the standards of what Visa *ought to be,* it would be a lie to deny a sense of failure. In spite of my pride in all that Visa demonstrated about the power of the chaordic concept of organization and all the things it has accomplished, I do not believe that Visa is a model to emulate. It is no more than an archetype to study, learn from, and improve upon. In terms of organizations as they ought to be, we did not get Visa half right. As an archetype of leaders of the future, I would be delighted to think I came anywhere near that level. But that is quite all right. *Failure is not to be feared. It is from failure that most growth comes, provided that one can recognize it, admit it, learn from it, rise above it, and try again.*

The important question is not whether an institution or an individual reaches the ultimate, but whether they aspire to reach it and constantly rise in the scale.

Chapter Eighteen

The Jeweled Bearing

God will not ask me why I was not Moses.
He will ask me why I was not Susya.

—Rabbi Susya

The moving finger writes; and having writ
Moves on; nor all your piety and wit
Shall lure it back to cancel half a line,
Nor all your tears wash out a word of it.

—Omar Khayyám

Early in 1984, the curtain came down on my performance as CEO of Visa. The business costume went into the closet and I went directly from the commercial theater to life on 200 acres of remote, ravaged land. It was shockingly difficult, an aching void emptied of things once craved—money, power, prestige, position—all achieved and now abandoned. The lifelong dream of pioneering a new concept of organization had been realized. There was pride and gratification in knowing what it had been, what it now was, and what it might become. There was also a sense of failure about what it ought to be. The world was marveling at Visa's success. To me, its flaws were all too apparent. Well, so be it. Life flows on. Bishop Butler had the right idea: "Things are as they are and will be as they will be, why then should we desire to be deceived?"

One by one, I picked up the frayed ends of more beautiful threads—nature, literature, grandchildren, art, contemplation, humility—and slowly wove them deeply into the fabric of being. Gradually the void filled, pain eased, and ten drastically different, but wonderful years emerged.

In the ninth year of that decade of seclusion, Thee Ancient One, Old Monkey Mind, and I had our glorious day together ending with a splendid storm, and Waldrup's book, *Complexity,* the story of new science emerging at the Santa Fe Institute in New Mexico.

Morning brought a clear sky and a world dripping from rainfall and filled with sparkling sunlight in the aftermath of the storm. At the breakfast table with Ferol, I excitedly shared my amazement that concepts now emerging in science were surprisingly similar to organizational concepts that I had been working with for decades. She laughingly remarked:

"You haven't been this wound up since you had those crazy notions about a global device for the exchange of value twenty-five years ago. Come down off the ceiling, call the people at the Santa Fe Institute, and find out what's going on."

"No way," I replied, "It's okay to think about, but it was hard enough to put all that aside once. I'm not going to get caught up in it again."

I whistle up Baron, our German shepherd, and set out on a walk through the woods. This day belongs to Baron, Old Monkey, and me, to reflect and reconnect with reality and nature as it is, not as the scientists in the labs claim it to be. Their claims lie in the rational corner of the mind. That small place where the trickster measurement creates mechanistic, particulate thought. In that world, we can never be more than "thing." Well, I'm not feeling like "thing" this morning. I feel more like "becoming."

Baron has no adjustment to make. In his German shepherd mind, he is always whole and at one with the world. Overjoyed at the sight of the walking stick, he leaps straight up, expressing in every way, "Yeah! Let's live a little." His nose is high, straight into the wind, as he roves from side to side, perceiving what lies in the dense woods ahead. From time to time, he lowers it to the grass to examine traces of creatures that passed in the night. His ears are twitching with sounds beyond my ken. The mental map he creates of the morning is one I can never know.

We are stopped in our tracks by a cacophony in the mouth of the canyon a quarter-mile ahead. It takes a few seconds to realize it is a pack of coyotes in conversation about something we can't discern. Their vocal range is extraordinary. In the dark of night, I have mistaken them for a screaming child, a moaning cow, or an injured dog. What images they are communicating to one another and to Baron's mind, I can't imagine. What an adventure it would be to borrow his nose for a day and connect with the world in his way. It's beyond imagining. Another of the countless ways of knowing that lie beyond human perception.

Baron races ahead, and returns, barking and whining to urge me on. We circle the pond, climb to the summit of the ridge, and sit for an hour, enjoying the immense panorama of forested hills, village, valleys, farms, and ocean. I pick up a stick and begin scratching at the forest debris beneath my feet.

Billions upon billions of self-organizing interactions are occurring second by second in the square yard of soil, each interconnecting, relating, creating, and shaping self and others. Every particle is inseparably interacting and relating to others, and they to still others, unto the remote reaches of the universe and beyond—beyond knowing, but *not beyond awareness, respect, and love.* The mystery of it all is overwhelmingly beautiful. Were it fully explained, what would be the point of life? Could there even be life? I am lost in the wonder of it all.

Baron has had enough sitting. He tugs at my pant leg and we rise to work our way down the ridge for a bit of lunch. At the house, on the message machine I hear the sound of an unfamiliar voice. "This is Steve Millard." The voice claims we met once years before, gives a telephone number, and requests a call. I can't remember a meeting. After ten years of isolation and an unlisted telephone number, calls from strangers are rare. Probably another hustling salesman. I reach for the erase button, then pause. Something in the voice has aroused my curiosity. I dial the number and am soon connected.

"You may not remember," he explains, "but five years ago we met once for lunch. I tried to persuade you to do some consulting. You made it clear that you had no interest in consulting. For some reason, you popped into my mind this morning and I decided to call. We're forming another company and your experience could be helpful. Could we discuss it?" A vague recollection of the meeting comes to mind. I am annoyed, anxious to end the call, and less than gracious.

"Nothing has changed. I severed all connections with business nine years ago. There is no chance whatever that I would do any consulting." He laughs and replies.

"I thought you may have changed your mind. I don't want to intrude, but somehow felt compelled to call." Memory sharpens as Steve reminds me that during our lunch we had discovered a mutual love of literature. We had happily talked away half the afternoon about things we were reading.

"Have you read anything lately that has caught your interest?" Steve asks.

"I just finished a book called *Complexity*. It's about a handful of scientists speculating about the nature of complex, adaptive systems. It's extraordinary, for whole paragraphs and sentences of the book echo what I have been thinking and arguing about with respect to organizations for..." He cuts me off mid-sentence. "I don't believe it! This is extraordinary! You're talking about the Santa Fe Institute. I've been there many times and am thinking about joining their board. The chairman, Jim Pelkey, is a friend of mine. He lives in Atherton, not ten miles from your place." The hair begins to rise on my arms and the back of my neck as he continues, "You simply have to meet him. I'll arrange lunch." And he did just that. One never knows when one might step on one of the tiny, jeweled bearings on which life can turn.

***

Within the week, Jim Pelkey, a venture capitalist, and I are at lunch sharing his experience with the institute and mine with Visa. He insists I must visit the institute and become involved. I thank him for the invitation but decline. In the week that follows, it is as though the early days formulating patterns of thought about a global device for the exchange of value are repeating themselves. My mind is leaping into the future. It is not so much the science they profess to study at the Santa Fe Institute that intrigues me, but the institute itself. What is the nature of the organization—its structure, its governance, its conceptual beliefs? Does its nature, structure, and behavior reflect the emergent science it studies? Is it possible the institute could be a vehicle for disseminating new concepts of organization?

Nothing in the next week resolves the turmoil, nor can the extraordinary synchronicity of events be put from my mind. An inner voice experienced at pivotal points in my life will not be silent. Recollection of the only explanation I could offer when leaving Visa returns: "I simply want to open my life to new possibilities." The humor does not escape me. If these are the "new possibilities, "they were infernally slow coming.

Ferol and I agree that nothing is to be lost by an open mind and a trip to the institute. Let things evolve as they will. If it comes to nothing, well, nothing is where it began. I call Jim to say that we will go, explaining that the structural aspects of the institute interest me most. If he will provide copies of organizational documents, the history of the institute, and make arrangements to speak with founders about their concept of the organization and its purpose, I will be happy to go, providing we agree there are no commitments, one way or the other. He agrees.

Several days later, Ferol and I fly to Albuquerque, New Mexico. The drive up the valley from the airport to Santa Fe is somberly beautiful. Mountains to the east, barren, dry land in the valley, the vast bowl of the sky and towering cumulus clouds on fire from the afternoon sun remind us powerfully of our childhood mountain home.

Meetings over the next few days are disappointing. The structural concept of the institute is seventeenth-century. It seems little different than a thousand other institutes, with the exception that it promises to be multidisciplinarian in pursuit of its supposed "new science." I have no desire to engage in academic study and publish ponderous papers about complexity theory in the midst of crumbling societies, a disintegrating biosphere, and starving people.

Whether the smallest discernible bit of matter is a wave or a particle seems akin to old religious arguments about how many angels can dance on the point of a pin, and in the midst of critical social problems, just about as useful. Thought of becoming enmeshed in such a situation seems increasingly wrong. Yet the ideas that have dominated my life have been aroused and feelings that they might someday find acceptance is unsettling.

At a break in a meeting at the institute, a young man appears, introducing himself as Joel Getzendanner, vice president of a foundation in Chicago. He wants to discuss how Visa came into being and the concepts on which it is based. He keeps me up far into the night probing my beliefs, eventually asking "Where do you think the epidemic of institutional failure will lead?"

"We are on the knife's edge between two probabilities and will not remain there long," I reply. "One is that institutional failure will continue to escalate, leading to increasing inequity and social carnage. In an effort to control societal problems, there will be ever greater centralization of power—regression to much more dictatorial institutions, both political and commercial—that could last for decades. Such repression cannot endure. It will, in turn, collapse, leading to even greater social carnage. Maybe then, there may be enough change in individual and societal consciousness to allow chaordic concepts of organization to emerge and be accepted.

The other alternative is that with collapse of "change float" and the explosion of the capacity to receive, utilize, store, transform and transit information, changes of internal consciousness may emerge much more quickly than we might now imagine. If enough people change their mechanistic, internal model of reality, new concepts of organization could emerge much faster than has ever occurred before. It so, it might lead to constructive, orderly transition from old organizational forms to new. However, I do not believe that will happen. The first probability is by far the more likely."

"But that's just not acceptable, "he replies.

I tease him with a smile. "You must have a marvelous telephone. Evolution has never rung anyone I know to ask for consent."

***

Ferol and I flew home, persuaded that the trip to Santa Fe had been a waste of time. Within weeks, however the foundation once again intruded into my idyllic life to paraphrase the challenge that led to Visa, and throw it in my face.

"Why don't you ask yourself the same kind of question that led to Visa: 'If anything imaginable was possible, if there were no constraints whatever, what would it take to create massive institutional change throughout society?' You did it once. Why not try again? If you do, we would be interested in looking at it."

It was a ridiculous request. Yet it fascinated Old Monkey and me. Week after week, we prowled my library, bought more books, pored over hundreds of pages of past notes. In time, it came down to four things.

Examples

At least a dozen extremely successful, new examples of chaordic organization, similar to Visa and the Internet, would have to evolve. They must emerge in such different fields as education, government, social services, commerce, and the environment, as well as in all nations and cultures, so that no one could argue the concepts were not universally applicable. They must breach all existing organizational boundaries, linking people and institutions in diverse fields. Opportunities to create such organizations must be discovered and methods and resources brought to bear to bring them about. People simply will not abandon old concepts of organization and methods of management in favor of new ones until they see a substantial number of such organizations obtaining superior results in correcting the vast systemic problems that plague society.

Models

Four-dimensional physical models of such structures would need to be created, so that people have something tangible to examine, relate to their existing organizations, play with, and enhance. Chaordic organizations cannot be portrayed in two dimensions on a traditional organization chart. They are more akin to the organization of neurons in a brain. Yet even the three dimensions of physicality are not enough. The fourth dimension, the spiritual and ethical dimension, something we have largely lost sight of in existing organizations, is essential. How to physically embody and portray that dimension will be one of the great challenges.

In addition to the physical models, computer models would need to be created, collapsing time and graphically demonstrating in thirty minutes how, based on clarity of shared purpose and principles, complex enabling organizations self-organize, evolve, and result in order impossible to achieve by engineering, or command and control. People must see the thirty-year evolution of Visa, the Internet, and other such organizations in thirty minutes.

Intellectual Foundation

The examples must be supported with an impeccable intellectual foundation. Whether we like it or not, whether it is a good thing or not, science is the religion of the twenty-first century, and academia is its church. The economic, scientific, political, historical, theological, technological, and philosophical rationale for such organizations would have to be documented and synthesized. Much of the work has already been done, however, it is not yet complete. It lacks coherence and clarity. Far more important, neither the language nor metaphors necessary for massive dissemination and understanding have yet evolved.

Organization

A global organization would have to emerge, linking in a vast complex of shared theoretical and experiential learning, people and institutions of every persuasion concerned about institutional failure and committed to doing something about it. It must self-organize in accordance with the principles it espouses and, itself, be one of the successful examples of chaordic organization. The purpose of the organization should be the development, dissemination, and implementation of new, more chaordic concepts of organization. Were the global organization properly conceived, it would organically dissolve into the fruits of its labor.

I told the foundation of the four conditions. And I also told them there was absolutely no chance any of the four could happen. They did not agree. In time, it led them to make an absurd proposal. If the foundation would make an unconditional grant to cover expenses, would I contribute my time to investigate, as freely and broadly as

I liked, whether or not the four objectives were indeed impossible, and if I should change my mind, what might be required to set them in motion? Would I be willing to discuss it with the board of trustees of the foundation?

"No, I would not," I told them. "An asthmatic, hard of hearing, sixty-six year old man who has lived in isolation and anonymity for nine years is not going to accomplish anything. It would be a waste of your money and my time. It has been an interesting exercise, but it makes no sense to go on."

***

A week later, as Ferol and I happily prepare to welcome the family for a holiday at the ranch, I am sitting in a comfortable chair in the study. Outside, a lynx appears, concentrating on a freshly dug gopher mound in the green grass of the undulating hillside below the study window. The binoculars bring it within a few feet. It is a poem of coordination and concentration. Each paw is raised sequentially in imperceptible, liquid motion, moved forward and inserted toes-first into the grass, then angled to rest silently on the Earth.

In slow motion, the lynx flows forward, six-inch tail motionless, eyes unblinking. It slowly shifts weight onto its haunches in a half-crouch, muscles in back and forequarters rippling under the sleek coat. If there is a more perfect manifestation of The Essence That Is, I've never seen it. Too quick for the human eye, it leaps. A gopher, kicking dirt as it backs from the burrow, is impaled on curved claws. Lunch is served.

> Old Monkey is fascinated and can't leave it alone. Lynx happens but cannot be done. The essence of lynx is beyond measurement, design, engineering, or knowing. It is not chaotic. It is not controlled. It is an orderly pattern lying between chaos and control. It is a harmonious blending of both. Lynx is not a thing of the rational mind. It is in the realm of spirit, intuition, feeling, and wisdom. If we knew everything about every atom of its structure, and about

> every particle of every atom, we would know nothing about lynx. Lynx is an inseparable, interacting relationship between earth, grass, light, air, gravity, rodent, heat, man, and countless other things. Each, in turn, is another interacting relationship between countless others, unto infinity. Lynx is atoms formed and reformed in countless ways throughout eternity. Lynx is time and time is lynx. Lynx is universe and universe is lynx. Man is atoms formed and reformed in countless ways throughout eternity. Man is lynx and lynx is man, formed of one another. Who can know the composition of the next minute? Certainly neither lynx nor man.

The next morning I am sitting in the same chair, as seven grandchildren happily play in the grass and flowers where yesterday lynx dined on gopher. I can't put the foundation's proposal from mind. If we can't conceive of institutions as more than machines, if they can't be brought into harmony with the spirit of grandchildren, lynx, and land, if the epidemic of institutional failure continues to accelerate, if social and ecological carnage get out of hand, it could happen within the next two or three decades. My grandchildren and their children will be caught in the middle of it. I could still be alive. They might find out their grandfather was asked to try to do something and refused.

"Why didn't you do it?" they would be certain to ask. What would I say?

"Too old? Not enough time? Too difficult? No money? No power?" Such answers are excuses, not reasons. It is a conversation I do not care to contemplate. The image that has appeared to me at every high and low point in my life returns, more vivid than ever. Someone raises their arms to the heavens crying,

"Why me, God?" The bemused reply is ever the same,

"Why not?"

A week later, I am at dinner with the president and the trustees of the foundation. They have listened with interest and asked a great many questions. Whether it is a subconscious wish to be relieved of responsibility, or desire to make certain they understand the full extent of the risk is not clear, but I finish by saying, "Were I a trustee of the foundation, I could not, in good conscience, approve such a grant, for the chances that anything can come of it are too small to calculate. However, the decision is yours. If you wish to make the grant, I'll make the effort." And so they did.

***

In April 1994 I set out on an adventure more improbable than Visa, and incomparably more important, searching out people concerned about pervasive social and ecological problems and committed to doing something about them. I asked the same questions over and over again of everyone I met.

"Is there some pervasive cause we're not getting at underlying so many intractable societal problems? Is there an epidemic of institutional failure? What is the connection between the two? Are the dominant organizational metaphors and concepts any longer relevant? Do you think there is critical need for massive institutional change? If there is such a need, are the four objectives the right objectives? Do you think there is any chance they can be set in motion within five years?"

If the response was positive, I would add, "If an effort were undertaken by responsible people to realize those objectives, would you care enough to join with them to help bring them about?" Before parting I would ask, "Who do you think I should talk to that I have not met? What do you think I should read that I have not read?"

It led to shelves of books and articles. It led to hundreds of extraordinary people, inner-city leaders, scientists, corporate CEOs, Native Americans, authors, software and communications experts, educators, entrepreneurs, politicians of every persuasion, economists, environmentalists, theologians. It also led to a great many less specialized souls of exceptional understanding and wisdom.

Some were negative, some indifferent, some bewildered. But most were interested. Some were excited and anxious to begin. Invitations to speak began to arrive from diverse groups—the Life Insurance Marketing Association, the Arabian Gulf Business Awards Convention in Bahrain, Rabbobank executives in the Netherlands, environmental organizations, universities, government entities, school systems, trade associations of all kinds, futures institutes, corporations, medical associations, and a bewildering variety of others.

Audience response was unlike anything I had previously experienced. Most would settle into deep silence as they struggled to absorb and understand the Visa story and the concepts underlying it. At the end, questions were always intense and prolonged, at times lasting for hours. Later, people would crowd around asking endless questions. Had I written a book? Where could they learn more? How could they help? When would an effort to set the objectives in motion begin? How does one set about creating such organizations? Can existing organizations transform themselves or must they be replaced? How can someone begin such work within a command-and-control organization? How does one set about changing one's internal model of reality? Where is this way of thinking taught? There seemed an insatiable hunger for new concepts—for renewed hope—for a more creative, constructive path to the future.

It was difficult to accept the reaction. Thirty years of often bitter experience during which I had encountered an abundance of flattery, opposition, and deception had left me inclined to be cynical and cautious. But what possible motive could so many strangers have for engaging in deception? What motive could they have for concealing their real thoughts? There was nothing I could do to help or to harm any of them. Why would they waste their time? To what purpose? My conviction that the four objectives were impossible began to waver.

Fascinating patterns began to emerge. Most women seemed to understand the concepts quickly, deeply, and intuitively. People raised in Eastern cultures or religions were also swift to understand. Native peoples had no trouble at all. Exceptions to the patterns were numerous and pronounced, but the patterns were unmistakably there. Those who had the most difficulty with the concepts were usually Caucasian men in positions of power in Western societies. People just like what I had been.

We were the ones who had created the old concepts. We were the ones who fought to sustain them. We were the obstacles to be overcome. Our internal models of reality would require the most rigorous transformation. No wonder mine had been such a difficult lifelong struggle, one far from over. Not happy thoughts at all.

> Such thought soon had Old Monkey and me wandering back to the notion of organizations. In a strange way, is every institution the same? Do they have a giant they refuse to acknowledge that accompanies them everywhere they go? Is their giant the mechanistic, industrial age concepts of organization and management? No matter how much we shuffle control

and responsibility back and forth from one industrial age form of organization to another—government or private enterprise, democracy or socialism, monarchy or republic, planned economy or free market, national or municipal government, nonprofit or for-profit—our social and environmental problems continue to escalate. No matter how we try to solve them with industrial age techniques, the problems reemerge in different form and dress, more complex and virulent than ever.

Something is deeply, fundamentally wrong. No matter how many technological miracles we perform, no matter how sophisticated the virtual worlds we create, no matter how many atoms we crack, no matter how much genetic code we splice, no matter how many space probes we launch, no matter how strenuously we try to suppress our problems with industrial age techniques, things grow progressively worse.

In truth, there are no problems "out there." And there are no experts "out there" who can solve them if there were. The problem is "in here," in the consciousness of you and me, in the depths of the collective consciousness of the species.

When our consciousness begins to understand and grapple with the destructive industrial age concepts of organization and management practices to which it clings; when it is willing to risk loosening the hold of those concepts and the lust to control they inevitably bring; when it is willing to embrace new possibilities; when those possibilities engage the minds and spirit of enough people, then and only then will new patterns of organization emerge, ripe with hope and rich with possibilities. At bottom, it is a wrong concept of organization and leadership based on a false metaphor with which we must deal. Until we do, the problems that crush the young and make grown people cry will grow progressively worse.

With time, came doubt about my conviction that the four objectives were impossible. Was there some chance, however small, that they could be set in motion? If not, might pursuit of them bring forth better alternatives? Old Monkey jumped on it.

"Okay, old man, now what? You've always claimed that possibility can never be determined by opinion, only by attempt. Do you call the foundation and say there is some small chance the objectives might be realized and wash your hands of it? Do you write to all those people whose interest you've aroused, thank them for their time, and tell them 'goodbye and good luck to you'? Do you stop answering the telephone and ignore the mail? Those grandchildren are not going away. What are seven grandchildren worth anyway? And their children, and their children's children?"

"Damn you, Old Monkey."

Questions came one after the other. Is this why I was so badly bloodied fighting my battles with institutions? Is this why I had endured the years with Visa, never able to identify "self" with "president"? Is this why I walked away for reasons never fully understood? Is this why I've already had my "retirement"—twelve years of bliss with nature, books, and family? Were my 67 years merely preparatory?

If something was trying to happen and wanted to use me, I could say yes or no. That's what free will is all about. If "no," life would be pleasant, comfortable, at times, idyllic. If "yes," it would mean day and night labor filled with stress, criticism, disappointment, and virtually no chance of success. But, if I held back would I be in denial of my becoming? *A life worth living can't be made of denial. It must be made of affirmation.* In time, the essential question emerged.

Is this what my life is all about? There it was, as simple and plain as that. There was no conceivable answer to the question. *But, there was insatiable desire to find out.* It was time to move on, wherever it led, whoever my companions, whatever the results, for as long as I could endure.

Chapter Nineteen

Out of Control and Into Order

This is the true joy of life, the being used for a purpose recognized by yourself as a mighty one; the being thoroughly worn out before you are thrown on the scrap heap; the being a force of nature instead of a feverish, selfish little clod of ailments and grievances complaining that the world will not devote itself to making you happy.... The only tragedy in life is being used by personally minded men for purposes that you recognize to be base.
—George Bernard Shaw

The next day brought deep blue skies and magnificent sunshine. The private park we had been creating for more than a decade was never more beautiful; our splendid home on the hill never more enticing; the views over valley, village, forests, and ocean never more stunning. As the family scattered across the 200 acres to enjoy their bit of paradise, I could not forget how I had labored through the years to plant thousands of trees. Even the fastest growing evergreens would not reach maturity in my lifetime.

Hundreds of nuts from huge black walnut trees surrounding the small Utah cottage where I had been born had been sprouted in pots, then planted as saplings throughout the ranch. They would not reach full maturity for a century. Redwoods would take even longer. In my imagination, I could wander at will under the magnificent canopy they would make, though I would never live long enough to experience it. Nor would my children or grandchildren.

The thought that someone, someday, without ever knowing how it came about, might actually experience what the land ought to be was more than enough to bring contentment to the effort.

In a very real sense, each of the black walnuts from the ancestral tree contained no more than the *idea* of a black walnut tree, waiting for the conditions by which it could sprout and slowly realize its becoming. If seeds of the concepts of organization that had been growing in Old Monkey and me were planted in enough minds and nurtured by enough spirits, could they someday intermingle with seeds of similar ideas planted by others and grow into a forest of societal change? What difference if it took a hundred years, or two hundred, or even three.

A paragraph from *The Scottish Himalayan Expedition,* by W.N. Murray puts it best. The last two lines are often attributed to Goethe, the German poet, philosopher, and scientist, one of the great spirits of the past few centuries.

> Until one is committed there is always hesitancy, the chance to draw back, always ineffectiveness. Concerning all acts of initiative and creation there is one elementary truth the ignorance of which kills countless ideas and splendid plans. The moment one commits oneself, then providence moves too. Multitudes of things occur to help that which otherwise could never

occur. A stream of events issues from the decision, raising to one's favor all manner of unforeseen accidents, meetings and material assistance which no one could have dreamed would come their way:
"Whatever you can do or dream you can, begin it.
Boldness has genius, power, and magic in it."

Within a year and a half after the adventure began, it was devouring my life. It was like 1969 all over again, multiplied manyfold.

Invitations to speak poured in from a bewildering variety of organizations in dozens of countries. Other foundations volunteered funds to help pay travel and other basic expenses. Two young university professors came forward to ask if they could devote a year of sabbatical leave, to learn and to help. A young man of means offered to work for nothing for the same purpose. Groups of people came forward asking for help in using concepts within existing organizations and in forming wholly new ones. Magazine articles emerged, along with overtures to write books and make films.

It was impossible to accept more than a few of the opportunities, or to know who was deeply interested, and who merely saw an opportunity to serve self-interest. At one point it seemed prudent to form a not-for-profit organization in order to accept tax-free grants from foundations and other gifts to build more capacity. It did not take long to realize I had no desire to head another organization, whether for-profit or not-for-profit, though it took some time to be rid of the responsibility and let the organization find its own way, uninhibited by a reluctant leader.

It has ever been my belief that, in the deepest sense, one can never own anything until it is given up, freely, completely, without regret or remorse. Only then, can it never be lost or taken from them. Four years into our new adventure, the ranch in its entirety, our dream home, every acre, every building, every tree, spring, and pond, every piece of equipment, was put on the market and sold without regret or remorse. Thus, it became ours forever, and we were free to open our lives to the possibilities then emerging.

***

As the years passed, there was opportunity to explore the concepts of chaordic self-organization with thousands of people from hundreds of organizations in dozens of industries—health care, education, religion, energy, agriculture, forestry, philanthropy, software development, finance, ocean fisheries, welfare, the military, global warming, and conservation. In every case, there was no lack of knowledge about either the problems or what to do about them. At bottom, the problem was the same. There was no existing organization, in fact, no concept of organization capable of linking together the immense complex of organizations and people necessary to getting it done.

In none could the most compelling problems be solved at the local level. Nor at the regional, national, or even global level. They were too complex to be fully understood at any single point and evolving too rapidly for any mechanistic, centrally devised plan to have any hope of success, even if it could be devised. Any solution would require a complex of effective, interdependent actions at every level, conducted with cohesion and coherence, yet free of command and control.

This is best illustrated by part of a speech made to hundreds of such organizations, modified only to fit the specifics of their circumstances. The excerpt that follows was delivered to hundreds of doctors at the annual convention of one of the largest medical associations in the United States. After sharing the Visa story and underlying concepts, I told a small story.

> My work has led to a little-known system of health of which you may not be aware. In this system, every individual has a lifetime health care account. The medical history of each individual is electronically encoded in a health transaction card, encrypted so that it is available nationwide only to qualified providers of medical services selected by the individual. Emergency facilities are equipped

to override the encryption in the event an individual is incapacitated.

Each provider of health care has electronic equipment custom-designed for their practice, yet compatible with the overall information structure. Thus, 95 percent of the system is incrementally owned and operated by tens of thousands of health-care providers and vendors in free and open competition with one another. Yet it functions as a unified whole through common standards and cooperatively owned elements, such as a central switch to which everyone has access. An ever-increasing amount of health information and care is provided through inexpensive, interactive voice-data-video equipment in the home and at an increasing number of community locations open to the public.

The system has accumulated an immense amount of online, de-identified, patient data, invaluable for analysis of health trends, preventive measures, development of new drugs, and tracking of epidemics or terrorist attacks. An abundance of information is electronically available to patients so that they can make informed choices for maintenance of their health. The system provides insurers and funders an immense variety of data, allowing them to custom design authorization and payment procedures to balance costs, losses, and the level of service in competition with one another. The value of the data alone provides more than enough income to operate the system and finance its evolution.

The system provides a lifetime customer account into and through which money flows electronically from a variety of sources—insurance companies, government, employers, personal earnings, and charitable institutions. Funds are fully invested, yet accessible for health care at times or for purposes determined by the account holder in accordance with the reasonable constraints of the provider of funds. Funds are accessed by the same electronic encoded card that carries patient medical data. Each medical transaction is instantly authorized prior to performance of services. Payment is electronically made when service is rendered at a cost of less than two pennies per transaction.

Government retains the authority to tax and redistribute income or otherwise set public policy in order to ensure a minimum level of care to each person, but is not involved as a direct provider, owner, or controller of the system. Individuals have responsibility for and control over their own health and care, as well as the money required for that purpose. They have access to reliable, low-cost medical care around the clock, seven days a week, wherever they may be or care to go. They initiate all transactions. It is a customer-driven system.

There is no need to continue this description because some of you are no doubt wondering if you're being misled; whether the system really exists. Every element of what I just described exists right now, right here in the United States, as well as in many other countries. Everything required is state-of-the-art, off-the-shelf hardware, software, and communication equipment that is plummeting in price. More is being engineered at ever-reducing costs at a pace far beyond our capacity to put it to productive use. Every element of the kind of organization and management required has been pioneered, has come into being in other fields, and has produced the results described. There is nothing to be learned, invented, or tested. It is all at hand, right here, right now!

Why then does such a system still lie dormant in the field of health? The answer is not complicated. Who would you trust to own and control such a system? The federal government? The American Medical Association? HMOs? State government? Major insurance or drug companies? A stock corporation? (Each question is inevitably met with a chorus of "no" from the audience.)

If you think carefully about every existing form of organization, I doubt there is a person in the room who would trust any of them with the direction of such a system, and rightly so. Only with the evolution of a chaordic organization in which all relevant and affected parties have an equitable voice in governance; in which the whole does not control the parts and the parts do not control the whole; in which competition and cooperation are harmoniously blended; only then, will a universal, safe, low-cost system of health evolve.

You don't have a health-care problem. You have an institutional problem, and until you deal with it, things will get progressively worse.

Can such a thing be done in the field of health? First, a few facts. Sitting in this room are hundreds of the most intelligent, highly educated people in our society. You are the most technologically sophisticated people in the world, certainly when it comes to medical intervention. Most of you are among the most caring people in the world, else why would you have entered your profession? Your work is the most liberally financed in our nation—publicly, privately, charitably, and individually. For more than a century, you and your predecessors have been among the most highly respected, trusted people in the world.

Any one of you will set out virtually anywhere in the world with a small rectangle of blue, white, and gold, polyvinyl-chloride in your pocket with complete confidence that you will be transported, housed, fed, clothed, and entertained, with all the complex information that requires—currency conversions, language translations, and financial settlements—handled within seconds with complete privacy and 99.99 percent accuracy.

How can it be that you cannot provide anything remotely comparable if I walk down the hall or across the street between medical practitioners, hospitals, or laboratories, let alone have the temerity to become ill or involved in an accident in another town or country?

How can it be that you can understand and deal effectively with the most intricate, complex, systemic structure that trillions of years of evolution could create, a human body, yet remain in the dark ages when it comes to organizing yourselves into an effective, systemic structure for the benefit of those you purport to serve, even when doing so would serve your interests equally well?

How can it be that you tolerate rising rates of preventable medical error resulting in death or serious injury that would cause you to rise up in arms were it to happen in any other segment of society?

I hope you will forgive me for raising such deeply troubling questions. They are not raised in criticism of you as an individual medical practitioner, your medical association, or even health care as a whole. Lord knows, you need no more of that! I raise them because of a powerful belief that deep within your seemingly intractable problems is an incredible opportunity; because embedded in your industry are values essential to a more liveable world; because you have the ability, resources, and training to swiftly deal with your organizational problem and create something extraordinary.

Have you the will to do it? Or more correctly, for I am a patient, have we the will to do it? Now that is a very different question. A question only you can answer, for if it is to happen, the leadership must come from within the healthcare industry, and from within those who come forward to take the lead in such a new order of things.

***

The message delivered to the medical association has been delivered many times to large groups of educators. After sharing with them the Visa story and the organizational concepts on which it is based, I pretend to have discovered in my travels around the world, an educational system with which they may not be familiar.

In this system, every individual, from birth, has a lifetime electronic learning account into which money flows from a variety of sources including taxes, family, friends, employers, charitable institutions, lenders, and scholarships. The funds are under the control of the individual or, if under age, parents or guardians, but can only be used for educational purposes established between the account holder and the sources of funds.

The funds are accessed by an electronic transaction card acceptable at any qualified provider of learning services. Every transaction can be electronically authorized and paid at any time agreed between the learner and provider of learning services whether in advance, periodically, or upon completion of the service, at a cost of less than two cents per transaction.

Learners have the choice of all-inclusive, site-specific schooling, or construction of a unique education by combining courses, educators, classes, and self-instruction delivered either electronically or personally, at the home, at computerized centers or at traditional, site-specific schools, or at any combination of the three. Learning services are purchased by each individual or through purchasing groups formed in voluntary concert with others. Prices generally move freely by supply and demand, although they can be set by public policy where essential.

Funds derived through government power of taxation are allocated in any manner determined by public policy to be fair and equitable, however, they are not centrally collected and redistributed with more than half burned up in bureaucratic processes, as is now the case. Taxpayers merely transfer that portion allocated to learners in their own family to their respective educational account. That part taxed from the more affluent, or from corporations to be provided to the less affluent, flows electronically from taxpayer to the account of the nearest economically deprived learners. The cost of administration, collection, and redistribution of resources and other bureaucratic paraphernalia has dropped from more than half of funds collected to less than ten percent. It is expected to decline to less than five.

The system provides a variety of measurements of achievement, some of which are objective, some subjective, and others based on tracking achievements of learners as they transition from schooling to lifetime work-learning and full participation in society. The system has become incredibly data rich, with all learners and their families having electronic access to the performance of all providers of learning services and the relative success of their students. Government, employers, and providers of learning services now have available vast amounts of organized, undeniably accurate, common data with which to make decisions.

The account is negotiable at any authorized provider of learning services, whether K-12, undergraduate, graduate, vocational, or employer. The account is not age-specific, thus the learner can proceed at an optimum pace and is relieved of the stigma of lockstep age requirements. However, it is subject to minimum requirements for levels of achievement within prescribed periods as a condition of access to the funds.

Individuals are free to make decisions about whether to follow a purely academic path, or lifetime work-learning, whether through apprenticeship, military service, public service, self-employment, or corporate enterprise. At any time, they are free to move between academic and work-learning, taking their account with them. Funds from public sources gradually decline and are replaced by funds from employers as learners make a transition from adolescence to adult participation in their life's work. Comparable degrees are awarded, whether achieved through the traditional academic path or through public or private work-learning.

The enormously expensive, site-specific warehousing of bodies for the purpose of learning, and the huge bureaucracies that formerly digested nearly half the money destined for learning have evolved into a flexible, integrated system resulting in a much higher valuation of learning and greater compensation to effective providers of it.

When audiences of educators are asked by show of hands to whether they think I am deceiving them, or whether such an educational system actually exists, the response is very much the same as that from audiences in the medical field. Once they realize that all requisite technology is state-of-the-art, off-the-shelf communications, hardware, and software; that every element of the kind of organization and management required has been pioneered, has come into being in other fields, and has produced the results described, they rarely have difficulty understanding, *at the intellectual level,* that they have an organizational problem, not an educational problem. Nor do they have trouble understanding that no existing form of organization could or should be trusted with the ownership, governance, and evolution of education *as they know it ought to be.* Questions are usually insightful and intense, often, when time permits, lasting for hours.

The same has been experienced in hundreds of groups in dozens of fields where there have been opportunities for such an exchange. But, with few exceptions there is a problem. It runs headlong into their perspective; their mechanistic, internal model of reality, which prevents the change of consciousness that such new concepts of organization require. What most seem unable to do is accept it in the depths of their being—*to get it in the bone.*

> In the years since the fork in the road appeared and Old Monkey pushed me down "the one less traveled by, "we have long puzzled over the nature of leaders who have had a profound effect on the direction of society. Mother Teresa, Buddha, Nelson Mandela, Gandhi, Christ, Mohammed, Martin Luther King, Galileo, Lao-Tzu, Newton, Thoreau—the list goes on and on, from every continent, in every field of endeavor, throughout history.

Few came from positions of wealth and power. Few were born to families of fame or fortune. Few were great orators. None were elected to do what they did. None had permission. Most were met with contempt and derision. Yet, somehow, their lives had profound effect on human consciousness.

What they had in common was uncommon ability to get beyond how things were, how they are, and how they might become, and immerse themselves in how they ought to be. But, even that was not the essential thing that made their lives so compelling. *It was their conviction that the world as they believed it ought to be already existed and the will to live their lives in accordance with that belief.*

They did so not in pursuit of fame, money, power, or personal gain, but because they could not do otherwise, because they had become *what they ought to be.* It gave their lives such authenticity that it drew others to them and gave what they then had

> to say compelling force and effect. *The way they lived their lives educed similar behavior that lies buried in everyone, waiting to come forth.* They went before to show the way.

The years since the fork in the road have provided an opportunity to explore a great many other societal problems and how chaordic concepts of organization might be applied to them. It would take another book to describe the multitude of opportunities that have appeared. Space permits but a few brief examples.

***

In the midst of the furor that led to complete energy deregulation in California, then other states, opening the field to the corporate plunder of Enron and a good many others, I was approached by an energy economist with a California state agency. He and others soon made me familiar with the enormously complex grid of suppliers, producers, generators, transporters, distributors, retailers, users, and regulators that had evolved to supply our insatiable demand for energy.

It had all the characteristics of the bank card mess of the late sixties. The internal strife was immense, pitting one segment of the industry with another in constant conflict for dominance. Each segment had messiahs preaching one gospel or another—government monopoly, unrestrained competition, state regulation, vertical integration, local control, regional integration, and a host of others—nearly all driven by greed and self-interest. The system was breaking down and the needs and desires of individual energy users were lost in the maelstrom.

A small group of individuals came to understand that the situation was custom made for the kind of organization in which I deeply believed. An effort was made to bring others to the same realization. It was not to be. The old ways had not yet exhausted their credibility and new leaders did not emerge.

***

The demise of family farms and healthy, decentralized production of nutritionally sound food in the face of chemically produced, genetically altered, tasteless, nutritionally dangerous food is another opportunity, a situation that cries out for an organization within which family farms could both cooperate and compete as they build their own global brand and distribution system.

***

The enormously wasteful, ineffective complex of public and private producers of geo-data is another opportunity. Each hoards what it knows and uses the data selectively, at times dishonestly, to advance the interests of traditional organizations. The situation cries out for a transcendent organization within which they could both cooperate and compete, to synthesize knowledge of the Earth in a dependable manner for the benefit of both people and planet.

***

The world of philanthropy within which thousands of not-for-profit organizations spend more half their time, energy, and money competing with one another for foundation grants is another opportunity. In many cases, such organizations burn up more than three-quarters of their gifts from individuals soliciting more. The foundations that make the grants routinely spend eight to ten percent of the money they have available in processing grant requests. Thus, at least 60 percent of philanthropic resources are consumed in "the doing of the doing" and never get near the people for whom they intended to do good.

The not-for-profit, nongovernmental world of organizations is arguably the fastest-growing segment of the economy. As a whole, it would dwarf Visa and all other organizations. Yet, it is completely fragmented and its voice lost in the din of private-enterprise propaganda. There are 10,000 not-for-profit organizations working for the preservation of sea turtles alone. The world of philanthropy and nongovernmental organizations cries out for an enabling organization within which cooperation and competition can be blended, resources efficiently used, values harmonized, and unified voices emerge.

***

The list goes on and on: welfare, social security, global warming, ocean pollution, preservation of species, communications, software development, fisheries; each with a need for a concept of organization that enables independent, effective action as the smallest scale, right on down to the individual. One that also allows self-organization and self-governance to ensure effective action at any subsequent scale right on through to the global. An organization within which coherence, cohesion, and order could emerge on which every part could rely without need for knowledge or control of others.

Nature has been organizing in that manner forever. Every individual is a living manifestation of it. Every brain engaged in reading this book is so organized. Society, ever so slowly, is beginning to understand. The collective human mind may one day come to see that the mind, in and of itself, is the best model for the societal organizations it so assiduously works to create. When it does, and when it acts in accordance with that understanding, we may yet come to know what miracles are all about.

Chapter Twenty

The Emergent Phenomenon

The ideas of the past, although half destroyed, being still powerful, and the ideas which are to replace them being still in process of formation, the modern age represents a period of transition and anarchy.

—Gustave Le Bon

As Old Monkey and I traveled further down "the road less traveled by," we began to understand how little we really knew about what was happening. The concepts and ideas were not ours. They were emerging everywhere, in a variety of forms, described in countless ways. They had a life of their own. They belonged to evolution. *The "I" that is not "me" was inexorably revealing its eternal nature;* a "we" of such diversity and complexity that it is beyond knowing or even imagining, let alone controlling. But not beyond understanding. A phenomenon was emerging in which my life and Visa were but tiny fragments.

Visa is far from alone as a distributive, enabling organization. Many others are operating on every scale. Many are global. The Internet is a magnificent example of self-organization within which competition and cooperation are blended. It also epitomizes both intended and unintended consequences. Once the child of government intended for a limited purpose, it quickly escaped its boundaries and became something wholly unintended. Not unlike Visa, it has become a transcendent global enterprise in which no part knows the whole, the whole does not know all the parts, and none has any need to. Like Visa, it is not a model to be emulated, but one to be studied and improved upon, for it too has flaws.

The Internet grew so rapidly and in such unexpected ways that participants never had time to think through and create a governance structure in harmony with its architecture. Some effort has been made in that direction in the past few years, but with limited success. It has no effective means to deal with its own excesses, whether pornography, commercialization, spam, viruses, invasion of privacy, or fraud.

***

The World Weather Watch is another example of a distributive, enabling organization with no central ownership or control. It links together a global complex of weather stations, satellites, communications facilities, and computers that enables every television station, radio station, and newspaper to both cooperate and compete in providing ever more reliable weather reports and projections. Through its programs, members coordinate and implement standardization of measuring methods and techniques, common telecommunication procedures, and the presentation of observed data and processing information in a manner understood by all, regardless of language. The information it provides is equally invaluable to airline traffic control systems, shipping lines, and government disaster planning. Again, no part knows the whole, the whole does not know all the parts, and none has any need to.

***

The air traffic control system is similarly structured. In the United States alone, there are more than 50 million aircraft departures each year, in every kind of weather, headed for hundreds of thousands of different airports scattered around the world. The system is equally available to the lone pilot of a tiny, single-engine, homebuilt aircraft, the captain of the largest jetliner, the pilot of a corporate jet, or the pilots of any of the thousands of aircraft filling every niche in between. Yet it is virtually unheard-of for an aircraft using the air traffic control system to land at the wrong airport.

No individual organization or government owns or controls the vast network of people, computers, communication lines, and other resources that comprises the air traffic control system, yet trillions of dollars worth of aircraft and cargo are entrusted to it, and billions of people entrust it with their lives without hesitation.

***

Alcoholics Anonymous, the best system ever devised for dealing with the problem of alcoholism, is another example of chaordic organization. Every chapter of AA self-organizes and manages its own affairs in accordance with a clear purpose and a dozen or so "traditions." The organization chart shows local groups on top and headquarters on the bottom. The headquarters is a core office with a small staff that does little more than provide literature, information, some level of communication, and coordination of chapters. They are the keepers of the flame. As the fourth tradition states,

> With respect to its own affairs, each AA group should be responsible to no other authority than its own conscience. But when its plans concern the welfare of neighboring groups also, those groups ought to be consulted. And no group, regional committee or

individual should ever take any action that might greatly affect AA as a whole without conferring with the trustees of the general service board. On such issues, our common welfare is paramount.

It is interesting to note the use of "should" and "ought," never "must," or "shall."

Any individual who has a drinking problem is welcome at any chapter of AA at any time, but has no obligation to attend more often, or do more when in attendance than they choose.

***

In the commercial world, the Mondragón Corporación Cooperativa in the Basque county in Northern Spain is an excellent example of chaordic organization. The Mondragón system grew out of the vision of a young Catholic priest, Don José María Arizmendiarrieta. Beginning in 1956 as a tiny factory manufacturing paraffin stoves, it has grown into the leading industrial group in the Basque country and the seventh largest in Spain with 2003 sales of 9.655 million euros in its industrial and distribution activities, 9.247 million euros of administered assets in its financial activity, and a work force of 68,260. It is a cooperative business group of 218 companies and entities organized in three sectors: financial, industrial, and distribution.

The entirety is unified by ten basic principles to which all parts subscribe. This "genetic code" of the enterprise determines the nature of its growth and evolution:

1. Open membership
2. Democratic organization
3. Worker sovereignty
4. Instrumental, subordinate nature of capital
5. Participation in management
6. Wage solidarity
7. Cooperating between cooperatives
8. Social transformation
9. Universal nature
10. Education

These are not a public relations vision statement or code of ethics to be waved when convenient as a disguise for avarice and ambition. Each has been educed through an extensive, democratic process and thoughtfully elaborated in writing into a belief system that not only guides the form, governance, and conduct of the participant organizations, but the lives of the people who are involved as well.

Does it work? The Mondragón system has consistently been among the most stable and profitable in Spain. If you get chaordic organization even half right in commercial organizations, profit becomes a barking dog begging to be let in.

***

At the smallest end of the scale is the primary example of chaordic societal organization, one with which everyone is familiar: the family. Every healthy family is chaordic by its very nature. It is there that the greatest exchange of nonmonetary value takes place. The things we do because we care, for which we expect no recompense and keep no records. I know of no parents who use mathematics to make up a balance sheet to prove to themselves which child they love more. Nor do I know of any who use such techniques to make certain that no one receives more than they give, or gives more than they receive, or what the "profit" of their joint enterprise is, or how it should be distributed. Of course, there always have been and always will be some families conducted on other principles. But few enlightened people would consider them healthy.

There is no need to go on with endless examples. Once one is accustomed to a chaordic way of thinking, consciousness changes and such organizations become manifest everywhere, if not wholly, at least partially. Once such perception arises, the world with all its problems begins to make sense, and what to do about it becomes less puzzling.

Enough of the more constructive possibilities of such organization. What about the dark side? One of my deepest beliefs is that everything with capacity for good has equal capacity for evil. Chaordic self-organization is no different. It is emerging everywhere, good and bad, whether we are conscious of it or not.

A little more than three years ago, two highjacked aircraft were deliberately flown into the twin towers of the World Trade Center and a third into the Pentagon. But for the courage of a few passengers, a fourth may well have destroyed the White House.

Terrorism is one of the dark sides of chaordic organization. No one owns it. No one controls it. It has no global headquarters. Its adherents are driven by beliefs so powerful that many will voluntarily go to certain death for the opportunity to take a few hated people with them. When any part of terrorism is attacked, it dissipates, self-organizes in different form, emerges with new adherents in unpredictable ways, more virulent than ever.

The same is true of the organization of the traffic in illegal drugs, gambling, prostitution, and other forms of organized crime. It was no different with illegal traffic in alcohol in the United States during the days of Prohibition.

A great many insurgents and a few armies have used self-organization with great effect, as we learned (or failed to learn, as the case may be) in Vietnam, Afghanistan, Iraq, and a host of other places. Efforts to suppress such organizations with industrial age, centralized, command-and-control organizations have been futile, just as they have been futile in attempting to deal with such chaordic problems as global warming, ocean pollution, deforestation, destruction of species, and depletion of topsoil.

> In our ruminations about great leaders, Old Monkey and I could not ignore powerful leaders who have induced abominable behavior—Hitler, Stalin, Pol Pot, Idi Amin, and a host of others—now and throughout history. What they had in common is all too easy to see: lust for power, wealth, fame and fortune, along with willingness to ruthlessly use force and barbarity to bend others to their will. What differentiates the despotic leader from the beneficent leader is values: the purpose and principles from which they derive their internal being; their consciousness; their internal model of reality. Corrupt leaders believe in a world *as they want it to become, not as it ought to be,* and that world is also in existence, buried in everyone,

> waiting to be aroused. In truth, they are not leaders. It is a travesty to call such people leaders, for they compel, not educe behavior. They are not even managers, for they have gone so far down the dark side of management they are tyrants, pure and simple.

The more one explores both the bright and the dark side of the emergent phenomenon, the more the questions we must answer become apparent. Are we to cling to the archaic, increasingly irrelevant, industrial age, internal models of reality and the organizations and leadership they have spawned, or can we consciously understand the chaordic organizational patterns that have existed throughout nature since the beginning of time and are struggling to emerge in societal systems? Can we consciously create the conditions by which chaordic concepts grounded in beneficent purpose and principles can emerge and thrive, or are we to stand unconsciously by as barbarous purpose and violent principles dominate their emergence?

As they emerge, will they be as corrosive of the human spirit as the old forms, or more in harmony with it? Will they continue to increase the already obscene maldistribution of wealth and power, or will they redress it? Will they be as destructive of the biosphere as the old forms, or will they support and enhance it? Old Monkey and I have no answer to such questions, but of some things we are certain.

Individual change of consciousness and a different internal model of reality is the bedrock, the foundation without which beneficent institutional change is impossible, and with which it is inevitable. To do so is not the prerogative of famous leaders. They are, for all their accomplishments and notoriety, accidents of time and circumstance.

The answer to these great millennial questions is resting in the heart and soul of every person alive today, especially the young, waiting to be beneficently educed or tyrannically aroused. What will be our consciousness, our perception, our values, our internal model of reality?

Will it be chaordic, pacific, equitable, and just, as it ought to be? Or will it be mechanistic, violent, inequitable, and unjust, as it might become? What will be our becoming?

If you are unwilling to examine your present consciousness, your internal model of reality, your perception of how you were, how you are, how you might become, and how you ought to be, you are making a grave mistake. No one is without influence. Everyone has choices to make about where they will lead and where they will be led. No one is without power to choose wisely and well. *After all, if you think you can't, why think?*

If you are in management in any organization, commercial, political, or social, and unwilling to go beyond such self-examination to look deeply into how your organization was, how it is, how it might become, and *how it ought to be,* not only economically, but socially, ethically, and morally, you are abrogating your responsibility as a leader and making a grave mistake.

If there is a corporate CEO or senior executive officer who does not have some of the company's best people with adequate resources deeply exploring chaordic concepts of organization and leadership, who is not testing them in significant ways through a variety of projects, that person is failing to lead; failing to go before and show the way and making a grave mistake.

The same holds true of those who hold power within political, social, and nongovernmental organizations. For those in education, particularly at the college and university level, the failure to understand, explore, and experiment with such concepts is inexcusable.

Can such a massive change of consciousness occur? Of course it can! In the great sweep of history, it often has. Will it occur in time to ameliorate the epidemic of institutional failure that is everywhere apparent and minimize the resulting environmental and social carnage that is enveloping us all? Ah, that is another question entirely. As always, Old Monkey and I turn to the classics for guidance, for they have never let us down.

***

Aristotle argued that for a community to function properly all citizens should be within the sound of a single voice. He could not have dreamed that modern communication would make of the world but a single village composed of countless villages at hundreds of scales—from communities of four or five to a community of billions—and even beyond that to a community of trillions of life forms, all within the sound of a single voice.

Just as we are citizens of a city, province, or nation by right of birth so too are we citizens of the world, for we were most certainly born there also. We are no less citizens of corporations, churches, and countless other organizations by right of choice. If we do not develop new and better concepts of organization and leadership wherein persuasion prevails over power, reason over emotion, trust over suspicion, hope over fear, cooperation over coercion, and liberty over tyranny, we shall never harness science or technology in the service of humanity, let alone in the service of all other creatures and the living Earth on which we depend.

Instead, with the great levers of science and technology we shall socially, economically, politically, and physically continue to tear this world apart. While that will bring bitter pain to us and shame to our ancestors, it will be a legacy of agony and evil beyond comprehension to our grandchildren, their children, and their children's children. To the universe, it will be an event scarcely discernible, let alone worthy of note.

The American writer, Norman Cousins, put our dilemma succinctly two decades ago when he wrote

> A great technological ascent has taken place without any corresponding elevation of ideas. We have raised our station without raising our sights. We roam the heavens with the engines of hell—whatever mankind's success in intermediate organization, he has failed to make an organization of the whole. His finest energies have gone into interim projects. He has made a geographical entity of his world without a philosophy for

ennobling it, a plan for conserving it or organizations for sustaining it.

In his book, *Celebrations of Life,* Rene Dubos, the world-renowned scientist and philosopher, wrote

> It is fortunate that practical necessities will compel local solutions to global problems.... The ideal for our planet would seem to be not a world government, but a world order in which social units maintain their identity while interplaying with each other through rich communications networks.

In his book *The Third Wave,* futurist Alvin Toffler suggests that ahead lies

> a matrix of organizations with common interests, densely interrelated like the neurons in a brain.

How are we to discover these new ideas of community, these new concepts of organization? One can find no better answer than the words of Camus.

> Great ideas come into the world as quietly as doves. Perhaps then, if we listen attentively, we shall hear the faint fluttering of wings, the gentle stirring of life and hope.

Some will say this hope lies in a nation, others, in a man. I believe rather that it is awakened, revived, nourished by millions of individuals whose deeds and works every day negate frontiers and the crudest implications of history. Each and every one builds for all.

We are at that very point in time when a four hundred year old age is rattling in its deathbed and another is struggling to be born. A shifting of culture, science, society, and institutions enormously greater and swifter than the world has ever experienced. Ahead, lies the *possibility* of regeneration of individuality, liberty, community, and ethics such as the world has never known, and a harmony with nature, with one another and with the divine intelligence such as the world has never seen. It is the path to a livable future in the centuries ahead, as society evolves into ever-increasing diversity and complexity.

Unfortunately, ahead lies the *equal possibility* of massive institutional failure, enormous social carnage, and regression to that ultimate manifestation of

Newtonian, mechanistic concepts of organization, dictatorship, which, in turn, would have to collapse with even more carnage before new concepts of organization could emerge. It matters not a whit whether such regression to tyranny is in the hands of governmental, commercial, or religious organizations.

Or have we—have we at long, long last—evolved to the point of sufficient wisdom, spirit, and will to discover the concepts and conditions by which chaordic institutions can find their way into being? Institutions with inherent capacity for their own continual learning, order and adaptation; institutions in harmony with the human spirit; institutions with capacity to co-evolve harmoniously with one another, with all people, with all other living things, and with the Earth itself, to the highest potential of each and all.

I simply do not know the answer to that question, but this I do know. At such times, it is no failure to fall short of realizing all that we might dream: The failure is to fall short of dreaming all that we might realize.

545

We must try!

Acknowledgments

It should be apparent to the reader that this book is more about concepts and ideas than people, events, or sources. It would require a book of different nature and size to mention all the people or events that led to Visa or to the contents of this book. The few that appear in the story are not there to set them above others, but as representative of the multitude I have encountered along the way who are deserving, but did not become part of the story.

From childhood, I have been an incessant, eclectic reader and buyer of books. For sixty years past, I have lived and worked in the midst of thousands. It is impossible to know the influence of each on the evolving concepts and ideas that led to Visa and events since. Let the few citations that found a natural place herein stand for thousands that could have served as well, but did not come so readily to hand.

About the Author

Dee Hock is founder and CEO emeritus of VISA. In 1991, Hock became one of thirty living Laureates of the Business Hall of Fame, and in 1992 was recognized by *Money* magazine as one of the eight individuals who most changed the way people live in the previous quarter century.

Index

A

accounting, management, *279, 282, 283*
accounts, lifetime, *502, 504, 506, 508, 510, 512, 514, 517*
adversity, coping with, *348*
advertising, credit card marketing, *142*
affirmation, vs. denial, *494, 496*
agreement, organizations, *123*
air traffic control systems, *526, 528*
Alcoholics Anonymous, *528, 530*
Altimira Hotel, first meetings of the national executive committee, *194, 196*
American Bankers' Association, money and payment system committee (MAPS), *304, 306*
American Express, antitrust charges, *363*
Bank of America credit card authorization system, *304*
emergence of credit card competitors,
Antonius, Marcus Aurelius,
  facing the day,
  men's badness,
Aristotle, community structure, *539*
Arizmendiarrieta, Don José María, Mondragón Corporación Cooperativa, *530, 532*

autonomy, voluntarily surrendering, *230*

B

Bacon, Sir Francis,
  accepting new concepts, *315*
  discovering vice and virtue, resistance to change, *436*
Baker, Donald, Department of Justice, *340, 357*
Bancomer, BankAmericard in Mexico, *365*
bank members,
  defining rights and obligations of individual, *237, 239, 241*
  participation in National BankAmericard International (NBI), *228, 230*
Bank of America, BankAmericard, *106*
  winning their accord, *214, 216, 218, 219, 221, 223, 226*
Bank of America Service Corporation,
  credit card licensee operating problems, *154, 157, 159, 161, 163*
  worldwide licensees, *365*
bankers,
  credit card experience, *146, 148*
  introducing NBC credit cards to, *119, 121*
banking, nature of, *177, 179*
Barclaycard, BankAmericard in England, *365*
Barclay's Bank, Visa name change, *410, 412*
Baron, walking with, *468, 470*

BASE 1 (Bank Authorization System Experimental), creating the system, *315, 317, 319, 321, 323, 325*
BASE 2, transaction clearing system, *451*
BASE 3, merchant processing software, *451, 452, 454*
Bateson, Gregory, information, *309, 311, 313, 315, 327*
behavior,
   educed, *87*
   healthy organizational, *173, 175*
birds, watching, *9, 10*
Black's Law Dictionary, *249*
Board of Directors,
   approval to create BASE, *317, 319*
   National BankAmericard International (NBI), *275, 277*
   open meetings, *441, 443, 445, 447, 449*
bonsai, continuity of life, *416, 418*
boundaries, computers and changing, *130*
broom handles, credit card mailers, *132, 133*
Butler, Bishop, the desire to be deceived, *468*
bylaws, amending NBI, *277, 279*

C

cafe, old Joe's, *34, 35, 37*
Camus, great ideas, *541, 543*
capacity to receive, utilize, store, transform and transmit

information (CRUSTTI), *325, 327, 329, 332, 334, 336*
cards, keypunch, *146*
Carlson, Maxwell,
   accepting decision to leave NBC to head NBI, *265, 267*
   advice on gaining approval of member banks, *230, 231*
   'borrowing' employees, *106, 108*
   committing NBC support to the new organization, *188, 190, 192*
   first meeting, *82, 84*
Carte Bleue, Visa name change, *412*
Celebrations of Life (Dubos), creating a new world order, *541*
change,
   institutional, *306, 478, 481, 482, 484, 536, 537*
   international organizing committee resistance to, *370, 372*
chaordic, defining, *22, 24*
chaordic organizations,
   concept of, *297, 299*
   cultural changes in adapting to, *462, 464*
   examples of, *481*
   existing, *532*
   encouraging, *537, 539*
   terrorism, *533*
   theology of, *212*
chaos, complexity, *20*
Chargex, BankAmericard in Canada, *365*
   international organizing committee meeting in San Francisco, *393, 395, 397*

Chase Manhattan, emergence of credit card competitors,
check clearing, Federal Reserve System, *306*
checks, money float, *150, 152, 154*
church, serving the sacrament, *34, 35, 37*
Citicorp, emergence of credit card competitors,
citizenship, world, *539*
Clausen, Tom, Bank of America, *231*
Clinton, John, Barclay's Bank acceptance of Visa name change, *412, 414*
committee,
    American Bankers' Association money and payment system (MAPS), *304, 306*
    chief executive officer organizing, *231, 233, 235, 237, 239, 241, 243*
    creating a new organization, *192, 194*
    formation of a national, *165, 166, 168*
    the international organizing, *368, 370, 372, 381, 384, 385, 387, 389, 391, 393, 395, 397*
    of seven, thrashing out problems between Bank of America Service Corporation and credit card licensees, *157, 159, 161, 163*
commonality, organizations, *123*
reaching a point of, *418, 420*
communication, rumors, *140, 439*
community,

corporations, *173, 175*
   evolution to a global, *283*
   proximity, *40, 41*
   structure, *539*
competition, and cooperation, *424, 427*
credit card provider,
complexity, language and societal diversity, *329*
Complexity (Waldrup), *18, 468*
computers,
   BASE 1, 2 and 3 system, *321, 323, 325, 451, 452, 454*
   credit card transactions, *177, 179*
concepts,
   accepting revolutionary change, *517*

community, *37, 40, 41*
debit cards, *460*
opposites, *10, 12, 15*
organizational, *247, 249, 252, 254*
organizations, *173, 175, 297, 299*
separability, *6*
connections,
   between man and machine, *4, 6*
   and relationships, *31*
connectivity, complex, *18, 20*
consciousness, change of, *537, 539*
control,
   total, *10, 12, 15*
corporations,
   community, *173, 175*
   defining the persona of, *252, 254*
   cost, socialization of, *260, 263, 265*

counterfeiting, new Visa logo experiment, *429, 431, 433, 435*
Cousins, Norman, organization of the whole, *541*
creation, exponential reduction of time, *152*
credit cards,
    counterfeit, *144, 146*
    early processing mechanisms, *140, 142*
    emergence of competing,
    evils of, *119, 121*
    primary function of, *181, 183*
    shredding personal, *73*
    unsolicited, *111*
crime,
    chaordic organizations, *533*
    credit card, *144*

Cronkhite, Jim, meeting of credit card licensees with Bank of America Service Corporation representatives, *154, 157, 159, 161, 163*
CRUSTTI (capacity to receive, utilize, store, transform and transmit information), *325, 327, 329, 332, 334, 336*
cuff links, Ibanco motto, *391, 393, 395, 397*
cultural float, *152*
Cummings, Bob,
    introduction to, *106, 108*
    working with, *111, 113, 115, 117, 119, 121, 123, 125, 128, 130, 132, 133, 136, 138*
currency, guarantees, *177, 179*
cycles, balanced, *50*

D

de Jouvenal, Bertrand, society and government, debate team, success, *50, 52, 54*

debit cards, concept of transition from credit cards to, *460*

denial,
  accepting change, *377, 379*
  vs. affirmation, *494, 496*

Department of Justice, the duality issue, *342, 344, 346, 348, 355, 357, 359, 361, 363*

deposit, the lost, *95, 97*

Digital Equipment, creating the BASE 1 computer system, *323*

Dillon, Jack,
  credit card licensee problems resolution at Bank of America, *214*

national executive committee, *194*

dimensions, models with four, *481*

Discover Card, antitrust charges, *363*

diversity, language and societal, *329*

DNA, CRUSTII, *327*

Dostoyevsky, Fyodor Mikhailovich,
  fear of change, *381*
  fear of the new, dreams, pursuing, *498, 543, 544*

Drexler, K. Eric, Engines of Creation, *332*

duality, problems with freedom of choice, *338, 340, 342, 344, 346, 348, 350, 352, 355, 357, 359, 361, 363*

Dubos, Rene, Celebrations of Life, *541*

duck hunting, with Ralph, *44, 46*

E

economy, the global, *420, 422, 424, 427*
education, lifetime learning accounts, *510, 512, 514, 517*
educe, defined, *87*
Einstein, Albert, I=DC(2), *329*
Emerson, Ralph Waldo,
   seeking paradise, *99, 101*
   trusting self, *212, 319*
energy,
   industry chaos, *518, 520*
   wasted, *60, 62, 64*
Engines of Creation (Drexler), nanotechnology, *332*
Enron, deregulation of the energy industry, *518, 520*
equality, mantra confirming, *233, 235*
evil, chaordic organizations, *533*
evolution,
   principles of, *327*
   technology, *332, 334, 336*
examination, self, *537*
experiments, counterfeiting the new Visa logo, *429, 431, 433, 435*
expertise, scientific, *68*
experts, clerical staff as leaders, *133, 136*

F

failures,
   epidemic of institutional, *20, 22, 476, 478*
   successful business, *77, 451, 452, 454, 456, 458, 460, 462, 464, 466*

family, chaordic organizations, *532*
Faragher, Bob, launching of FBC credit card program, *133, 136*
farming, global brand and distribution opportunities, *520*
Federal Reserve System, check clearing, *306*
fees, maximums for member banks and Bank of America, *458, 460*
Ferol,
　dealing with personal threats, *346*
　high school, *50, 52*
　meeting, *41, 44*
　Sante Fe Institute, *474, 476, 478*
　university bound, Firstcard, Seattle First National, *106, 108*
float, compression, *150, 152*
follower, defined, *87*
foundation, intellectual, *482*
Frost, Robert, taking the road less traveled by, *363*
future, possibilities, *543*

G

gain, capitalization of, *260, 263, 265*
genetic code,
　CRUSTII DNA, *327*
　Mondragon Corporacion Cooperativa, *530, 532*
　organizational, *200, 203*
geo-data, information sharing opportunities, *520*
Getzendanner, Joel, epidemic of institutional failure, *476*

gift, Bob Cummings' generous, *138*
giving, art of, *50*
Goethe, pursuing your dreams, *498*
gopher, and lynx, *484*
grants, foundation, *482, 484, 486, 488*
growth, failure and, *466*
guarantees, currency, *177, 179*

H

harmony,
   organizations, *50*
   returning to, *15, 17, 18*
headquarters, office space configuration, *454, 456*
health care, lifetime account system, *502, 504, 506, 508, 510*
homilies, wisdom of, *29*
humility, and pride, *97*

I

Ibanco,
   logistics of changing name to Visa, *402, 404, 406, 408, 410, 412, 414, 416, 418, 420, 422, 424, 427, 429, 431, 433, 435, 436*
   Visa International motto, *391, 393, 395, 397*
IBM, creating BASE 1, *321, 323*
Icarus, banks as, *148*
imprinters, credit card, *140, 142*
information,
   age of mind-crafting, *422, 424, 427*
   the capacity to receive, utilize, store, transform and transmit (CRUSTTI), *325, 327, 329, 332, 334, 336*

float, *152*
and institutions, *350, 352, 355*
nature of, *309, 311, 313, 315*
ingenuity, human, *104*
institutions,
  chasm between function and reality, *37*
  conformity imposed by, *31, 34*
  float, *154*
  nature of, *168, 170, 173, 175*
interactions, self-organizing, *470*
Internet, evolution of the, *525, 526*

J
James, Fred,
  committee of seven, *163*
  national executive committee, *194, 216*
Johnson, H. Thomas, Journal of Cost Management article on management accounting, *279, 282, 283*
Johnson, Sam, national executive committee, *192, 194*

K
Khayyam, Omar, longevity of the written word,
Koheleth, satisfaction with self,

L
ladder, climbing the corporate, *80*
language, societal diversity and complexity, *329*
Lao-tzu, the good man's task,
Larkin, Kenneth, credit card licensee problem

resolution at Bank of America, *214, 216, 218, 219, 221, 223, 226*
international organizing committee meeting agenda in Spain, *387, 389*
testing the counterfeit Visa logo card on, *431, 433, 435*

laws, antitrust, *239, 241*

lawsuits,
American Express and Discover Card antitrust, *363*
Worthen Bank antitrust, *342, 344, 355, 357, 359, 361, 363*

Le Bon, Gustave, the modern age, *525*

leader, defined, *84*

leaders,
clerical staff as, *133, 136*
inner force that creates great, *517, 518*

leadership,
group endeavors, *101, 104*
monetized corporations, *265*
personal commitment, *241, 243*
self, *94*

licensees, worldwide Bank of America Service Corporation, *365*

licensing, proprietary credit cards,

life,
control, *10, 12, 15*
float, *150, 152*
gift of, *50*

Life Magazine, banks as Icarus, *148*

loss, socialization of, *260, 263, 265*

Lucretius, the nature of things,

lynx, and gopher, *484, 486*

M

Machiavelli, Niccolo De Bernardo,
    change, *379*
    new ideas, mailers, getting out the new NBC credit card, *128, 130, 132, 133, 136*
management,
    changing from command and control, *462, 464*
    Ibanco and NBI joint, *401, 402*
    of self, *88, 91*
    unorthodox methods, *75, 77*
mantra,
    the human equation, *233, 235*
    on thinking, *210, 537*
market research, counterfeit new Visa logo cards, *429, 431, 433, 435*
marketing, training in credit card mass, *111, 113*
MasterCharge, emergence of credit card competitors,
McDonald, Ron,
    borrowing Bob Cummings, *136, 138*
    interview with, *80, 82*
meetings,
    custom of holding open Visa, *436, 438, 439, 441, 443, 445, 447, 449*
    introducing NBC credit cards to bankers, *119, 121*
membership,
    interlocking Bank of America and MasterCharge, *338, 340*
    NBI conditions for bank, *273, 275, 277, 279, 282, 283, 286*
memories, early childhood to young adult, *27, 29, 31, 34, 35, 37, 40, 41, 44, 46, 50, 52, 54*

merchants, enrolling in NBC credit card program, *121*
metaphors, machine, *67, 68, 377*
Mexico City, international organizing committee meeting in, *381, 384*
military, study of U.S. Army command styles, *62, 64*
Millard, Steve, Sante Fe Institute, *472, 474*
Milton, John,
  to be free, *165*
  life's trials, *451*
Minsky, Marvin, nanotechnology, *332*
models,
  four dimensional, *481*
  need for new organizaitonal, *490, 492*

Mondragón Corporación Cooperativa, genetic code, *530, 532*
money, essence of, *177, 179*
motto, Ibanco (Visa International), *391, 393, 395, 397*
Murray, W.N., The Scottish Himalayan Expedition, *498*
musings,
  the capacity to receive, utilize, store, transform and transmit information (CRUSTTI), *325, 327, 329, 332, 334, 336*
  capitalization of gain and socialization of loss, *260, 263, 265*
  chaordic leadership of tyrants, *533, 536*
  community and nonmonetary

exchange of value, *50*
computers and changing boundaries, *130*
concept of community, *37, 40, 41*
connections between man and machine, *4, 6*
corporate organization, *247, 249, 252, 254*
defining lead and follow, *84, 87, 88, 91, 94*
essence of lynx, *484, 486*
evolution of 'float', *148, 150, 152, 154*
finding new solutions to age old problems, *492, 494*
four ways of thinking, *196, 198*
the global economy, *420, 422, 424, 427*
group endeavors, *101, 104*
inner force that creates great leaders, *517, 518*
institutional failure, *20, 22*
institutions and information, *350, 352, 355*
management accounting, *279, 282, 283*
mechanistic organizations, *67, 68*
nature of information, *309, 311, 313, 315*
nature of institutions, *168, 170, 173, 175*
nature or organizations, *121, 123*
opposites, *10, 12, 15*
pride and humility, *97*

wisdom, change and understanding, *372, 374, 377, 379, 381*

N

name, choosing an internationally recognizable, *399, 401, 402, 404, 406, 408, 410, 412, 414, 416, 418, 420, 422, 424, 427, 429, 431, 433, 435, 436*

nanotechnology, possibilities of, *332*

National Bank of Commerce (NBC), customers, selecting initial NBC credit card, *121*

early experiences at, *94, 95, 97, 99, 101, 106, 108*

introduction to, *80, 82, 84*

Maxwell Carlson's support, *188, 190, 192, 230, 231, 265, 267*

starting our own BankAmericard program, *113, 115, 117*

National BankAmericard International (NBI), bank member participation, *228, 230, 273, 275, 277, 279, 282, 283, 286*

CEO committee offer to head NBI, *247, 257, 258, 260*

duality and problems with freedom of choice, *338, 340, 342, 344, 346, 348, 350, 352, 355, 357, 359, 361, 363*

employee titles, *456, 458*

fee maximums for member banks and Bank of America, *458, 460*

first annual meeting, *299, 301*

from idea to reality, *269, 271*

office space configuration at headquarters, *454, 456*
nature,
　love of, *29, 31*
　subduing, *9*
noise, information, *327, 350*

O

officers,
　'borrowing' to work for clerical leaders, *133, 136*
　NBI Board of Directors, *277*
Old Monkey Mind,
　dialogues with, *20, 22*
　voice of, *2, 4*
　See also musings,
opportunities, to encourage chaordic organization, *537, 539*
order, spontaneous, *18, 20*
organization,
　a new global, *482, 484, 486, 488*
　new principles of, *203, 204, 206, 208*
　reconceiving the nature of an, *200, 203*
organizations,
　command and control, *64*
　credit card handling, *183, 185*
　enabling, *525, 526*
　evolution from hand-crafting to mind-crafting, *422, 424, 427*
　global, *367, 368*
　harmony, *50*
　linking complex, *500, 502, 504, 506, 508, 510, 512, 514, 517*
　mechanistic, *67, 68*
　nature and governance of, *121, 123, 125, 128*
　reality of, *173, 175*
　Sante Fe Institute, *474, 476*

See also chaordic organizations, organizing agent, role of international organizing committee as, *381, 384, 385, 387, 389, 391*
  success and compromise, *391*
outhouse, in the snow, *27*
ownership,
  issue of duality, *338, 340, 342, 344, 346, 348, 350, 352, 355, 357, 359, 361, 363*
  nonmonetary forms of, *282, 283*

P

Paget, Stephen, wonders of nature,
Paine, Tom, on principle, *218*
Pascal, Blaise, mutual dependence, passions,
Ferol, *41, 44*
  three great personal, *29, 31*
patterns, need for new organizational model, *490, 492*
peers, managing one's, *91, 94*
Pelkey, Jim, Sante Fe Institute, *472, 474*
perspective, changing perceptions, *196, 198*
philanthropy, improving non-for-profit systems, *520, 522*
power,
  corporate use and abuse of, *254*
  purpose, principles and people, *206, 208, 210*
Price, Andrew, launching of FBC credit card program, *133*
pride, and humility, *97*

principles,
  of evolution, *327*
  evolution of, *125, 128*
  name change for Ibanco, *406, 408, 410*
  new organizational, *203, 204, 206, 208*
problems,
  finding new solutions to age old, *492, 494*
procedure, vs. purpose, *58, 60*
projects, time factor, *57, 58*
promises, employers and unkept, *73, 75*
proposal, foundation grant, *482, 484, 486, 488*
purpose,
  honoring principles and, *451*
  self-governance, *125, 128*

Q

questions, three compelling, *77*
'railroad letter', Department of Justice, *355, 357, 359, 361, 363*

R

rationalizations, power and wealth, *263*
reading, love of, *29*
reality, changing our internal model of, *379*
reconnecting, to life after Visa, *468, 470, 472, 474*
relationships,
  and connections, *31*
  flaws in fundamental, *22*
responsibilities, managerial, *88, 91, 94*
results, rules and procedures, *60*

retirement, 'on the job', *80, 82, 84*
rules, ignoring the, *57, 58, 60*
Rumi, Jalal, Uddin, true human beings,
rumors,
   credit cards, *140*
   Visa staff meetings, *439*
Rutherford, Mark, harmony, *399*

S

sales, bank authorizations, *144, 146*
San Francisco, international organizing committee meeting in, *391*
Sante Fe Institute, *468, 482, 484, 486, 488*
science, complexity, *18*
Seattle First National, Firstcard, *106, 108*
Seattle First National Bank, *80*
separability, concept of, *6*
sergeant majors, operating instructions, *62, 64*
Shaw, George Bernard, the true joy of life, *497*
Shelley, Percey Bysshe, poetry in our lives, *365*
Simmons, Dick, indoctrination of a new employee, *57, 58, 60*
Smilinich, Nancy, launching of FBC credit card program, *136*
society, a global, *420, 422, 424, 427*
software,
   development of merchant processing, *451, 452, 454*

See also computers; systems,
soup, 'rich man's', *27*
space float, *152, 154*
Spain, international organizing committee meeting, *384, 385, 387, 389*
statutes, corporation-for-profit,
Stewart, Sam,
   formation of a chief executive officer organizing committee, *231, 233, 235, 237, 239, 241, 243*
   role in resolving credit card licensee problems at Bank of America, *221, 223, 226*
subordinates, managing, *91, 94*
success, breaking the rules, *57*
Sue, Bernard, Carte Bleue, *414, 416*
Sumitomo Bank, Visa name change, *410*
Sumitomo Card, BankAmericard in Japan, *365*
Sunday school, superintendent of, *35, 37*
superiors, management of, *91, 94*
Susya, Rabbi, being true to self,
systems,
   adaptive, *20*
   American Bankers' Association committee on money and payment (MAPS), *304, 306*
   creating the Bank Authorization System Experimental (BASE), *315, 317, 319, 321, 323, 325, 451, 452, 454*

credit card authorization, *304*
the 'Dirty Coffee Cup', *323, 325*
distributive, enabling organizations, *525, 526, 528, 530, 532, 533, 536*
electronic neural networks, *420, 422, 424, 427*
global brand and distribution opportunities, *520, 522*
improving not-for-profit, *520, 522*
lifetime accounts, *502, 504, 506, 508, 510, 512, 514, 517*
need for institutional immune, *464*
sales draft clearing, *142, 144, 146*

T

teamwork, performance, *101, 104*
technology, nanotechnology possibilities, *332*
terrorism, chaordic organizations, *533*
The Scottish Himalayan Expedition (Murray), *498*
The Third Wave (Toffler), future organizations, *541*
The Zoo, National Bank of Commerce, *117*
Thee Ancient One, lessons learned from, *4*
working with, *15, 17, 18*
thinking, four ways of, *196, 198*
Thoreau, Henry David, building castles,

threats, dealing with personal, *344, 346, 348*
titles, NBI employee, *456, 458*
Toffler, Alvin, The Third Wave, *541*
tools, worshiping, *41*
trademarks, for Visa logo, *408, 410*
tradition, resistance to change, *462, 464*
training, teller, *94, 95, 97, 99*
transactions, floor limits, *144*
trees, planting, *497, 498*
tyranny,
   nature of, *15*
   regression to, *543*
tyrants, chaordic leadership of, *533, 536*

U

unemployment, coping with, *71, 73*

U.S. Army, command styles, *60, 62, 64*

V

value,
   monetized, *50*
   nonmaterial, *41*
   nonmonetary exchanges, *40, 50*
Visa,
   changing the logo on the card, *427, 429, 431, 433, 435*
   organizational structure, *291, 293, 295, 297*
   trademarks for, *408, 410*
voice, inner, *2*
Voltaire,
   evil,
   geometer, *399*

W

water, 'walking', *27*
Weber Junior College, *50, 52, 54*
Wells, H.G., ethical governments, *436*

wisdom,
  change and understanding, *372, 374, 377, 379, 381*
  evolution of data into, *350, 352, 355*
  of homilies, *29*
wolf, taking the, *355*
work, poor, *95, 97*
world view, systemic, *282*
World Weather Watch, *526*
Worthen Bank, lawsuit charging antitrust violations, *342, 344, 355, 357, 359, 361, 363*